NICK DRAKE

NICK DRAKE

PATRICK HUMPHRIES

BLOOMSBURY

TO SUE, FOR IT ALL

First published in Great Britain 1997
Bloomsbury Publishing PLC,
38 Soho Square London W1V 5DF

PICTURE SOURCES
Scott Appel: pages 3 *bottom*, 7 *bottom*
Larry Ayres, Santa Barbara, California: page 3 *top*
Island Records: page 5 *top*
Marlborough College Archives: pages 1, 2
Jeremy Mason: page 4 *bottom* 8
Keith Morris: pages 4 *top*, 5 *bottom*, 6, 7 *top*

A CIP catalogue record for this book is
available from the British Library

ISBN 0 7475 2976 0

10 9 8 7 6 5 4 3

Typeset by Hewer Text Composition Services, Edinburgh
Printed in Great Britain by Clays Ltd, St Ives plc

CONTENTS

FOREWORD

The idea of writing a book about Nick Drake is one which I resisted for many years, not least because I worried that it might be an unbearably depressing task. Eventually, though, all roads really did lead to Nick Drake, and having pondered the family connection – my uncle was the doctor who brought baby Nick into the world – I began to see a certain symmetry. Perhaps I could discover something about Nick's life and not just dwell on the last few years leading up to his death.

While I was researching my biography of Richard Thompson, Nick's name was mentioned regularly, and I began to think that perhaps the moment had come. When I mentioned the idea to Joe Boyd, while interviewing him about Richard, Nick and Richard's producer cast his eyes heavenwards, patiently explaining that I was not the first to come to him with this idea and that he was weary of cooperating on projects which never came to fruition. His response was simply: we'll talk when you've got a publishing deal. But publishers are like policemen – there's never one there when you need one – so it took time. One British publisher rejected the detailed proposal and chapter breakdown, explaining that they didn't consider there was sufficient market for 'a book on Nick Cave'.

By the time I had found a publisher with sufficient faith and vision – a genuine debt of gratitude here to Penny Phillips of Bloomsbury – both Joe and Nick's sister, Gabrielle Drake, had decided not to cooperate, which meant I was unable to quote from Nick's lyrics. This did, of course, make my task a less straightforward one, but by that time I had gone too far to turn back.

Slightly daunted, I went through the journalistic motions with little hope of much success. In the event, I was quite overwhelmed by the response: there seemed to be dozens of people who had known and remembered Nick Drake, simply waiting for someone to ask them about him. New undreamed of angles started to emerge, and a strange, unfamiliar picture of a very different Nick Drake began to develop. Far from being depressing, the project became exciting, even uplifting. The fondness of his schoolfriends for the young Nick was particularly contagious, and I began to feel I had a mission to give this young man his life back.

Nick's parents are now dead, but I very much wanted to use their words, not just for the background to his early family life, but because, more than anyone else, they were in a position to shed light on the last few years, when his illness had taken hold. I am therefore indebted to T.J. McGrath for allowing me to use tapes of interviews he conducted with Rodney and Molly Drake in 1985; these gave me the backbone of Nick's story.

Joe and Gabrielle have both been interviewed many times and, where necessary, I have drawn on, and acknowledged, these previously published sources; otherwise their quotes come from interviews I conducted with them in 1994 for a magazine piece which never appeared. All other quotes, unless otherwise noted in the text, are taken from the dozens of interviews which I conducted exclusively for this book.

In the past, myth and rumour have attached themselves like barnacles to Nick Drake. Rock 'n' roll is notoriously unreliable: session logs have disappeared, corporate take-overs have seen archives vanish, correspondence has been ditched, original press releases shredded. Misquotes and misinformation proliferate. For too long Nick has been the victim of myth-making. In the end, out of twenty-six years, twenty-three were spent by and large happily, either with his family, at school and university, or beginning his recording career. It was only towards the end that, in his mother Molly's sadly chilling phrase, 'the shadows closed in'.

It would have been nice to have some of the story in Nick's words. As it is, he lives on not only in his music, but in the fond memories of the many whose lives were touched by his, and through them, I hope in this book. This is a life of Nick Drake, in the words of those who knew him. And if that is not enough, there is always, and always will be, the music.

Patrick Humphries
London, September 1997

INTRODUCTION

All morning the crowds seeped from the city centre, a constant stream trickling down to the Lough. The sun was high in the clear blue sky which hung over Belfast that bright spring day. It was a time before television, when cinema was a sideshow novelty and only radio whispered in soft waves across the air. The borders of Europe had remained unchanged, secure in their dynastic stability for centuries; the twentieth century had yet to make its mark on the map.

The year was 1911. King George V was still a month away from his Coronation and Queen Victoria had been dead for a decade. With her passing, Imperial Glory and absolute monarchy had also gone to the grave. Edward VII had succeeded his mother, and in marked contrast to the widow's weeds and mournful demeanour which had dominated the past four decades of Victoria's reign, his ten years on the throne were characterized by vivacity and bright colours.

Edward's funeral, in 1910, was to be the final occasion when all the crowned heads gathered. Men who held unquestioned power over the lives of untold millions in Russia, Austria-Hungary, Germany and France stood together, heads bowed, as the corpulent King was wheeled past. There had not been a land war in Europe since Great Britain had battled Russia in the Crimea over half a century earlier.

The first years of the twentieth century had ushered in a new era: an exciting time of flying machines and moving pictures and confidence that man – for it was still a masculine world – could harness and control the forces of nature.

In 1911 seven out of every ten tons of shipping which sailed through the Suez Canal were British. Gandhi was still practising law in South Africa; Stalin languished in a Tsarist prison; and Hitler was eking out a living as an artist in Vienna. For the majority of subjects of the British Empire, place-names such as the Somme, Auschwitz and Hiroshima were as yet unknown. It was the calm before the storm.

In Belfast – home of the massive shipyards which build the ships which sail the seas which bind the Empire together – the White Star Line has commissioned shipbuilders Harland & Wolff to construct the largest ship in maritime history. But the vessel the crowds flock to see launched will never sail through the Suez Canal, will never leave the Atlantic. RMS *Titanic* will never know safe harbour.

The ship which began life as an enormous metal skeleton, its massive bare bones welded together like something unimaginable and Jurassic, looms like a cathedral of steel over the city which witnessed its birth pangs. It will be a symbol of the pre-eminence of Empire, the pre-eminence of man. Following Blériot's conquest of the air only two years before, this floating palace will banish any vestiges of uncertainty. The White Star Line boasts that the *Titanic* demonstrates 'the pre-eminence of the Anglo-Saxon race in command of the seas . . .' and pays 'eloquent testimony to the progress of mankind and the conquest of mind over matter'.

It will take just sixty-two seconds, on the morning of 31 May 1911, for the 46,328-ton, 852-foot-long steamship to crash down the slipway and out into Belfast Lough. But before she is ready to undertake her maiden voyage there must follow nearly a year of fitting out and lengthy sea trials. At last, as she sails out of Southampton on 10 April 1912, she is deemed 'unsinkable'. With a crew of 885 and 1316 passengers on board, she sets out across the Atlantic. Riding with her are all the hopes of the world.

Cleaving through the chill Atlantic waters, *Titanic* is the visible conqueror of the last frontier, for her arrival in New York is set to herald a whole new era of unparalleled luxury travel and speedy communication between England and America.

At 11.40p.m. on the night of 14 April 1912, eleven storeys above the ship's deck, lookout Frederick Fleet calls down with the warning of an iceberg. Down below, first-class passengers have dined on oysters, consommé, salmon mousse, filet mignon, roast duck, roast squab, asparagus vinaigrette, Waldorf pudding and French ice-cream. The ladies have retired and the gentlemen are finishing their cigars and brandy in the lushly appointed smoking room on the promenade deck.

Just before midnight four stewards sitting gossiping on Deck D notice the silver set out for breakfast rattle slightly, but the steady rhythm of the *Titanic*'s four mighty engines resumes, and she sails on. Below decks Mrs J. Stuart White, about to turn off her light, feels the ship appear to 'roll over a thousand marbles'. Others hear what they later describe as a distant ripping sound, 'like someone tearing a long, long strip of calico'.

Those still out on deck see what looks like a ship closing in, its sails full open; but none of them doubts that it is too far north for sailing vessels to be abroad on the chill Arctic waters. As the majority of passengers sleep on, the iceberg which looms over a hundred feet above the *Titanic*'s deck yet seems set to pass by harmlessly on the starboard side, slices a 300-foot gash in the liner. Within four hours the world's greatest liner has slipped beneath the surface of the ocean and into legend.

The shock of the disaster, as well as its swiftness and the scale of losses, lent the sinking of the *Titanic* mythic significance. She had been heralded as unsinkable – the ship which would link the proud achievements of Empire with the opportunities offered by the new world; but now all such hopes had been dashed. In accordance with Board of Trade regulations, the *Titanic* carried twenty lifeboats to accommodate 1178 persons. On her maiden voyage she had carried over two thousand passengers and crew.

In all, the loss of the *Titanic* claimed 1500 lives. Barely two years later the First World War had gutted Europe, and households in Belfast and London had become accustomed to reading over breakfast of casualties on a similar scale, losses sustained in a matter of hours on the Western Front.

It is hard to imagine how the sinking of the *Titanic* could have been any more portentous. The pride of the British merchant fleet, lost on its maiden voyage, sinking in the icy isolation of the Arctic night, beneath a still, moon-filled sky. It was as if a five-star hotel had been plucked from Mayfair, all its lights blazing, and up-ended, foyer first, into the freezing ocean. But by all accounts there was no panic as she began to descend. Passengers roused to gather on the boat decks only began to appreciate the enormity of the situation as the Arctic frost bit into their sleepy fug.

The band did play on, but memories vary as to what was played. The precious few lifeboats were lowered to the accompaniment of ragtime music; as they pulled away from the sinking ship 'Nearer My God To Thee' floated across the silent night; and as the boat deck

finally sank from sight, survivors heard the Episcopalian hymn
'Autumn'.

On that frosty spring night, high up on the northern extremities of
the map, an era slowly and symbolically passed away. The massive
ship, nearly twice the height of the Great Pyramid, had taken years to
emerge into life but only hours to slip beneath the North Atlantic.
The electric lights were soon extinguished as the waters flooded over
them, and the pitiful complement of lifeboats, lit only by moonlight,
were left bobbing, uncertain and alone, on the vast, silent, empty
ocean.

During 1995 the Royal Naval College at Greenwich hosted an
exhibition about Dr Robert Ballard's expedition which had discovered the wreck of the *Titanic* in 1985. Among the artefacts which had
haemorrhaged from the ship there were surprisingly few mono-
grammed 'Titanic'. Tableware and cutlery – expected to serve for
any of the company's vessels – were stamped simply with the more
prosaic 'White Star'. But the knowledge that these items had been
salvaged from the seabed, having lain four miles below the waves,
undisturbed for more than eighty years, set off a shiver from across
the decades.

The *Titanic*'s bell had survived and been found, the one which
Frederick Fleet had rung from his crow's-nest on that doomed night.
And there it was, safe now in its glass case, brought up from the
depths, shined and secure for all eternity. Even at the end of a century
grown old and weary with larger and more inconceivable tragedies,
the impact of the *Titanic*'s loss still resonates.

There remains something quaintly romantic and chillingly sym-
bolic about the loss of the *Titanic*. No disaster was ever better
equipped to sail into myth than that ship's demise, and it haunts
us still. I think of it again each time I think of my late uncle, James
Wallace Lusk. My mother's older brother, Uncle Jim was a doctor,
and when she was very ill he sat and wrote a memoir of their lives
together. Jim and Hester grew up, along with their brother Ian and
sisters Peggy and Madeline, the children of John Brown Lusk, a
minister of the Glascar Presbyterian Church for forty years when he
died in 1939.

Among the memoir's closely typed pages are photographs of the
faces my mother and uncle had known as children. They are
unmistakably from another time, faces with more in common with
the distant, dusty world of the young Queen, Victoria, and of

Tennyson, than the era of Edward VII and Rupert Brooke into which my mother and uncle were born. I remember my Aunt Madeline talking, before she too was taken, of an abiding memory she shared with her brother Jim; and sure enough, there it was in his memoir:

'The Titanic had been launched from Harland & Wolff's yard in Belfast . . . Aunt Isabel was housekeeper to Lord Pirrie, the chairman of the firm, and got us tickets for the launch and I saw the great Titanic slide into Belfast Lough dragging huge piles of enormous chains to slow her entry into the water. I also remember seeing Lady Pirrie clad in long silken robes and an enormous feather boa, cleaving her way through the crowds like one of her husband's liners.'

So there he was, my Uncle Jim, on the day the *Titanic* inched into the water. Half a lifetime later, and far from Belfast Lough, Uncle Jim was to touch on my life again. For James Wallace Lusk was the doctor who delivered Nick Drake into the world . . .

The only conversation I can remember having with Uncle Jim about music concerned his high opinion of Val Doonican's talents as a singer. Music – rock 'n' roll music – wasn't something that you talked to your uncle about. And though his music is soft and gentle, acoustic and folk-oriented, Nick Drake is rock 'n' roll. That is something my uncle might have had a problem with. His was a life formed by a childhood in rural Ireland during the adolescent years of this century, far removed from the neon chaos of London and the music industry.

On returning from Burma after the war, Uncle Jim became a GP in Weymouth in Dorset, and spent much of his spare time fashioning a book – *A Fresh Look At The Brontës And Their Ancestors In Ireland*. Brontë biographer Phyllis Bentley described the fiction of the sisters as 'a Yorkshire tune played on an Irish harp'. But it was a book by Dr William Wright, *The Brontës In Ireland*, published in 1893, which first revealed the extent to which the Irish ancestry of the novelists played a role in the creation of their fiction.

Delving further into the Brontë background in Northern Ireland, Uncle Jim unearthed strange patterns of behaviour in the Brontë family over three generations. These discoveries, and his comments as the doctor who knew Nick Drake as a small boy, may perhaps have some bearing on Nick's short, sad life: 'The causes of mental disturbances are usually multiple,' wrote my uncle, 'and in addition, the patient reacts to his own disturbance in his own way. One also may think of the patient suffering from society, and society may suffer from the patient.'

Journeys into the mind are now commonplace, but at the time Uncle Jim began his medical studies Freud had yet to enter the mainstream. His world, and that of Nick's father, Rodney Drake, sprang from a sense of tradition and moral certainty: a belief in the right of Empire and the duty of the British to serve that Empire. For men born as the twentieth century turned, there was little doubt and few questions.

In a letter written a few years before he died, my uncle asked me if I knew the work of a singer called Nicholas Drake; remembering the conversation about Val Doonican, I was relieved that I didn't. But he wrote again about this singer when a record called *Fruit Tree* was released, and it was then that the connection was made. A connection between a man born into the strict sepia world of an Edwardian manse and a lost child of more uncertain times.

Thanks to my uncle, James Wallace Lusk, there is a long unbroken link from the launching of the *Titanic* to the life of Nick Drake – a life begun in a Burmese hospital and ended in a quiet Warwickshire village.

The gravestone lies beneath an oak tree, just off the path which leads from the church to a gate into the open fields surrounding the village of Tanworth-in-Arden. The churchyard overlooks a curl of hill, the clipped fields sweeping into woods beyond. The horizon is topped by trees, and then dips down towards Danzey Green and Pig Trot Lane. The canvas-coloured headstone is weathered and worn, the inscription faded and, after little more than twenty years, surprisingly hard to read. But edging close and squinting, you can discern the epitaph: 'Nick Drake, 1948–1974. Remembered with love.'

The passing years have seen Nick joined by his father Rodney (1908–1988) and his mother Molly (1915–1993). To the casual visitor, the Drakes' grave is simply another family plot, bordered by those of the Winwood family, of Mary Kathleen Whitehouse, the Tibbles family and Edward Rogers. There is something strangely comforting and consoling about a stroll around an ancient English country churchyard in the sunshine. There is some of Philip Larkin's 'awkward reverence', but there is also history in every square foot of turf.

On a sunny day in mid-October, the graveyard of Tanworth-in-Arden's parish church is silent and undisturbed. The only sound is that of the wind, lightly whispering through the leaves of the oak, tinged with autumn brown, which are slowly falling to carpet the graves. St Mary Magdalene is no bad place to end your days. Little disturbs the calm of the village. No car alarms shatter the serenity. And from inside the church the sound of Bach floats across the quiet churchyard; eternal music cascading gently into the silence.

Just above the organ's keyboard is a plaque which reads: 'The sesquialtera stop was given in memory of Nicholas Drake and his music by his family in 1977.' Chris Langman, who was playing the organ that day, interrupted his Bach to demonstrate the stop. 'It's not the most obvious choice,' he said as the empty church echoed to the high, keening sound. It was an eerie, solitary, ricocheting note. A lonely sound.

Outside, in the fresh autumn air, lie buried hundreds of souls, many whose whole lives were bordered by the boundaries of this tiny Warwickshire village. St Mary Magdalene has provided the final resting-place for many since it was built in 1330, and Nick Drake's is not the only famous name: the motor-racing champion Mike Hailwood is also remembered here. The graves are kindly tended; the grass, trim and neatly cut, does not intrude upon the solemnity of death. The leaves are raked, to leave the headstones clear and visible.

The cult of death snakes around rock 'n' roll like bindweed in the garland of a May Queen. But the grave of Nick Drake is not the graffiti-scabbed resting-place of Jim Morrison. The flowers around the headstone did not grow here; they are freshly cut, brought by someone who loves his music and was touched by his life. This is the grave of an only son, a lost boy, laid to rest in the village where he grew up: the only home he really knew.

Tanworth-in-Arden is picture-postcard pretty, a cameo of Middle England. The church's guidebook speaks regretfully of 'unfortunate alterations' in 1790. There is a war memorial and a general store, an off-licence and a garage, a church school and a pub. Inside the Bell, people drawn by the music of Nick Drake often sit over a pint or a coffee, reflecting on what they have seen in the churchyard. But here in the pub another erstwhile Tanworth resident is the focal point: a notice informs the casual visitor that Jack London, British and European Welterweight Champion, 1926–1935, was the landlord from September 1939 to December 1972.

It was from Tanworth that Nick Drake set out on his short voyage into the outside world, and to Tanworth that he returned to die. It was only when my wife pointed it out that I saw the barely legible inscription, curiously located, almost hidden, on the back of Nick's headstone: 'Now we rise and we are everywhere.' The words have a

Biblical ring, a familiar scriptural feel, and it was only later that I realized they came from Nick's 'From The Morning' – the final song on the last album released in his lifetime.

Standing by his grave that autumn day, it struck me how short a distance Nick had actually travelled. But what a journey he had made. Largely ignored in his lifetime, with combined record sales barely reaching 20,000 copies, after his death Nick Drake has become the focus of a fascination which shows no sign of abating. And yet the mystery still remains: just what is it about this shy, introverted singer-songwriter, who made only three albums, that still draws people to his work?

Why, when they have their own idols and eloquent spokesmen, are the children of Nirvana and Oasis drawn afresh to Nick Drake? To begin to understand that, you have to go back to another place and another time. From the leafy tranquillity of the Warwickshire countryside to the steamy Far East. To the far reaches of the British Empire, to a city perched on the edge of Burma, close to the Indian Ocean, where Nick Drake was born half a century ago.

BOOK I:
BEFORE

1

Teak first drew the British to Burma. A heavy, durable timber, it was much favoured in the building of ships at a time when the British needed more and more vessels to service their expanding Empire. Even when the wooden hulks gave way to steel dreadnoughts, Burma still had plenty to offer far-away Britain, not least the fruit of its rubber trees. Rich in teak forests, and with rubber plantations stretching to the far horizon, Burma enriched the Empire.

In 1824 a Burmese invasion of Bengal had led to fears of further incursions into British-ruled India, but the two nations managed to maintain their uneasy alliance for another sixty years until, in 1885, Burma's King Thibaw decided to confiscate the assets of the Bombay Burmah Trading Corporation (BBTC), the leading Anglo-Burmese firm which would later employ Nick Drake's father, Rodney. This sequestration led to a full-scale invasion by 10,000 British and Indian troops, and by 1886 Burma had become a fully integrated part of the British Empire.

Long before Nick Drake was born there, and long before his father worked in the country, Burma was already the subject of fiercely divided opinion. Rudyard Kipling had written of his love of Burma in the poem 'Mandalay'. George Orwell hated the place with a vengeance, having spent 'five boring years' there between 1922 and 1927, as an officer in the Imperial Police. Burma may have disgusted Eric Blair, as Orwell was then known, but it inspired some of his best writing, notably the short stories 'A Hanging' and 'Shooting An Elephant'. In 1934 his first novel, *Burmese Days*, though enthusiastic about the country and its landscape ('It was a good life while one was young and need not think about the future or the past'), displayed real venom towards the petty snobbery and pinched racism of the expatriate British Empire-builders.

For the British inhabitants of Burma during the 1920s and 1930s it was a good life. Servants kept the mundane at bay during the day, while the evenings were spent socializing and fulminating against progress and native independence with those of a like mind. There was a prosperity in Rangoon and other capital cities of the British Empire which kept the expats buoyant. Back at home you might have been born to trade and struggling for acceptance, but in Burma you were unquestionably part of the ruling class. It could be an idyllic and undemanding life, with no reason to change. The Empire had survived a mutiny in India in 1857 and no other nation had since had the temerity to challenge decisions made in Whitehall on its behalf.

If you came from the top drawer, the product of a public school, the far-flung reaches of the Empire were a good place to finish your education, in the teak or rubber trade, or the Army. Clive and Livingstone, Rhodes and Wellington – these were the gods of Empire, in whose shadow you walked.

By 1937, though, another sun rising further to the East was beginning to cast shadows. Long-time British residents in the Far East had never paid much attention to the threat of Japan, dismissing the barbarities meted out by its army to the Chinese since 1931 as like against like. The British Empire surely had no reason to fear the tiny, rather jaundiced-looking troops of the Emperor Hirohito. Here was racism they would live to regret.

Just before eight o'clock on the morning of 7 December 1941, two years and three months after Hitler unleashed the Nazi blitzkrieg on Europe without warning or declaration of war, Japanese dive-bombers zeroed in on the American fleet at Pearl Harbor. Within half an hour over two thousand Americans lay dead or dying, and the European conflict had exploded into a global war. Just three months later the Japanese had subjugated the Far East, and the Empire of the Sun had spread its tentacles from the tip of the Soviet Union all the way to Australia, thousands of miles across the Pacific.

Before Pearl Harbor, Burma had been seen as a safe outpost of the British Empire, the likelihood of war reaching its inhabitants remote. Even as Nazi tanks trampled across Poland, Belgium, the Netherlands and France in the spring of 1940, the residents of Rangoon were untroubled by the war which raged half a world away from them. Others scoffed at such lassitude, and a rhyme, popular in the officers' messes of the Far East, ran:

'Where was I when the war was on?'
  I can hear a faint voice murmur,
'Where was I when the war was on?
  In the safest place, in Burma.'

Within three days of Pearl Harbor, the British territories of Singapore and Hong Kong had been bombed, and Japanese troops had landed in Malaya. By 12 December the war was inching towards Burma, and Victoria Point, the Burmese town nearest to the Thai border, was evacuated. Rangoon itself was bombed during the following December, and as the Japanese swept along the Malay Peninsula, Burma's rich rubber and teak plantations offered a succulent prospect.

As Singapore – 'the Gibraltar of the East' – fell in February 1942, the full extent of Japanese barbarities became apparent. On capture, prisoners were bayoneted or beheaded. Survivors were treated contemptuously by their Japanese captors, who believed they had sacrificed all honour by allowing themselves to be taken alive. A living hell followed, in the steaming jungles of the Malay Peninsula, where the Japanese built their prison camps.

As the Japanese swept on, bombing Australia, taking Java and the Dutch East Indies, they seemed unstoppable. Early in March 1942 Japanese troops entered Pegu, forty miles from Rangoon, and within days General Alexander ordered the evacuation of the city. Burma fell soon afterwards.

By July the country was occupied by the Japanese, who sought to build a railway connecting their forces in Burma with those in Thailand. For over a year 46,000 Allied prisoners of war laboured on the line which became known as 'The Railway of Death'. By the time the last sleeper was laid, 16,000 POWs and 50,000 Burmese labourers had died of starvation, brutality and disease. It was said that every sleeper laid along the 258 miles of track had cost one prisoner his life.

As the Japanese thrust deeper into Burma during the spring of 1942, my Uncle Jim led a group of British subjects and loyal Burmese out, by car, train, raft and on foot. He was doctor and leader to the straggling column for two months as they made their escape, sometimes only hours ahead of the advancing Japanese. In his journal he wrote of professors and bankers, planters and policemen, all fleeing. As the detritus of the European community in Burma lay all about them, they knew they were witnessing the end of something and that, inconceivable as it had seemed a few months before, this Empire too might fall.

Rodney Shuttleworth Drake was born at his parents' home in Redhill, Surrey, on 5 May 1908. The Drakes were a medical family and his father, Ernest Charles, was a surgeon who had trained at St Bartholomew's Hospital in London. At the age of fourteen, Rodney followed family tradition by going to Marlborough College, but he left the school just a few months after his seventeenth birthday. He trained as an engineer and later took the long voyage out to Burma, to work for a British firm dealing principally in teak.

Rodney fitted in well in both Burma and the company, and his name occurs frequently in A.C. Pointon's official history of the Bombay Burmah Trading Corporation. It was in Rangoon that he met Mary Lloyd, known as Molly. On 14 April 1937 – a quarter of a century to the day since the *Titanic* had sunk – they were married in the cathedral in Rangoon. Molly was twenty-one years old, Rodney almost twenty-nine.

During early 1942, caught up in the chaos as the Japanese armies cut a swathe across Burma, Rodney and Molly Drake, along with others employed in Burma, were evacuated to BBTC's headquarters in India. By the end of the year Rodney had taken over sawmills at Poona and Jhelum.

Nick's older sister, Gabrielle, was born in Lahore, while the Drakes were stationed in India. One of her earliest memories is of living in an inventive house built by her father. Rodney had been sent a sawmill from America, and in addition to erecting this he used the enormous packing cases to construct a home for the family.

Within three years Rodney was back in Burma. He returned to Rangoon just weeks after its liberation in May 1945, to inspect what remained of the milling capacity after the long years of Japanese occupation. BBTC officially resumed trading on 1 January 1946, with the intention of returning the company to its pre-war eminence. But things had changed in Burma.

Despite initial cooperation with the Japanese, whom they saw as a means of overthrowing British imperialism, the Burmese nationalist movement had eventually fought alongside the Allies against the

Japanese. But with the war over, and buoyed by the granting of independence to India in 1946, the nationalists once again took up arms against British imperialism. With weapons supplied by the British to fight the Japanese, the Burmese began their fight for freedom. Soon struggles within the movement led to a civil war in Burma, with fighting between nationalist guerrillas and communists continuing until Burma was granted full independence, on 4 January 1948, some five months before Nick was born.

Like other British companies, BBTC was concerned about the effect Burma's independence would have on trade. It fell to Rodney Drake to formulate a plan, and early in 1949 he put a proposal before the Burmese Government to terminate BBTC's responsibilities in exchange for 'a form of payment for all it would surrender'.

Walter Snadden worked alongside Rodney in Rangoon in 1948, and nearly half a century later he still remembered Nick's father fondly as 'one of the old school'. Rodney, he said, was 'an Englishman of the past, of the colonial past, and well respected'.

On 19 June 1948, while the eyes of the rest of the world were on the divided city of Berlin, where an Allied airlift was bringing supplies to the starving population, my late uncle, Dr J.W. Lusk OBE, MD, ChB, the Drakes' family doctor in Burma, delivered Nicholas Rodney Drake, at the Dufferin Hospital in Rangoon.

Nick's birthplace was the one exotic and faintly exceptional thing about him. A scion of the English upper middle classes, the Drake's second child was born where his parents' business had taken them. Those who dealt in Empire business, whether in commerce or on active service, were well used to a life of dislocation.

Rodney continued to work in Rangoon, supervising the gradual hand-over of mills to the Burmese Government. In 1949 he travelled to Borneo to negotiate with the North Borneo Trading Company over the possibility of expanding BBTC's operations into their territory. The Drakes left Rangoon in 1950, when Rodney was made Company Manager in Bombay, but by 1951 he had decided that it was time to take his wife and children back to England.

The following year he joined the Wolseley Engineering Company, in Birmingham, installing his family in a small village half an hour's drive from the city. The company Rodney joined, and of which he became Managing Director in 1953, manufactured cars. In later years he would remember that in 1900 his own father had bought a car from the pioneering Herbert Austin – then of the Wolseley Sheep

Shearing Machine Company – and driven it all the way back to
Redhill: 'quite a feat in those days'.

Coming back from the bright sunshine of Burma to the grey
austerity of Britain in the immediate postwar years must have been
a shock. During the war Britain's cities had been pummelled by Nazi
bombs and rockets while it stood alone against Hitler's aggression,
and by 1950 the nation was counting the cost. Determined that
returning troops would not suffer the humiliation which had greeted
returning survivors of the Great War, the new Labour government
embarked on a massive wave of public spending. Money was poured
into houses, schools and hospitals. In the chill winters of the Attlee
government, the Welfare State was painstakingly constructed, brick
by brick, from the bomb craters and blitzed buildings of a Britain
which had won the war but was already in danger of losing the peace.

It is questionable how much of this change impinged upon life at
Far Leys, the large comfortable house in the Warwickshire village of
Tanworth-in-Arden, where the Drake family settled on their return
from Burma. What we do know is that this beautiful little village
would remain home to the Drake family for as long as Rodney, Molly
and Nick lived.

2

Sitting sleepily amid the green, rolling Warwickshire hills, Tanworth-in-Arden is a rural idyll which the twentieth century seems to have passed by. Visiting Tanworth in the sunshine, as traffic thunders along the M42 in the distance, far away enough not impinge on the calm, you half expect to see Miss Marple hastening to investigate a murder at the vicarage, or Mrs Miniver preparing another batch of jam for the church Bring & Buy.

The centre of Tanworth is a tiny village green, in the middle of which stands the parish War Memorial. The green is bordered on one side by the Bell Inn, and on the other by the parish church of St Mary Magdalene. Even the present incumbent, Canon Martin Tunnicliffe, is baffled as to why a small village like Tanworth should merit such a disproportionately large place of worship. A new school now stands next to the church, the cottages by the Green are perhaps more conspicuously gentrified, and the village garage boasts names other than that of nearby Rover; but otherwise little in the village appears to have changed in the forty-five years since Rodney Drake brought his family back from Burma to settle in this tranquil corner of England.

Barely a dozen miles away is Stratford-upon-Avon, the birthplace of William Shakespeare. Shakespeare too left to find his fortune in London, but returned to end his days in the Warwickshire village of his childhood. Nowadays the contrast between Stratford and Tanworth could not be greater. Stratford is virtually a Shakespeare Theme Park, stuffed with Bardic mementoes, tea rooms and Ye

Olde Antique Shoppes. Tanworth remains undiscovered, its few pilgrims drawn by the music of Nick Drake.

Just a handful of miles north of Tanworth begins the scabrous urban sprawl of Birmingham. The coal-black industrial heart of Britain is the nation's second city, but lacks London's charm and glamour. Motorways circle the city, turning it into a concrete compound, caught in the Spaghetti Junction of spiralling concrete loops which carry traffic past the city. Aptly enough, given the city's engineering tradition, this was the first place in Britain where the car took priority over human beings. It was to here that Rodney Drake travelled to work each day.

Far Leys, the beautiful brick-built house in Tanworth where the Drakes settled in 1952, was bought from a Mr Stanton, a BBC director of music, who had purchased the property during the 1940s. The house stands back slightly from the road, on a lane on the outskirts of the village. Although large, it had the friendly feel of an extremely comfortable, rambling, family home, rather than an air of great elegance. At the front a wooden gate with the house name painted on it, stood open, while at the back french windows opened on to a small terrace and then the garden: a huge expanse of lawn surrounded by shrubs and trees which merged into the countryside beyond.

One hint of exoticism which the Drake family imported to Tanworth was their Burmese maid, who came to Britain with the family to act as nanny to Nick and Gabrielle. Otherwise, Far Leys was a typically English household, decorated and furnished by the Drakes in the traditional way. The house was cosy and homely, not ostentatious or particularly stylish; pieces of furniture collected during their life together were kept for their familiarity and comfort. It would remain their family home for forty years.

Gabrielle has nothing but happy memories of growing up in leafy Tanworth. The Drakes were a close family, and from their parents both children inherited a love of music of all sorts. Molly Drake played the piano and sang, and once composed a whole suite of children's songs for Nick and Gabrielle. During the 1930s, when suave sophisticates such as Noël Coward and Ivor Novello, Al Bowlly and Jack Hylton, were giving the American crooners a run for their money, Molly had even turned her hand to a little amateur songwriting. It is generally accepted that Nick inherited his musical gifts from his mother, but Gabrielle remembers that Rodney also composed, once writing an entire comic operetta about an Englishman who was based out East.

In 1985 Gabrielle, by this time an actress, told *TV Times*, 'It was an idyllic childhood,' adding: 'It was exciting living abroad, but the really wonderful thing was coming back to England – seeing snow for the first time and being able to drink water straight from the tap. I remember thinking that was extraordinary.'

When, that same year, the American writer T.J. McGrath interviewed Rodney and Molly Drake at Far Leys, he asked them about Nick's childhood. 'Well,' said Rodney, 'he was always very fond of listening to music.' The voice is bright and well-enunciated, a voice of authority, upper-middle-class, worn and shiny like a much-used cricket bat. The pride in his only son's achievements shines through.

'As a baby he was always conducting,' added Molly, 'whenever the music started. He always said he was going to be a famous conductor.' Rodney remembered Nick being frightened as a child by a piece by Sibelius, *The Swan Of Tuonela*. Written in 1895, the tone poem had its origins in the Finnish epic which tells of the young hero Lemminkäinen, who journeys to the North Country in search of a wife and dies in the attempt, but is brought back to life by the magical powers of his mother. Sibelius used a solitary cor anglais to represent the swan, which glides on the black waters that surround Tuonela, the land of the dead.

'He was very fond of classical music. He listened to a lot . . .' Rodney continued sadly. 'I don't know about the early days, but going right to the very end, the night before he died, he was listening to one of Bach's Brandenburg Concertos.'

When I asked Gabrielle Drake about growing up with Nick, she spoke of the sheer joy of their childhood together at Tanworth: 'We came to live in England when Nick was about four and I was eight . . . My dad was offered a job in Birmingham, and if you served out in the Far East, you had to retire earlier, so he knew he was looking for somewhere to settle over here. We were a very close-knit family, a very happy family. I had a most wonderful childhood . . . Nick and I were sort of opposites, we never had rivalry. I always used to think that Nick was a great deal more talented than I was. I was devoted to him. As we grew up, I became terribly proud of him.'

Once settled in Tanworth, Nick and Gabrielle grew up, safe and prosperous, insulated and content, in the calmly Conservative Britain of the 1950s. Gabrielle remembers Nick composing songs even at this very early age: 'When he was three or four, two of his great passions were cowboys and food. I can remember two songs he wrote then, one was a song about a cowboy in a book, called "Cowboy Small": "Oh Cowboy Small, Oh Cowboy Small/All the other cowboys, call Cowboy Small". The other song was about celery and tomatoes.'

Prime Minister Harold Macmillan took the opportunity of a booming economy to remind the nation that they had 'never had it so good'. Consumer durables were the tangible proof, and cars, television sets and record players were beginning to be visible across the strata of British society. Further highly visible evidence of the boom came with the advent of commercial television in 1955. Besides breaking the BBC's stranglehold, ITV offered the public the opportunity to view, in their own home, advertisements telling them just what was available out there to buy. Many feared it was the end of civilization as they knew it. But for the Conservatives, such manifest prosperity ensured an uninterrupted span of government lasting from 1951 until 1964.

The Empire which Rodney Drake and myriad other loyal servants had so diligently served was withering. The demands for independence which followed the end of the war had persisted long into the 1950s, and Macmillan was enough of a realist to discern the 'wind of change' sweeping through the African continent. The final flourish of Imperial dignity, and the stagnant end of Empire came in 1956, when Nick was eight. A joint Anglo-French invasion set out to destabilize Egypt's President Nasser, following his nationalization of the Suez Canal. It ended in a humiliating defeat.

The Suez débâcle occurred the same year that John Osborne's *Look Back In Anger* opened in London. Railing against the values around which men like Rodney Drake had built their whole lives, the play was a clarion call to disaffected 'Angry Young Men', and the effect was seismic. Nineteen fifty-six also marked the first British sighting of an alien from a planet called Tupelo, Mississippi. It was the year the writing was first sprayed on the wall, the year the English middle classes were all shook up by the two-pronged attack of John Osborne and Elvis Presley.

Little of this sneering, urban rebelliousness percolated to secluded Tanworth-in-Arden. Asked about Nick's youthful musical influences, Gabrielle grimaced: 'Well, we are talking about our childhoods, and of course it sounds ridiculous now, but someone like Russ Conway was a great favourite of Nick's, because Nick used to play the piano a lot as a little boy. We both had piano lessons.'

Rock 'n' roll was barely tolerated by the BBC. The Drake family listened in to an old-fashioned radio which eventually wound up in Nick's bedroom, and the music which issued forth was safe and unthreatening: Pearl Carr & Teddy Johnson, Frankie Vaughan, Russ Conway, Ruby Murray . . . For Nick and Gabrielle, Saturday morning was a favourite time to cluster round the radio, for *Uncle Mac's Children's Favourites* on the Light Programme. For two hours, songs like 'Champion The Wonder Horse', 'Robin Hood', 'Nellie The Elephant', 'A Windmill In Old Amsterdam' and 'Sparky's Magic Piano' kept the nation's infants mesmerized. It was all very consoling, seated safely at the knee of Auntie BBC.

British cinema in the 1950s was no less cosy. Thousands of schoolboys like Nick Drake grew up with a fiercely nationalist film industry. Incapable of dealing with the painful legacy of a lost Empire, it dwelt instead on the celebration of a war well won. Films like *The Dam Busters*, *Reach For The Sky*, *The Wooden Horse*, *The Cruel Sea* and *The Colditz Story*, seemed so much more reassuring than the ugly questions posed by Teddy Boys, Elvis Presley and the botched imperialism of Suez.

Well into the seventies the final cinema performance of the night would conclude with the audience standing, more or less to attention, for the National Anthem; but by then the comforting, flickering, black-and-white images of steaming mugs of cocoa and duffle-coats were already period pieces. Gritty Northern realism had subverted the mainstream: the male icons of the mid-sixties were Albert Finney and Tom Courtenay, not Richard Todd and Kenneth More. The new role models questioned and challenged the status quo, rather than epitomizing established values.

Rock 'n' roll also created ripples in Britain during the late fifties, but the stone had been dropped a very long way away and the ripples were still very faint. Few authentic rock 'n' rollers appeared in Britain during that decade – Buddy Holly and Eddie Cochran were the best-remembered. Jerry Lee Lewis's tour was cut short after it was revealed that he had married his thirteen-year-old cousin, and Elvis never made it beyond Prestwick Airport in Scotland, where his plane touched down to refuel while taking him home from military service in Germany.

The soundtrack of *South Pacific* remained at the top of the UK LP charts from their inauguration in 1958 until March 1960; another popular long-player featured numbers from George Mitchell's *Black & White Minstrel Show*. For all the hip, café-society image of the nineties' Easy Listening revival, the real sugary root of that ghastly phenomenon lay in the singalong pulp which constituted the pre-Beatles, musical dark ages.

Home-grown rock 'n' roll – on television and in the still thriving
variety halls – was essentially a novelty act, a bill-filler put on to
placate teenagers between juggling and comedy acts. For all the
inroads made by Cliff Richard & The Shadows, Johnny Kidd &
The Pirates, Joe Brown, Billy Fury and producer Joe Meek, 'all-round
entertainment' was still the name of the game in Britain as the fifties
lapped, like a slow tide on a pebble peach.

In the spring of 1957, at the age of eight, Nick was sent away to prep
school at Sandhurst in Berkshire. Until then he had lived at home and
attended local primary schools, but for the next five years, holidays
apart, Eagle House School would be home. He did well at the school,
becoming a prefect, and eventually, in his final term, Head Boy.
Already Nick was proving to be an 'outstanding' athlete, and gained
his colours as a 'fine wing three-quarter' for the rugby XV. He was in
the school choir, and at thirteen, even appeared in the school play,
playing 'Jack Pincher, a detective' in the old favourite *The Crimson
Coconut* by Ian Hay.

Twenty-six years after Nick left Eagle House, his former headmaster, Paul Wootton, wrote that he remembered Nick 'for his fine
voice as a leading member of the Chapel choir'. Mr Wootton also
mentioned 'another master . . . who just may have had some
influence on the career in music of Nicholas Drake. This French
teacher earned fame, particularly among the boys, for having come
second in the Eurovision Song Contest with his song "Looking High,
High, High".'

Rodney Drake remembered a school report from Eagle House,
which he found not long after Nick died: 'He was a very strong
character at school, they always said in the reports we got . . . His
first school, he left it when he was just under fourteen, and he was
Head of that school, and they said he was a very strong character. In
the report, which I've still got, the Headmaster said: "Nobody knows
him very well." '

At the end of the Christmas term of 1961 Nick Drake left Eagle House
for the last time. After the Christmas holidays he would follow in the
footsteps of his father and grandfather and travel the sixty or so miles
from Tanworth down to Wiltshire, to study at Marlborough College.
As much a product of his heredity as of his times, Nick thought it only
natural to attend a fee-paying public school.

The Duke of Wellington was disingenuous when he claimed that 'the battle of Waterloo was won on the playing fields of Eton'. Like all subsequent military victories, it was won in the slum lean-tos and back-to-back squalor of British cities; in the hamlets and shires of rural England. The officers who blithely but bravely led their troops over the top may well have learned their pluck at Eton (or Marlborough, Harrow, Rugby or Dulwich), but the 'poor bloody infantry' certainly didn't.

The public-school ethos, based almost entirely on a belief in 'playing the game', drew its strength from tradition and continuity. And so it was always understood that N.R. Drake would follow his father and grandfather to Marlborough. It may seem incongruous that someone as enshrined in rock legend as Nick Drake should have had such an establishment upbringing, but quite simply, that is what he was born to. Ironically, Paul Weller, a recent convert to Nick's work, chose to attack the institution which bred Nick in 'Eton Rifles': 'What chance have you got against a tie and a crest,' he snarled on The Jam's 1979 hit.

It was in January 1962 that Nicholas Rodney Drake entered Marlborough College, which would be his home until July 1966. Having heard so much about the isolation and introspection which blighted his later years, I was more than a little surprised, when talking to his friends and contemporaries from Marlborough, that their abiding memories of Nick Drake were, without exception, of a shy but happy and convivial friend.

'My memories are that he was tall, very gentle, a guy who smiled a lot; a guy who seemed to be enjoying himself.' (Simon Crocker)

'Nick was reserved. Quiet . . . Thinking back, how you remember people, when I remember Nick, I remember him with a great big smile on his face.' (David Wright)

'I remember Nick very clearly. He was a popular guy, quiet and understated. We were in C1 House together. He had flashes of being very, very funny, clever and charming. Not a swanker. A very respected guy.' (F.A.R. Packard)

Michael Maclaran, another friend of Nick's from Marlborough, gave perhaps the most vivid first-hand impression of his teenage friend: 'Nick was tall and stooped forward, holding his head quite low in his shoulders, as if there was always a cold wind blowing. He had a friendly smiling face and a Beatle haircut . . . He was always pushing the school clothing and appearance regulations to the limit, with raised seams on his grey flannels, trouser bottoms that were too tight or too flared, did or didn't have turn-ups and so on. However, he didn't do this in an extrovert way, and got away with more than some "rebel" types, to the quiet admiration of his peers.'

Nick's housemaster at Marlborough was D.R.W. Silk. Although he went on to become Warden of Radley College and President of the MCC, like James Hilton's immortal Mr Chips, Dennis Silk still has clear and fond memories of the hundreds of Marlburians who passed through C1 House. Thirty years after last seeing him, his face lit up at the mention of the teenage Nick Drake: 'My abiding memory is the degree to which everybody liked Nick. One can honestly say that he had not an enemy in the place. I suspect he had one face for the staff, and another for his chums, who found him very amusing. It was not what you would call a sparkling sense of humour, but a rather dry, ironic sense of humour.

'He was reasonably industrious, but his heart was not really in anything academic except English. A very dreamy pupil. Very. "Wake up, Drake." "Oh sorry, sir." Always very polite . . . But deep down, there was something we never got near to. And there was a whole way of life there that I can't claim . . . to have penetrated, although we always got on well.'

Marlborough College was founded in 1843 for the purpose of educating impoverished clergymen's sons. The school was housed in a Queen Anne-style mansion which, according to Marlborough archivist Dr T.E. Rogers, had been 'an aristocratic home until about 1751, when it became a very fashionable coaching inn on the London to Bath route. The coaching inn went bankrupt when the railways killed off the coach trade.'

The portents for Marlborough were ominous. Some of the school's early buildings were designed by the architect who went on to build Wormwood Scrubs prison. Like many of its predecessors, and successors, Marlborough was founded on a system which bordered on the brutal. Flogging and birching were commonplace, conditions spartan and ascetic; it was all part of the high-Victorian belief that mortification of the flesh helped enlighten the soul and elevate the moral spirit.

Hopes of a benign beginning for the school were almost immediately dashed by 'The Great Marlborough Rebellion' of 1851. In his definitive history *The Public School Phenomenon* Jonathan Gathorne-Hardy wrote: 'By 1851, Marlborough was like France in 1789 . . . Years of savage, unjust, but also inefficient tyranny were about to be overthrown.' Over a period of five days Marlborough pupils rebelled against the vicious regime of near-starvation and brutality. It was the most violent upset in the history of Britain's public-school system. Order was eventually restored, but as Dr Rogers noted, there were 'very Spartan conditions right up until 1975'.

Eminent Marlburians who preceded Nick at the school include the craftsman, poet and political activist William Morris; poets Siegfried Sassoon, Charles Sorley, Louis MacNeice and John Betjeman; Conservative politicians R.A. ('Rab') Butler and Henry Brooke; round-the-world yachtsman Sir Francis Chichester; and the travel writer Bruce Chatwin. During the 1920s the school was attended by one Anthony Blunt, later curator of the Queen's pictures, and later still the most infamous British spy since Kim Philby.

Betjeman loathed his days at Marlborough; the old dining room, he later recalled, always smelt of Irish stew. The school spanned the main road through Marlborough, and the road was straddled by a bridge known to pupils as 'The Bridge of Sighs', as it took them from the boarding houses into their classes.

During Nick's time the school's population was 800, all boys, all boarders, all away from home. Dennis Silk recalled the routine: 'Classes until lunchtime, classes after lunch on Monday, Wednesday, Friday. Half holidays on Tuesday, Thursday, Saturday, and after lunch on half days, games. So it was work, work, games, prep, house prayers, more prep, bed. We bored them silly.'

It was while at Marlborough that Nick really began to blossom and bloom. Here he was exposed to friendships and influences which would endure. Nick was one of a freewheeling group of pupils who shared a love of rock 'n' roll, smoking cigarettes and draught beer. There was a mutual antipathy to school regulations, lessons and homework. David Wright remembers listening with Nick to the Cassius Clay–Henry Cooper bout of 1963, on a transistor radio on top of the Mound, one of the many medieval sites which circle Marlborough.

Set amid the rolling Downs in the lush and still rural county of Wiltshire, Marlborough was another idyllic backwater. With a population of barely over 6000 in Nick's day, the town was quiet and untroubled. But by the middle of the 1960s, and to the delight of its schoolboy inhabitants, a mere three hours away, down in London, things were beginning to get seriously swinging.

At the school itself, Dennis Silk recalls, 'We used to have a House Dance with a local girls' school, the usual sort of cattle market, and I can remember one such occasion. It went like a dream. It was about 1964, when the House was still biddable, and we were still in charge. We had this dance, and ensured that no girls were hurt by being left on the side, and programmed dances, and every boy had to dance with every other girl at some stage of the evening. I can remember . . . lovely quiet music, "Sleepy Lagoon" and things like that, and my wife giving them dancing classes before.

'A year later, the dispensation had changed, and against my better judgement, allowed electronic music. No one could speak to anyone at all, the records were so loud . . . The whole atmosphere of the House had changed, and we were no longer in control, we were swept away by this amazing new liberating thing.'

The public-school ethos hardly lent itself to the dropped aitch rowdiness and two-fingered rebellion of rock 'n' roll. Public-school rock 'n' rollers are at best a footnote to any rock encyclopaedia: Genesis first convened in the hallowed halls of Charterhouse, the school which would later offer house room to World Party's Karl Wallinger. Harrow played host to Island's Chris Blackwell; Peter & Gordon and Shane MacGowan attended Westminster; Roxy Music's Phil Manzanera and This Heat's Charles Hayward studied at Dulwich College; Kula Shaker's Crispian Mills was at Stowe. But in general there wasn't much room for the hoity-toity in the hurly-burly of rock 'n' roll.

The Beatles had rewritten the rule book. Far from trying to hide their provincial origins, they revelled in them, and theirs were the first defiantly regional accents to be heard regularly on the upper-crust BBC airwaves. One of The Beatles' oddest gigs was at Stowe. At the height of Beatlemania in 1963, following a request from a pupil, the Fabs played to a sedate, seated audience of public schoolboys. But The Beatles soon came to embody the new classlessness of the sixties: suddenly it didn't matter where you were from – only what you did. Cockney photographers and pop stars became the new aristocrats.

Jeremy Mason was Nick's closest friend during his early days at Marlborough. The friendship was forged over cigarettes, and as the two teenagers puffed away on Disque Bleu in 'smoking holes' dotted around the college, the conversation invariably turned to the music they both liked: 'At that time, Nick played the saxophone and the clarinet. The alto sax I think it was . . . Which meant that a lot of the music we liked early on was definitely sax-based: One of the records we liked was called *Giant Steps* by John Coltrane . . . But I remember going to listen to a John Coltrane record with Nick at Liverpool

Street Station, which must have been on the way back to school. I
think it was called *Ascension*, which was one complete barrage of
sound, and we rather lost interest.'

Michael Maclaran also remembered music always being a priority
for Nick: 'We spent hours in common rooms and studies listening to
records (45s were 6/6d) and the Top 20 on Sunday afternoons.'

With no television in the House in Nick's time, and Film Society
shows limited to a couple each term, pop music was all-important.
Nick's housemaster, Dennis Silk, couldn't help but notice the intru-
sion of pop music in his house: 'It was as much as your life was worth
not to know what was in the Top 20. You lost face terribly.'

Cigarettes behind the bike sheds and listening to pop records were
crucial, but the public-school tradition of team sports was also an
integral part of Nick's life at Marlborough. David Wright recalls that
once on the sports field, Nick was an enthusiastic participant: 'One
thing Nick was very good at was running, he was very quick. While I
was playing cricket, which he wasn't remotely interested in, he was
on the athletics track. He was a very quick 100-yarder. And he used to
play rugby, on the wing, because he was quick.'

Cricket has became irrevocably associated with the English public
school, but the ponderous process of a cricket match held little allure
for Nick. He would sprint in track events or tear off alone on the wing
of the house rugby team, and on occasion he could even be found on
the hockey field; but, perhaps surprisingly, cricket never appealed to
him.

'In the summers we used to meet on the athletics track for training
and for competitions against other schools,' Michael Maclaran
recalled. 'No one liked to admit to having to train – it was assumed
that natural talent would get you through. But Nick had good
motivation and a competitive streak and achieved great success in
sprinting, with his long stride, high knee action and powerful build.

'Rugby was the main winter game, but I turned to hockey after
some rugby injuries and often played with Nick for Marlborough
Second XI. I think Nick played centre half, which was a key position,
and he could hit the ball hard and well. He may well have been
captain, because he had leadership qualities in a persuasive rather
than dictatorial way, as well as talent.'

Confounding the familiar image of Nick Drake as a withdrawn
and virtually catatonic individual, Michael Maclaran's recollection of
his 'good motivation' and 'competitive streak' paints the very
different picture of a vigorous, even ambitious teenager.

Nick's days at Marlborough were, by and large, happy ones. A bona fide rock 'n' roll rebel may have rejected the rowdy rugby field and striving for victory on the athletics track, but although he was shy and fairly quiet, Nick's instinctive sporting abilities enabled him to fit in quite happily. It was over short distances that Nick really excelled; not for him the sustained endurance of the marathon, rather the quick-burn glory of the sprint.

Dennis Silk: 'He was a very distinguished sprinter. He played on the wing, away from the hurly-burly. It meant very little to him that he was a super athlete. He could have done anything athletically. He was very well made, tall – very tall, as a teenager about six foot two – strong, very quick. When he caught the rugger ball, he could run round the opposition. Dreaming a bit, he sometimes dropped it . . . He played rugger, I suppose you would say, apologetically.

'Nick was a very poor cricketer, a joke cricketer. He found cricket rather amusing, but it would be six or out. He played in gym shoes rather than cricket boots. He was quite a good hockey player, and of course, Marlborough was the outstanding hockey school, and he played in the school team, as he did in the rugger side. But his real forte was sprinting. He was rather a stately sprinter. Very upright, not leaning at forty-five degrees . . . upright, and like a ship in full sail.'

As a member of C1 House, Nick was a member of the winning Senior team in the school's summer 1965 relay race. He also set a school record for the 100-yard dash which remained unbeaten for some years. The school magazine noted that: 'In the Open Team, N.R. Drake is developing into a very useful performer over 100 and 220 yards.' The same account of athletics activities at Marlborough noted that M.A.P. Phillips, Captain of Athletics, had achieved a long jump in excess of twenty-two feet, before concluding: 'N.R. Drake has been awarded his colours.' Seven years later Nick's exact contemporary, Captain Mark Phillips, would marry HRH Princess Anne.

Photographs of Nick during his years at Marlborough show a chubby-faced teenager, smiling – shyly but photogenically – at the camera. Invariably he is part of a group: whether displaying a rugged pair of knees in the 1964 photo of 'C1 Cock House Upper League Rugby Team' or, the following year, celebrating victory in both the 'House Shout' (a unison singing contest) and the Junior and Senior Relay Races. The N.R. Drake that stares at you from these photographs is no different from the boys around him, except that his rugby kit is noticeably cleaner. He sports a Beatle cut, the fringe of his thick, straight hair almost reaching his eyebrows, but in deference to school regulations, the back and sides are well clear of his collar.

He looks chubbier here than in the later, more familiar photographs, and a half smile is evident on the head emerging from the striped rugby shirt. We are so used to the image of Nick as a haunted and doomed figure, stalking the pop landscape of the early 1970s, that there is real shock value in these school photos. The face is recognizably his; the strangeness comes from seeing Nick in company, relaxed, smiling – in the mainstream of life and apparently enjoying it. In the later pictures Nick was always alone.

The year after Nick went to Marlborough, I followed my father and uncle by attending Dulwich College. Trying to pull together the strands of Nick's life, I found myself drawn back, rather reluctantly, to those public-school days. I was several years younger than Nick when I started, but lucky enough – and close enough – to be able to continue living at home. The similarities, though, were legion: the ritual formality of posed team photographs; the rigid etiquette of the school magazine; the dogged determination to preserve cherished traditions; the absolute refusal to concede that the world outside was changing.

Over the years I had grown familiar with the tales told of Nick by fellow-musicians and record company types, but talking to his schoolfriends for the first time, it seemed to me that they had known a quite different Nick. Musicians always admire Nick; they are often in awe of him and frequently perplexed by how he did what he did and who he really was. But listening to Old Marlburians talking, what struck me time after time was the warmth and genuine affection they had felt for him long before he was famous, or doomed.

Perhaps that old chestnut about the child being father to the man is more than usually valid when considering the life of someone who died so early. Nick survived only eight years after leaving Marlborough, and much of that time he was in the grip of an illness which all but blanked out his true self. Tempting though it is to blame the insensitivity of the archaic public-school system, or the trauma of being sent away from home at such an early age, for his eventual fate, all the evidence suggests that, for Nick, his schooldays really were the happiest days of his life.

The Officer Training Corps met weekly to drill Marlborough's young officers in the making. War Games were played, parades undertaken, and the habit of accepting and obeying orders was hammered into the teenagers as they marched around the parade-ground in musty uniforms. Simon Crocker was in the Corps band with Nick and remembers them both hating it: 'We managed to get out by going on a conservation detail at an old building called the Mount House in Marlborough. There were four of us, and we had to repaint it every year. They were the funniest afternoons . . . I just remember us spending the whole time laughing . . .'

Marlborough had suffered terribly during the First World War, losing more old boys than any public school except Eton. Between 1914 and 1918, 733 boys were lost, most barely out of their teens. Fresh-faced subalterns, straight from public schools like Marlborough, were hewn down in their thousands by German machine-guns during the Great War. The life of a Second Lieutenant on active service on the Western Front was estimated at a mere two weeks. Peter Parker's *The Old Lie* quotes old Marlburian G.A.N. Lowndes reflecting that early in 1915: 'It was uncanny to look across Chapel to the back row opposite and realise that within six months probably half the boys there would be dead.'

The unflinching public-school code of honour fuelled the patriotic zeal which swept the nation during the summer of 1914. One of the first to enlist at the outbreak of the war was the poet and old Marlburian Siegfried Sassoon, though he would later come to question its inevitability. Sassoon's education mirrored that of Nick Drake – Marlborough and Cambridge – and Nick's housemaster, Dennis Silk, was a friend of Sassoon's and an expert on his work.

Another old Marlburian poet who died in the conflict was Charles Sorley. Barely twenty when he was killed in 1915, his only collection, *Marlborough And Other Poems*, was published posthumously. The old school was the only life the teenager knew when he enlisted in 1914, but soon he had discovered another, more brutal, existence:

> When you see millions of the mouthless dead,
> Across your dreams in pale battalions go . . .

Sorley's was a short life, and only the poems he left behind distinguish him from the countless others who foundered in the Flanders mud.

Though as distant as the Hundred Years War to the generations who have grown up with McDonald's and the Internet, the First

World War cast a shadow over the twentieth century which was long and searing. Such was the scale of the slaughter that death reached in and touched every community. Visiting Nick's birthplace, I paused by Tanworth's War Memorial, to find inscribed nearly forty names of men from that one village and its surrounding fields who fell in the Great War. Think of the losses in that tiny Warwickshire village, and in all the other hamlets which linked up to form the nation in the early days of this century, and consider the waste.

Siegfried Sassoon's near contemporary, the poet and soldier Wilfred Owen, targeted the public-school lies which he believed had led thousands of the brightest and the best to their deaths on the battlefields of France:

> My friend, you would not tell with such high zest
> To children ardent for some desperate glory,
> The old lie: dulce et decorum est
> Pro patria mori.

Born in Shropshire, and killed at the age of twenty-five, just seven days before the Armistice of 11 November 1918, Owen is celebrated now as one of the key poets of the early twentieth century. The association with 'doomed youth' inevitably draws comparisons with Nick Drake, especially as Owen's work was likewise only really appreciated posthumously. Indeed, in a 1992 assessment of Nick for *Record Collector*, Chas Keep noted that Nick's original song, 'Strange Meeting II' took its title from Owen's poem 'Strange Meeting'.

While at Marlborough, Nick divided his spare time between the athletics field and his growing interest in music. At this stage his musical tastes were very catholic, as Jeremy Mason pointed out: 'He very much liked The Graham Bond Organisation. He loved "St James Infirmary" – there was a very good sax line in it . . . But the record he really liked, and we played it absolutely into the ground, was *The Sounds Of '65* by The Graham Bond Organisation. This was *the* record, followed by Zoot Money & The Big Roll Band.'

Perhaps less surprisingly, Jeremy remembers Nick loving Odetta: ' "Auction Block" was his favourite. I knew none of these people, but another record we adored was Miles Davis's *Kind Of Blue*. Charlie Parker we liked. John Hammond we both liked: the one with him sitting on a motorbike. We thought he was pretty cool. We also bought a Segovia record together. Jimmy Smith was a great favourite of his. "Green Onions" by Booker T. & The M.G.'s he liked. We rather fancied Astrud Gilberto too, as I recall.'

Besides the popular Top 20 favourites which came courtesy of the pirate stations Radio Caroline and Radio London, Jeremy Mason explained how Nick began to develop an interest in the burgeoning folk, blues and R&B scenes: 'What people don't understand nowadays is that there seemed to be room to accommodate almost everything. At that time I had a passion for Jim Reeves at the same time as Bob Dylan – can you imagine? Old Jim was frowned upon at the time, but I had fourteen LPs of his! Nick was particularly keen on that Dylan album with the line "She wears an Egyptian ring . . .", Nick loved that – *Bringing It All Back Home.*'

Nick's growing interest in listening to records was accompanied by the desire to play music for himself. This interest soon grew into an obsession, and the ability to play an instrument – any instrument – was swift and instinctive. As well as the guitar, during his time at Marlborough Nick learnt the clarinet and alto saxophone. David Wright only remembers Nick playing the guitar towards the end of their schooldays: 'I presume he must have started music lessons on the piano, got bored, and taken up the clarinet when he was fourteen or fifteen. The clarinet was his instrument . . . Then, deciding, I imagine, that the clarinet wasn't very hip – it was all a bit Acker Bilk and "Stranger On The Shore" – he took up the sax.'

As well as the mainly classical pieces Nick played during his clarinet lessons, there were occasional forays into jazz; in particular, friends recall his fondness for Stan Getz's 'Desafinado'. Dennis Silk remembers that whenever jazz musicians came to play at the school, Nick was always there. However, an account in *The Marlburian* during the Lent term of 1966 was rather less relaxed about modern trends in music than Nick's erstwhile housemaster.

'Every week of every term, Marlborough's 6 resident and 13 visiting music teachers instruct 115 pianists, 16 organists, 3 singers, 13 students of harmony, 26 violinists, 3 violists, 13 cellists, 5 double-bass players, 18 flautists, 10 oboists, 4 bassoonists, 30 clarinettists, 8 horn-players, 15 trumpeters, 7 trombonists, 6 tuba players, 4 saxophonists, 3 euphonium players and 30 guitarists (330 in all). These numbers have changed surprisingly little over the years and the only interesting (or ominous?) change in recent years is that there are some thirty fewer pianists and thirty more guitarists, some of whom are tempted to attach amplifiers and speakers to their "machines" in order to convey their message without ambiguity to those who are hard of hearing.'

Written in the year that The Beatles released *Revolver*, The Rolling Stones *Aftermath*, and Bob Dylan *Blonde On Blonde*, the report adds: 'We are forced to the conclusion that boys are disinclined to listen to all but the most trivial music.' For 'trivial', read 'pop'. Within two years Nick Drake would himself be entering a recording studio for the first time.

Meanwhile he continued happily at Marlborough, remaining on good terms with the staff and the institution. Dennis Silk was aware that Nick kept in close contact with his parents too: 'He was obviously the centre of a very loving family. I don't know what they made of the pop music . . . but they must have worried. Father was very conventional, a delightful businessman, who adored his son. And the son adored him . . . They worshipped the ground Nick walked on, without spoiling him, and Nick adored them. So it wasn't a sort of rebellious youth giving hell to his parents . . .'

There were some rebellions, of course, but they were small, one might even say traditional. The days at Marlborough were familiarly mundane, and like most of his fellow-pupils, Nick leavened the dismal round of lessons and sports with sporadic interruptions for illicit pleasures. The most popular of these, back in the innocent mid-sixties, were cigarettes, puffed in quiet corners, and trips to the tearoom known as the Polly. David Wright recalls that, for the strong of heart, there was also the occasional jaunt to a town pub: 'Nick liked his ale. After lunch a bunch of half a dozen of us would go off to this pub in Marlborough, the Lamb, which had a sympathetic landlord, where you could go into the back bar, and scarper if someone came in the front.'

Jeremy Mason too has fond memories of Marlborough watering-holes: 'Almost every day after lunch, Nick and I used to go to a splendid place down the High Street, which had a bay window, so we could see if anyone was coming. And we'd sit there for our afternoon fag, smoking our Disque Bleu cigarettes. Saturday evenings we'd go drinking at a pub that's no longer there, called the Cricketers. The Buffalos had a room there – they were a bit like the Freemasons – and had this room, done up like a courtroom. It really was the most extraordinary place to begin your drinking career.'

The four and a half years Nick Drake spent at Marlborough were remarkable only for their ordinariness, and for their similarity to the schooldays of previous generations of British upper-middle-class males. The changes which were shaking the walls of cities outside, had as yet, left Marlborough largely untouched. But by 1965 the foundations were beginning to shake, largely due to the beat of Vox amplifiers and Rickenbacker guitars.

'We weren't rebels, that would give us too much credit,' admitted Arthur Packard, a Housemate of Nick's from C1. 'But we were interested in smoking cigarettes, John Player's – not marijuana – and nipping out for a drink, just a pint, at one of the local pubs. I suppose it was our attempt at a quiet revolution, not like the US campuses. We were slightly iconoclastic listening to Rolling Stones records, trying to grow one's hair slightly over the collar, sporting Chelsea boots, stuff like that.'

In January 1962, when Nick first entered Marlborough, The Beatles were a buzzing beat group, popular only in Hamburg night-clubs and Liverpool cellars; The Rolling Stones were still lolling around in their legendarily squalid flat in London's Edith Grove; and Bob Dylan was a chubby-faced kid who had barely begun writing his own songs. By the time he left the school in July 1966, the world had turned upside down: The Beatles were finishing their days as a touring band; The Stones had copyrighted snotty rebelliousness; and Dylan was reinvented as an electric Messiah.

It was a turbulent world where traditional values were being overthrown and institutions were foundering, but long on into the sixties the public schools remained little changed. Old Etonian Prime Minister Harold Macmillan watched his government brought down in the aftermath of the Profumo Affair in 1964; but the militant Schools' Action Union, the corrosive undermining of Lindsay Anderson's film *If*, the challenging of the established order by angry students – all this would wait until 1968, the year of revolution, by which time Nick Drake was long gone.

His contemporaries at Marlborough paint an achingly normal picture of the schoolboy Nick. Shy certainly, retiring even; but the mono-syllabic, almost catatonic figure of those final years, hunched on a Hampstead bench, strikes no chord with those who shared their formative teenage years with the boy from C1 house who had a penchant for French cigarettes, sprinting and Bob Dylan.

'You didn't think about the future then,' Simon Crocker recalls. 'You hardly thought about your bloody exams . . . You presumed you were going to go: school, university . . . and then there'd be something.'

3

Marlborough, like every other school in the sixties, was seething with spotty rock 'n' roll bands. The Beatles, The Rolling Stones, The Animals, The Searchers, The Yardbirds had kicked the door open, and in their wake came Marlborough's answer: Sex, Love & Society, Les Blues en Noir, The Four Squares – and, featuring Nick Drake on saxophone, clarinet and piano, The Perfumed Gardeners! Simon Crocker was a fellow Perfumed Gardener: 'The members that I can remember were Mike Maclaran, who played bass; me on drums and harmonica; Randal Keynes, who was the grandson of Maynard Keynes the economist – I think he played guitar and sax. He was the guy who introduced us all to Bob Dylan. A guy called Mike . . . on trombone. Nick played clarinet, saxophone and piano.'

The various Marlborough pop ensembles were always on the lookout for opportunities to perform, whether to assembled pupils and staff after a film show, in the gym, or as part of end-of-term celebrations. David Wright remembers playing bass on one such occasion, in a five-piece band featuring Nick on saxophone: 'We played in the Memorial Hall – Muddy Waters' "Hoochie Coochie Man" and "Little Red Rooster", Howlin' Wolf's "Smokestack Lightning". I do remember us doing "Gonna Send You Back To Walker", which was an old Animals B-side, any twelve-bar blues you can name. Our pedigree was The Yardbirds, The Stones.'

Simon Crocker also recalls playing Marlborough gigs with Nick: 'The thing was that Nick was absolutely the musical director. There was a bunch of us together, but Nick was the musical centre. He

played very good piano, very good sax and clarinet. Guitar was not
the big instrument then . . . We all agreed on numbers, but Nick
arranged them. Nick didn't want to sing . . . but the truth was, he was
the only one of us who could sing in tune. So he was kind of forced
into that leader-of-the-band role.

'Basically we took Pye International singles, Yardbirds albums,
Manfred Mann, Cliff Bennett & The Rebel Rousers, and copied all
that . . . The line-up did fluctuate, but the largest version of the band
we had was about eight people – saxes, trombone – and we did the
most amazing version of "St James Infirmary". That is the one tune I
remember us blowing the walls out, and everyone was amazed,
because normally at school there were four people playing popular
little tunes, and suddenly we had an eight-piece playing a really gutsy
"St James Infirmary".'

Jeremy Mason tells of a concert Nick played in the school hall
during their last term: 'He had a cold, I remember, and he suddenly
put down the saxophone and went over to the piano, and on his own
played a thing called "Parchman Farm", and it was an absolute *tour
de force*.' Written by Mose Allison, the song was inspired by the
Mississippi State Prison, where Elvis Presley's father, Vernon, had
spent nine months in the late 1930s for forging a cheque. Nick was
probably familiar with the 1966 recording made by Eric Clapton
while he was still with John Mayall, but there were also covers by
Georgie Fame, The Nashville Teens and Bukka White.

Beyond Marlborough's walls the new pop royalty was making its
mark, while within, competition for places in the various school
groups became fierce. Simon Crocker secured a gig with one group
'because I was one of only two kids at school who played the drums'.
As with any group, though, from The Rolling Stones to Oasis,
internal dynamics were as important as the music, and not all the
Marlborough bands were fashioned in complete harmony. Simon
remembers one such power-play: 'Chris De Burgh, or Chris Davison
as he was known at school, was a year behind us, and the thing I
remember about him is that he was small and he had a big guitar. He
was very keen, always wanting to join in, and rather cruelly we never
let him because Nick felt that . . . he was a bit too poppy, that he
wasn't quite right for the image of the band. I'm not surprised he's
done well – he was very good – but I remember him as being quite
pushy, and Nick wasn't pushy at all and he didn't like pushy people.'

Jeremy Mason too was aware of De Burgh 'always being turned
away from all the school groups because he was too short'; but he has

a final school memory 'of Nick Drake and Chris De Burgh on the same stage together, singing the old boys' song'.

Adept as Nick was on clarinet, saxophone and piano, he soon realized that if you were going anywhere in 1965 you had to get there on guitar. While still at Marlborough he splashed out £13 on an acoustic guitar, and with the help of David Wright, patiently added another instrument to his musical CV. 'He decided he was going to learn the guitar . . .' David recalls. 'I remember sitting down and teaching Nick C, A minor, F and G7th on the guitar . . . A few days later he was better at it than I was. He was a proper musician. He played by ear, and he was good.'

Already aware that his young charge 'was in love with music', Dennis Silk realized that all the music teachers were longing for him to play in the orchestra: 'Nick didn't want to disappoint them, and of course he was pretty keen on all music, but he was obviously gripped by the new music . . . You'd find him in his study sometimes, strumming away at his guitar.'

Jeremy Mason spent a lot of time with Nick at school and acknowledges that he was somewhat thoughtful, but he saw no sign of the isolation or crippling introspection which would kick in later: 'I can remember a couple of occasions when we'd go off on long walks – all motivated, I'm sure, by smoking cigarettes – along a railway line, where we got fairly intense. He was totally and utterly . . . ordinary. There was no manifestation, except this deep interest in music and slightly off-beat music . . . Dylan, who we both adored, was obviously another link.'

One of the strongest impressions Simon Crocker retains is of Nick's unassuming nature: 'I don't ever remember Nick contributing to the school magazine or anything. The thing about Nick was that he never pushed himself forward. He wanted to be in the background. He didn't want to be in the limelight. It wasn't that he was lazy, he was very industrious. But I think if myself and others hadn't hustled a band together, got the hall, got the equipment, made sure everyone got out of bed, it wouldn't have worried him . . .' Getting out of bed was a vital discipline because rock rehearsals, being rather frowned upon by the school authorities, were conducted very early in the morning in the Memorial Hall, in the hope that anyone who might object would still be in bed.

It seems strange that Nick didn't contribute to the school magazine, or indeed write anything much of his own at this stage, but

perhaps this too can be put down to his natural diffidence. Dennis
Silk remembers the odd poem, but nothing more substantial: 'He
loved his English. He wrote poems from time to time, but I never saw
one published . . . In his first year of specialization as an historian and
classicist, I taught him and occasionally they would write a piece of
poetry . . . I wish I'd hung on to them.'

Arthur Packard also sensed a deep modesty, but took it as an
indication that Nick was 'probably a lot more mature than the rest of
us . . . Thinking back on him, that expression "still waters run deep"
seems to describe Nick. He was funny, slightly zany, but underneath
that you sensed deep thoughts.'

Cloistered in school dormitories and studies at Marlborough, ears
pressed to transistor radios, the boys were tantalized by the sounds
crackling across the airwaves during the earth-shaking year of 1965. It
was the year the establishment acknowledged The Beatles, when
Prime Minister Harold Wilson, who modelled his style on the
youthful vigour of the late President Kennedy, made The Beatles
Members of the British Empire. It was also the year that the group
began to really think about making an album, rather than a string of
singles. Released in time for Christmas 1965, *Rubber Soul* marked the
first step away from simple love songs, particularly now that John
was contributing material like 'Norwegian Wood', 'Nowhere Man'
and 'In My Life'.

Rock historians have earmarked 1967 as the moment when it all
began to change, but I would submit 1965 as the year which laid the
foundations for a durable rock 'n' roll culture. This was when Dylan
kicked the stool away and hung folk music by going electric on
Bringing It All Back Home and *Highway 61 Revisited*. The Rolling
Stones, The Who, Simon & Garfunkel, The Kinks, Manfred Mann,
The Byrds, The Animals, The Small Faces and The Yardbirds were
taking pop in a new and exciting direction. Phil Spector excelled
himself with the Wagnerian 'You've Lost That Lovin' Feeling'; Berry
Gordy's Tamla Motown label was producing a seamless sequence of
hit records; and politics and pop were beginning to fuse together.

Nick was seventeen, and clearly aware of the changes which were
taking place, changes which were not just being felt in music, but in
fashion and film too. London was leading the world. Jean Shrimpton
shocked first Australia, then the world, by wearing the world's first
miniskirt, while David Bailey created the prototype of the classless
cockney photographer. In the cinema, the old stars were being swept

aside by the iconic Julie Christie, Tom Courtenay and Albert Finney; while the films themselves started to tackle issues like abortion, infidelity and homosexuality with a frankness which many found simply shocking.

The soundtrack to all this freewheeling frenzy, the music which played as everyone capered like crazy, was pop – or rock 'n' roll, R&B, jazz, folk-rock . . . Call it what you will, it was just too good to miss. And London was not that far from Marlborough for fit young men who didn't need much sleep.

Nick and David Wright soon became regular visitors to the clubs of swinging London: 'The Flamingo was where we particularly used to go,' David recalls. 'We used to hitch there after lights out, on the old A4 out of Marlborough. We'd get to Wardour Street . . . see the British R&B mob, the people we were really keen on. We'd stay there till daybreak, then get the bus to the A4 and hitch back in time for breakfast. It was fairly intrepid stuff.

'The two bands Nick and I saw and enjoyed more than any were Zoot Money & The Big Roll Band and Chris Farlowe & The Thunderbirds. But the best evening I ever had in the 1960s – Nick was there too – was the day that "Keep On Runnin' ", by The Spencer Davis Group, got to number one, in December '65. They were playing on the same bill as The Moody Blues, when Denny Laine was with them . . . in the days when they were a great R&B band, and The Mark Leeman Five. That night at the Marquee was absolutely sensational: there was Steve Winwood singing "Keep On Runnin' ", and it was announced from the stage that it had just got to number one, and there we were, in the Marquee!'

Jeremy Mason too has memories of illicit visits to London with Nick: 'Once we hitchhiked to London for the Flamingo all-nighter, and we had to be back in time for Chapel. It was all a bit risky. Once we saw Chris Farlowe – you can see Nick liking the way he sang. Another time it was Georgie Fame. In those days they had three rows of seats in the front, and everything else happened at the back. We thought we were pretty grown-up.'

Most of the clubs visited by the marauding Marlburians were in Soho, which in 1965 was like a slash of vermilion lipstick across the grey face of London. The pubs still closed at 11p.m., but Soho was rich in after-hours drinking clubs; and Soho was where the musicians gathered. Prostitutes also enlivened the streets, as David Wright recalls: 'Soho was so much fun in those days: it had the first pizza restaurant I'd ever seen, just up from the Flamingo. I remember Nick and I getting accosted by a lady of the street – we were fifteen or sixteen – and bartering with her, then running off with very cold feet.'

London exerted an equally strong pull during the school holidays, but without the need to rush back at dawn. David Wright remembers: 'We spent one wonderful New Year's Eve in London, getting absolutely legless in Trafalgar Square. My sister had a flat in Chalk Farm, and we pitched up there on New Year's Eve, 1965.'

Hitching down to London gave the seventeen-year-olds an opportunity to see in person acts they had enjoyed on record. Jeremy Mason vividly recalls finally getting to see Graham Bond: 'It was at the Manor House Hotel, Friday evening, 29 October 1965. Nick and I went to that together, I don't know how, because it was during term time, but we used to sneak off and go and listen to things. On this occasion we stayed at Gabrielle's flat. She wasn't there, and it was rather spooky – we were quite young. I'd never met her, and we were pretty pissed.

I remember Ginger Baker doing a drum solo – on a song called "Camels & Elephants", I think – and Nick was standing there watching, with a cigarette, and he was so impressed – I'll never forget this – he poured a pint of beer all the way down his front before he noticed.'

During 1965 and 1966 David Wright and Nick became close friends, and even during the long holidays from Marlborough, they spent much of the time together. 'I suppose we were drawn together by music, but also by the fact that we both came from the Midlands, so we saw each other in the holidays. He was in Tanworth and I was in Wolverhampton, so when we could both drive we saw quite a lot of each other.'

As they got older the two were able to venture further afield, and in August 1965 they set off to hitchhike around Europe for three weeks: 'Around France, Germany, Belgium and back again . . . [Nick] was barely seventeen. We got a train down to Dover, and set off with nothing but a thumb . . . We got down to Paris and then on to Avignon. The first night we slept in a cave, and then we just hitched and bumbled our way along the Côte d'Azur, having a great time. It was super, and I have visions of us sitting on the beach, and Nick got quite severe sea urchins. There was nothing particularly significant about that trip, but it was bloody good fun. We laughed all the way.'

Another abiding memory of the trip is of Sonny & Cher's protest song "I Got You Babe" playing everywhere they went: 'The reason I remember I Got You Babe is that you didn't hear much American pop music in France in those days – it was all accordions.' More ambitious plans were made, for travelling around the world after they left school, but the world had other ideas: 'We both had this wanderlust . . . and there was a plan to get a Land Rover, drive around the Mediterranean: down through Spain, Gibraltar, cross to Africa, right the way round. That was planned in 1965 . . . But by 1966, they'd shut the gates of Gibraltar, and by 1967 there was the Arab–Israeli war.'

That first trip to France, hitching during the summer of 1965, was followed by others, and over the next couple of years many of Nick's happiest times were spent in France. He was enchanted by that country and became familiar with a style of music which would subtly infuse his own work when he began recording. The *chanson* tradition imbues wistful, idealized love with a rueful charm, at the same time as recognizing despair. *Chanson* eludes definition – rather it is a feeling, a sense of melancholy which pervades the song like a wisp of Gauloise smoke.

Interpreted by Charles Trenet, Juliette Greco, Charles Aznavour, Jacques Brel and Edith Piaf, *chanson* is timeless and ineffably French. On moving to France, Petula Clark couldn't believe the impact of seeing Piaf in concert. Familiar with light-hearted English music hall and variety songs, she was stunned by the gritty realism and the honest, coruscating nature of the songs Piaf sang. The haunting existential beauty of Juliette Greco carried the *chanson* tradition into a new era. Stalking the bustling streets of St-Germain-des-Prés in the late forties, rubbing shoulders with Sartre and Cocteau, the black-clad Greco epitomized a new type of teenager.

Chanson embodied world-weariness, the realization that life was not sweet, but a rather bitter cup of black coffee. It was this air of melancholy and mystery which found its way into the songs Nick Drake would soon begin writing. Songs which, at their best, sat somewhere between the traditions of folk, the blues and *chanson*.

Throughout his life, Nick loved France. The landscape, the language, the food, the wine all held a strong attraction for him. As well as being home to the wistful, enduring art of *chanson* and the smoky sensuality of Juliette Greco, St-Germain-des-Prés provided a haunt for Jean-Paul Sartre. There in the smoky fug of the Café de Flore, Sartre mapped out the defiantly lonely life of the existentialist: 'Hell is other people.'

Sartre's work was widely available in paperback by the time Nick left Marlborough and went up to Cambridge, and his doomed anti-heroes were familiar to the postwar generation, as was the work of another of Sartre's contemporaries, Albert Camus. Camus, who died at the age of forty-seven in a car crash in 1960, was awarded the Nobel Prize for Literature, having become a landmark figure for a generation of disaffected young people with classic novels of alienation like *The Outsider* (*L'Étranger*). His *The Myth Of Sisyphus* was the last book Nick would read before his death.

The end of Nick Drake's education at Marlborough came in July 1966. He had switched from History and Classics to study English rather late in the day, but it seemed to suit him much better. He continued to play a full and robust part in the life of the school, at the same time as pursuing his own extracurricular interests, and this was recognized when he was made Captain of his House. His final months at Marlborough were also marked by distinction on the athletics track, when he had the honour of competing in the Wiltshire Junior Athletics Championship. Nick's housemaster wrote about him at the time: 'a most talented athlete, who was never really deeply interested in breaking records which were well within his grasp. He is probably one of the best sprinters we have had at Marlborough since the war, and yet he would much more often than not be found reading when he should have been training.'

Throughout his years at Marlborough, Nick had enjoyed the pubs of the nearby town. The local beer, Wadworth's from nearby Devizes, was a potent brew, and frequently Nick and Jeremy Mason, David Wright, Simon Crocker and Michael Maclaran would sneak off to the Bell in nearby Ramsbury, or pubs in Marlborough like the Cricketers or the Lamb, to drink beer, smoke cigarettes and put the world to rights. But none of Nick's friends or acquaintances from school remembers any evidence of drugs during their time there. David Wright: 'I don't ever remember any dope at Marlborough, but interestingly enough, I was chatting to a friend who was there the year after Nick and I left, which would be 1967, and it was around then.'

In his final term Nick took A-level exams again. He had sat some the previous year, but the results had been disappointing. This time around he brought his tally of passes up to four – History, English, Latin Translation with Roman History, British Constitution – and managed to improve his grade in English to a B, making a university place likely. The Marlborough College Register lists ex-pupil N.R. Drake simply as 'a guitarist, and composer of folk music for the guitar'.

In recommending Nick for a university place, Dennis Silk displayed an obvious fondness for him while suggesting that he had yet to achieve his full potential: 'Nicholas Drake is a boy who has taken a long time to mature scholastically. His IQ, measured when he first came to the school, was high enough to make us hope for a much more dynamic approach than he showed for several years. One always felt there were possibilities here and yet he seemed incapable of producing it . . .

'He is essentially a rather dreamy, artistic type of boy, very quiet, verging almost to the side of shyness. He loves English and this last year had a timetable especially prepared for him, by which he was able to spend a lot of time reading by himself. His whole written fluency developed enormously and people who had written him off were forced to eat their words . . .

'He was someone who everybody liked enormously here, despite his reticence and the difficulty of getting to know him well . . . In conclusion I would say that he is a genuine late developer who is only now growing into his academic potential. For a long time we have despaired of him but now I genuinely feel that given a chance to read English at the university he would prove a great success and in more spheres than the purely academic one. He could give a lot to the community as well as getting a lot. He is a most delightful person to deal with.'

Nick's final night at Marlborough was marked by a typical piece of teenage malpractice, and understandably Dennis Silk found him slightly less delightful that night: 'I can remember having a flaming row with Nick on his last night in school, when he was up at three o'clock in the morning drinking and smoking – everything that boys do on their last night at school which housemasters are paid to try and stop.'

To celebrate the end of A levels, Nick, David Wright and Jeremy Mason had sloped off into town, where they got spectacularly drunk on beer and wine. 'On the last night of term he got awfully pissed . . .' David recalls. 'And my abiding memory of Nick is with a bottle of sweet white wine, probably Graves, absolutely out of it, completely cold, by the Music Block.'

In an often-repeated quote, Nick is alleged to have described Marlborough as a place 'where the sensitive experience a horrified dissociation from reality that can sometimes never fade away'. The words are those of Steve Burgess, in a May 1979 profile of Nick for *Dark Star*, in which he seeks to equate his experiences of 'that evil

British institution known as boarding school' with those of Nick at Marlborough: 'I know that Nick and I were of a piece . . .' The truth is that Nick never expressed such an opinion – indeed all the contemporary evidence points to him having rather enjoyed his years at public school.

4

By the time Nick had completed his schooldays at Marlborough and was back at home in Tanworth in the early summer of 1966, The Beatles had released *Revolver* and Dylan unleashed *Blonde On Blonde*. Hazy and impenetrable as 'Tomorrow Never Knows' and 'Sad Eyed Lady Of The Lowlands' might be, they were the writing on the wall. Back at Far Leys again, Nick practised the guitar, sitting for hours in his bedroom or downstairs in the living room, endlessly tuning and retuning his guitar, formulating a style which would become his own, lost in a reverie of sorts.

There was more than a year to fill before he would go up to Fitzwilliam College, Cambridge, in the autumn of 1967. In the limbo between school and university, his friends were still those he had made at Marlborough, and it was to them that Nick looked to occupy the time. With his newly acquired driving licence, a tent and Molly's quaint little Morris Minor, Nick and three friends set off for France in July 1966.

One of Nick's companions was Michael Maclaran, who has clear memories of their journey: 'Driving a heavily laden and underpowered car was a nightmare, and included such dramas as losing both wing mirrors at once in a head-on near-collision and scraping the entire contents of a traffic island in our path as we ploughed on, wheels locked. At least the Morris's suspension was up to anything. After many weeks the car finally broke down nearing the top of a climb towards Grenoble. Short of mechanical skills, we stared under the bonnet. Someone spotted a broken spring, which was miraculously replaced by an identical one from a nearby piece of farm machinery.'

The hours Nick had devoted to learning the guitar had been well spent, for contemporaries began to notice just how proficient he had become on the instrument. 'Wherever we went, the evenings were often the same with groups of people gathering around bonfires under the stars, on beaches, in woods or at camp-sites, to hear Nick sing and play his guitar,' Michael Maclaran remembered. 'The venues included Remoulins, near the Pont du Gard, where we stayed with some of Nick's friends . . . They took us to the bullfight in Nîmes, but only after we had read Hemingway's vital work on the topic. There we hit a spectacular candlelight "Quatorze juillet" party in the woods, which was a two-day hangover. And at St Tropez, amongst the luxury yachts and private beaches, it was often getting light by the time last night's party was ending, and Nick would still be strumming away.

'Nick was a performer and yet despite the many people who would gather, most of them well lubricated, the sessions never became raucous singalongs; he didn't play to the crowd. Every string of his guitar seemed to be playing a complementary tune and his repeating melodies cast a mesmerizing spell. Very few left early for home.'

It was all quite idyllic – to be young and sleep under the stars in France on Bastille Day. To read Hemingway's *Death In The Afternoon* and *The Sun Also Rises*, and then to witness the bullfights of which the grumpy old master had written. St Tropez, made popular by Brigitte Bardot, was the premier summer vacation spot for the *demi-monde*. As millionaires' yachts bobbed in the tiny harbour, and the jet set sought their pleasures in the bars and boutiques, Nick and his three friends chitty-chitty-bang-banged their way along the French coast in Molly Drake's quintessentially English Morris Minor.

Jeremy Mason was in France that summer too: 'The year we left Marlborough, in the summer, Nick came down to France with his guitar. My parents had this house near the Pont du Gard, near Nîmes.' The faded colour photos of Nick during that holiday, taken near Nîmes, show a group of ghostly-white, almost transparent English schoolboys; the jet-blackness of their ubiquitous sunglasses only emphasizing the paleness of their flesh.

Provincial France was lagging a long way behind the perceived coolness of Britain and America, but it was, nevertheless, an awfully big adventure for English visitors only a few weeks out of school

uniform. Jeremy Mason: 'In those days, the tradition was to walk to
the main road, which was about a mile away. Very old-fashioned,
1966 Provence, and every evening all the young of the village used to
walk to the main road.

'Nick was a great hit. We used to sit on a wall at a junction of the
roads, and Nick would play, and I remember them all singing along –
"Michael Row The Boat Ashore", "House Of The Rising Sun" – all
that sort of singalong folk stuff . . . None of us spoke French terribly
well, but there was a bond formed, so much so that we were asked to
an enormous village fête. It consisted of long trestle-tables, where
Nick and I were persuaded to drink pastis without any water in it,
which we duly did. We got so drunk, we ended up running along the
tops of the tables and jumping into strange people's arms.

'We asked them all back to the house. I'd said: "Come back and
have a drink; Nick will play his guitar some more." But my mother
came downstairs to shoo them all away . . . She said: "I could hear
this cacophony of sound approaching, led by you and Nick."'

Another conversation with his mother – one that he and Nick had
one night towards the end of their holiday in France – stuck in
Jeremy's mind: 'That's when drugs came up: I don't think any of us
had anything to do with drugs at that time . . . But Nick sort of said:
"Oh, well, you know, it's one of those things one tries . . ." And I
remember a conversation we had with my mother, after dinner, doing
the washing-up. My mother got quite cross, and it's always been a
source of some irony. Nick was effectively saying it was all right to try
drugs . . . This was the summer of 1966, long before The Beatles
admitted to taking LSD or anything. It was obviously discussed, but
as far as I know, there were no drugs at school at all. We were just
into Disque Bleu cigarettes.'

Dylan may have been advising that 'everybody must get stoned',
but drugs and rock 'n 'roll weren't yet the close companions they
would soon become. Being busted for drugs still spelt the end of a
career, even for a pop star. The Beatles were still cuddly boy-next-
door mop-tops with MBEs. Even The Rolling Stones were deemed
largely harmless, rebellious perhaps, but not corrupters of youth via
the demon drugs. Most teenagers' knowledge of drugs was limited to
the mescaline trips recounted by Aldous Huxley in *The Doors Of
Perception*. LSD was still legal, but the most widely acknowledged
drug song was Peter, Paul & Mary's whimsical 'Puff The Magic
Dragon'.

On his return from France in the autumn of 1966, Nick spent a

short time in Tanworth before setting off for London to stay with his
sister, Gabrielle. It was the year when *Time* magazine officially
declared London 'Swinging', England had just won the World
Cup, and we all lived in a yellow submarine. Anything, and everything, suddenly seemed possible.

David Wright, Nick's close friend from Marlborough, was also in
London at this time: 'I think he came to London at the same time as
me, October '66 . . . I remember him telling me how the night before
he first came down to London, his parents had taken him aside for a
pep talk about drugs, and he found it hilariously funny that within
twenty-four hours of arriving in Chelsea he was sitting in this flat
rolling up a joint.'

Nick's time in London that year was brief. He was back at Far Leys
for Christmas, and shortly afterwards set off on his most important
trip to France. In January 1967, accompanied by his Marlborough
friends Simon Crocker and Jeremy Mason, Nick travelled across the
Channel, nominally to improve his French. Simon Crocker: 'Nick's
parents had always got on well with my parents, and I was being sent
to Aix-en-Provence to university, and when they heard this they were
casting around for something for Nick to do, and basically Nick said:
"Oh God, they want to do something with me. Shall I come to Aix?"
And then, when Nick was going, Jeremy said: "Oh well, I'll come as
well."

'We caught the train from Victoria. Nick had come down to
London a couple of days before and was staying in a flat near
Knightsbridge with a guy called Mike Hacking, who was one of
the real cool cats at school. He was about a year ahead of us, and it's
that time when a year is very important, and he wore a big old leather
overcoat and he had an older girlfriend. We got on the train and . . .
thought, what the hell are we doing? We had nowhere to live . . . we
were booked into the Faculty of Foreign Students at the University
of Aix–Marseilles, and that was it. None of us had ever really been
away that much. We were relatively unworldly. It was a really big
adventure for us.'

It was the year of flower power and the Summer of Love, and Nick
spent the first four months of 1967 deep on the South Coast of France,
nestling next to the Mediterranean, with the enticing coast of North
Africa just a boat ride away. There were other distractions too, as
Jeremy Mason remembers: 'We were going to the Foreign University
at Aix. I was by now deeply in love with a frightfully unsuitable girl,
and that probably had something to do with why I didn't follow Nick

down one or two paths. We got to Aix, and our parents, for some extraordinary reason, had not fixed up anywhere for us to stay. They had been told that once we got to the university it would all be arranged. We went to the university, and they were completely uninterested . . . They fixed us up for three nights with a family. Simon and I were in one room, and Nick had to stay with a granny in a flat down at the end of the road.'

To be young, free and single in 1967 was exhilarating. Nick, Jeremy and Simon, with no great inclination to attend lectures, enjoyed a freewheeling lifestyle in tune with the times. Aix was as good a place as any to spend the first, faltering months of the year which would alter everything. Jeremy remembers going to one lecture: 'On French colonial life or something. We then got a flat in a part of town that is now very, very chic it was just off the Place Vendôme, which is the centre of Aix. They let us use these flats because the block wasn't finished, so we were able to rent them cheaply. They were beautiful apartments . . . Nick and I shared a room. So we went and bought a gramophone, I bought some pictures for the wall, stuck up some postcards and proceeded to try and exist.

'It was an odd place, quite a lot of rich people. Somebody who was there with us was a chap called Roddy Llewellyn, who's become quite well known for having a fling with Princess Margaret. He was the only one with a car. We went to the odd club, but there was always an undercurrent, because Aix has quite an Arab population, and there were always slight problems in the nightclubs with the Arabs at that time – very minor, teenage stuff really, but there had been one or two quite nasty incidents. We appeared to spend a great deal of our time playing pinball at a café called Deux Garçons. We didn't really do anything. We slept a great deal of the time. I took up drawing, which I still do.'

Simon Crocker: 'The idea was to go and learn French, which was the last thing we did. Nick spoke better French than us. There was a £50 limit, which was all you could take outside the sterling area. Aix at that time had a really strange, mixed bunch of people . . . The English gravitated to each other, and this guy's parents had a house in St Tropez, and we went there and just busked. All we did was play twelve-bar blues. Nick used to play instrumentals.'

To hone his playing and to earn a few extra francs, Nick would busk with his guitar around the cafés in the centre of Aix. Jeremy acted as 'bag man': 'He played, and I collected the money. I don't remember what he played, and it may only have been a few times . . .

It was a funny time, a mixture of a nightmare time and an interesting time . . . We spent a lot of time in this smart café eating other people's bread; we never appeared to have any money . . .'

Nick persevered with his guitar-playing, and while in Aix took the first serious steps towards writing his own songs. Among his earliest known compositions were 'Birds Flew By' – which he never lived to record – 'Time Of No Reply' and 'Strange Meeting II', both of which appeared posthumously.

'I certainly don't remember Nick writing anything at Marlborough,' says Simon Crocker. 'We did instrumental stuff, but they were tied on to blues things. I do remember him writing in Aix, because I can clearly remember holding a microphone while he sang into the tape recorder . . . It was when we went to Jeremy's parents' house, which was somewhere near Avignon, that I became really conscious of him writing his own songs. I remember that weekend was certainly the first time we recorded some of his songs – Jeremy did have that tape, but lent it to somebody and it got lost – and they were certainly the basis of two songs on *Five Leaves Left*. I wouldn't swear to it, but I'm pretty sure "Time Has Told Me" was one of them.

'That was the first time one became aware that he was, you know, a songwriter . . . It wasn't surprising, but one was surprised at how good they were. Up until then we'd all been doing cover versions, just mucking around, and here was Nick obviously doing something seriously.

'I don't remember him ever talking about writing songs. My memory is that it was just something he did . . . He was there, playing all the time . . . it was just one of those things: "Oh, Nick's done a song. It's rather good. Let's hope he's got another one." I never really thought of asking him about them. I don't think he had any specific plan about what he was going to do with them. I don't think he thought that someone from his kind of background would necessarily go on and make it his career.'

Hitching back to Aix from his parents' house in Avignon, proved a difficult journey for Jeremy: 'Nick and I stood outside Avignon for about four hours, getting no lifts whatsoever. He said: "The only thing to do is split up – nobody's going to pick the two of us up. You go first and I'll sit on the other side of the road." It was a nightmare. I was picked up twice by homosexuals, one of whom I had to escape by getting out while the car was moving . . . and as I picked myself up, Nick went by, with a bird in an open-top car, with the guitar stuck in the back.'

Back in Aix in one piece, and desperate for cheap entertainment, Jeremy remembers that a seance was suggested: 'Childishly, we had a very big session, which Nick did get very involved in. He got carried away by this and discovered something from the table-turning . . . some uncle he didn't know existed. He actually rang his parents from a café – which in those days took three hours – to ask, did this uncle exist? Why did I not know about him? He became very involved with that, and went off and did it with other people as well. But they had an incident which frightened him off, and he stopped.'

Simon noticed a gradual change in Nick while they were together in Aix: always shy, he seemed to grow even more contemplative in France during the first months of 1967. 'I don't remember him becoming moody or difficult . . . He became more serious I think, and to a degree lost some of his light-heartedness. But that is partly because, in the English crowd there, there were some guys who burned the candle at both ends, and Nick was quite taken with them, I think. They were the well-cool cats, the Chelsea kids, sons of rich Chelsea people. They were pretty hip . . . There was a kind of split in Aix . . . and Nick did get sucked into the slipstream. And certainly, yes, that was the camp where there were more drugs. I don't think there were any excessive . . . it was recreational. I don't know, but it wouldn't surprise me if there had been acid around.'

After three months the holiday was coming to a close, and Jeremy feels sure that towards the end of this period a sea change took place in Nick: 'While I waited for this girl to come down from England, which was the disaster of my life, Nick decided to go to Morocco. I'm not quite sure who he went with, but I think it was a Swedish chap who I met in London . . . And Nick disappeared for two, three, maybe four weeks . . . Then he came back, and I think he was much more drug-orientated . . . We had an old guitar he smashed up and set light to, and he hung it from the ceiling and looked it at it like "Wow, man!"'

Marrakesh was an oasis of liberation for European visitors. Joe Orton was infamously attracted to the city by the Arabs' relaxed attitude to homosexuality, while the easy availability of kif drew busloads of hippies keen to score some dope. Jeremy is convinced that in Marrakesh Nick fell in with The Rolling Stones and their party. Mick Jagger, Keith Richards and Brian Jones were certainly in Morocco in March 1967, which fits in with Jeremy's timescale. In Tangiers, The Stones stayed at the El Minzah Hotel, where the pale, gaunt forms of Jagger and Richards were lovingly photographed by

Cecil Beaton. The Stones' party on that turbulent trip also included Anita Pallenberg – who arrived with Brian Jones and left with Keith Richards, Marianne Faithfull and art dealers Robert Fraser and Christopher Gibbs, who had been busted along with Mick and Keith at Redlands, Keith's Sussex home, on 12 February.

'I'm pretty sure Nick did take LSD,' Jeremy told me nearly thirty years afterwards. 'I came in one evening, and we had a balcony with a sliding glass door, and my bed had been moved to block it. Presumably he'd heard, or somebody had said, that one has the temptation to throw oneself off balconies . . . I myself never took drugs, but there was a lot of talk of it around. I didn't, though not because I thought it was bad – I didn't give it any thought whatsoever. But this, I think, is where we parted company in the end, over this. Not in any sense with animosity . . . as far as I was concerned we were friends until the end.'

However, Richard Charkin, who was with Nick in Morocco and has very clear memories of much of that trip, doesn't remember LSD being on the agenda: 'I don't think Nick took acid in Morocco. I would say not. I certainly didn't, and I'm sure if he'd had some we'd have shared it. That was March, April 1967.' While Nick was in Aix filling in time between school and university, Richard Charkin was in Paris doing pretty much the same: 'Paris was pretty cool then, particularly if you were English – Donovan and all that. Coffee and dope were cheap.' A friend of his called Mike Hill came up from Aix to Paris with Nick in tow, and introduced him to Richard, who recalls: 'We drove down to Aix and decided to go to Morocco together, in this Cortina GT. There were four of us: me, Mike, Nick and some other guy . . . We drove all the way, from Aix, through Spain down to Gibraltar and across to Tangiers . . .

'Nick was very nice, a nice, quiet guy who played guitar a bit. In Tangiers there was an amazing crowd in the street, and the rumour was that The Stones were there, and indeed we saw Keith and Brian, who were with Cecil Beaton, the photographer. We worked our way round, went to Meknes, Casablanca, Rabat, Marrakesh, and while we were in Marrakesh, Jagger was there with Cecil Beaton; they were recording these guys. So that was very exciting. Then one evening we were in some restaurant in Marrakesh and Jagger was there with a couple of the girls, and we persuaded Nick, who was very shy, to go and play for them, which he did. I can't remember what – the usual Dylan and Donovan probably. And they were more than polite . . .

'After Marrakesh we decided to go to Chad, which wasn't a very bright idea for four young lads who knew not what they were doing, and shortly after leaving Marrakesh we left the road unintentionally . . . We then had to get towed to a place called Meknes, the car was a bit of a right-off, we didn't have much money, and the guy at the garage was, surprisingly, perfectly happy to repair it without asking for too much money upfront. All he wanted was to have a photo of us with the car, for a before-and-after photo . . .

'We went back after a couple of days to pick up the car, and all he wanted was another photo, and would we play a song for him? So Nick played a song, and he was quite ecstatic . . . We paid a small amount of money and drove off. We got to Tangiers to go back, and were surrounded by police . . . we had appeared in the local Meknes newspaper as The Rolling Stones. They knew there were a bunch of English rock stars around – and there weren't many Europeans there – and the fact Nick played the guitar just convinced them. So they tried to bust us for dope.'

Back in Aix after Morocco, Nick tied up the loose ends and prepared to return home to Tanworth. He was no longer the shy teenager, fresh out of public school, who had set off only four months before. The observations of friends who had known him since school and saw him daily in Aix certainly suggest that something had changed. Perhaps it was during those early months of 1967 that Nick Drake first experimented with drugs. David Wright recalls him rolling a joint in London during October 1966, but it seems probable that in France four or five months later he began to dabble more deeply in drugs. It was in Aix that Jeremy first felt that Nick was becoming immersed in a drug lifestyle. And it was toward the end of his stay there that Simon noticed him beginning to run with a different crowd: 'the camp where there were more drugs'. But balancing all this is the verdict of Richard Charkin, who went to Morocco with Nick and is convinced that he wasn't taking LSD at that time.

Anyway it would be foolish to attribute the problems which later dogged Nick, simply to teenage forays into drugs. Back in the late sixties and early seventies, youthful flirtation with drugs was the rule rather than the exception. The real question is whether putative experiments – particularly with LSD – might have affected the chemistry of a mind that was waiting to be tripped off-balance. Whatever the reasons, it seems clear in retrospect that towards the end of those rootless months in Aix an already shy and introspective boy turned even further in on himself.

'There was certainly dope around in Aix – we are talking about the late sixties. Dope was everywhere. Christ, we were only just across the border from North Africa!' Simon acknowledged. But he went on to suggest that rather than the obvious, chemical causes, a number of subtle and more complex shifts in Nick's life may have caused the dislocation: 'The change in Aix was . . . when he'd been at school, like all of us, we had relatively sheltered lives, and suddenly we were out in an unstructured life, and of course it was the time when everything was opening up anyway . . . All the barriers were coming down . . . about what was acceptable: the sex, the drugs, the rock and roll . . . And I think all of us found that difficult to handle ourselves. Our generation had to learn to cope with these new circumstances, which were wonderful on one hand, but also threw up new problems.'

On his return from France Nick spent some time with his parents in Tanworth, and then, still with five months in hand before he was due to start his studies at Cambridge, he once again gravitated toward London. Tanworth seemed very quiet and parochial after his adventures in Aix and Morocco, and the lure of London, swinging and psychedelic, was irresistible.

Nick already knew London fairly well, and his elder sister was living there, in a flat where he could stay. Determined from the age of six to pursue an acting career, Gabrielle Drake had trained at RADA and was now busy paying her dues. Film work came early in her career, but was largely forgettable: she was a bridesmaid seduced by Peter Sellers in *There's A Girl In My Soup* (1970) and went topless in 1972's prurient *Au Pair Girls*, described by one film encyclopaedia as a 'feeble and dated attempt at a sex comedy'. But it was in the theatre that Gabrielle established her reputation, appearing in West End productions of *Jeeves* and *Noises Off*.

It was some years before she attracted wider attention in BBC TV's *The Brothers*, a Sunday-night soap opera which ran between 1971 and 1976. She played Jill Hammond, a popular character who was killed off in a car crash, provoking calls from outraged viewers. Gabrielle also appeared in the popular TV drama *The Champions* and an acclaimed adaptation of Oscar Wilde's *The Importance Of Being Earnest*. Cult-TV aficionados have fond memories of her as Gay Ellis in *UFO*, Gerry Anderson's first live-action drama. Gabrielle's profile peaked between 1985 and 1987, when she appeared in the long-running, four-times-weekly soap opera *Crossroads*, as

Nicola Freeman, 'the expensively dressed, sophisticated managing director of the Crossroads Motel'. Such was her success that on 9 April 1987 she was the subject of *This Is Your Life*.

While staying with Gabrielle in London during the early summer of 1967, Nick fell in with a rich crowd of hip young aristocrats centred around the Astors and Ormsby-Gores – children of the landed gentry who were drawn by the colourful opportunities on offer in London. The mutual fascination of the aristocracy and the rock establishment is an enduring one, but late-sixties London is where it first took root: the late Alice Ormsby-Gore was Eric Clapton's fiancée and Guinness heir Tara Browne was friendly with The Beatles, while other scions of the Guinness dynasty were close to The Rolling Stones.

The real exoticism of that period was concentrated in certain select London enclaves, where butterflies like Mick and Paul and Jimi fluttered. For teenagers like Nick Drake's Marlborough contemporaries, exposure to drugs was frequently second-hand, or at best tentative, attempts to score often resulting in a couple of pound notes exchanged for a knob of Oxo. But in London, with sufficient funds and the right contacts, almost anything was possible.

Julian Lloyd, whose photograph of Nick wrapped in a blanket appeared on 1994's *Way To Blue* compilation, knew Nick in London in 1967, and thirty years later talked about the period to Mick Brown in a *Daily Telegraph Magazine* piece. It was 'a life centred on scoring black hash at eight quid an ounce, buying twenty Embassy and a packet of Rizla papers, then getting terribly stoned and laughing a lot, followed by a companionable silence'.

5

'I think he might have had quite a wild time at Cambridge,' says Dennis Silk, 'the restrictions of Marlborough being removed, and him loose in town with his guitar, without his housemaster going round saying: "Drake, for God's sake put that bloody instrument away."'

Nick went up to Fitzwilliam College to read English in October 1967. After the tightly communal, strictly timetabled life of boarding school, an institution like Cambridge University must indeed have been a liberation for Nick, and thousands of students like him. There was no one looking over your shoulder, no rotas and lists to tell you what to do or when to do it.

There is something timeless about the melted-candle beauty of Cambridge. The city which has been home to spies and scholars, musicians and mathematicians, choristers and clerics, seems to maintain its other-worldly charm in the face of progress. There is still the beatific charm of an afternoon spent lazing on the Backs, the green stretch which borders the River Cam as it slips, silver, past colleges in the clouds. Willows weep silently over the river banks, but even the boisterous cries of undergraduates cannot overwhelm the quietude of the Cam as it winds its way down to Grantchester.

Rupert Brooke – another golden boy whose life bears similarities to that of Nick Drake – was educated at Rugby and Cambridge. A socialist poet and radical, he died at the age of twenty-seven in 1915, before he could reach Gallipoli, but not before he had done much to brush away the dust and cant of the Victorian age. His best-known poem, 'The Old Vicarage, Grantchester', was published posthumously in *1914 And Other Poems*, and in its poignant questions Brooke spoke for all the young men who sailed away to the mud of Flanders and the bloody beaches of Gallipoli:

> Stands the Church clock at ten to three?
> And is there honey still for tea?

Cambridge has been a university town since 1209, but for all its air of tranquil permanence, life bubbles away beneath the surface. In Market Square the market flourishes today as it has since the early thirteenth century. Among the fruit and veg and clothes are stalls selling joss-sticks, bootleg albums and shawls, much as they did in Nick's day.

From all over the country they came in the sixties, as they had always come, and on arrival they put away childish things and settled down to become students and put the world to rights. For relaxation, there were college cinema clubs, or the Arts Cinema on the corner of Market Square. Here, through clouds of cigarette smoke, the imaginative leap was made from the cinema of childhood to the foothills of the avant-garde. Cambridge all-nighters blended the anarchy of the Marx Brothers with the solemnity of *The Seventh Seal*, while tired late-teenagers grappled with the symbolism which came thick and fast by the celluloid mile.

This was a time before videos, computers and compact discs; before cashcards, mobile phones and mixed colleges. But the conversations were liberating and ideas were cross-fertilizing. To the distaste of some and the delight of many, in the turbulent year after Nick Drake's arrival in Cambridge abortion and homosexuality were finally legalized by Harold Wilson's Labour government.

Key texts of the time were Joseph Heller's *Catch-22*, Colin Wilson's *The Outsider* and Tolkien's *The Lord Of The Rings*. For additional cred, there were the grey-spined Penguin Modern Classics: Hermann Hesse's *Steppenwolf*, Jack Kerouac's *On The Road*, Franz Kafka's *The Castle*, Mervyn Peake's *Gormenghast* trilogy. Poetry had to a large extent been supplanted by rock 'n' roll, but no self-respecting 'head' left their digs without a well-thumbed copy of *The Mersey Poets*, and Yevtushenko ('Do not tell lies to the young. . .') was widely quoted.

This was the city to which Nick Drake came, the year The Beatles released *Sgt Pepper's Lonely Hearts Club Band*. Richard Charkin, who had been with Nick during his month in Morocco earlier in the year, went up at the same time. He laughed when he remembered how they met again: 'Come October '67 I'm in my room at Trinity College, Cambridge, there's a knock on the door and it's Nick. The astonishing thing is that in a month of living together in Morocco, he had never said that he was going to Cambridge. That's quite bizarre, but it was very symptomatic.'

Nick certainly seems to have enjoyed the Cambridge experience, at least some of the time, at least at the beginning . . . Simon Crocker, his old friend from Marlborough, visited Nick during his second term and found him in extremely good heart: 'We both went up to university in the autumn of '67. I went to Bristol, Nick went to Cambridge. In the second term there was an exchange between the Bristol revue group which I was in, and the Cambridge Footlights, and I remember Nick turned up after the show at Cambridge and said: "Right, let's go" – he had this old motorbike, and we spent the night roaring around Cambridge – "Let's have some fun." He was in great spirits.'

The Cambridge University Footlights Club, which was founded in 1883 as a forum for university entertainers, came into its own during the 1950s. Peter Cook, the John Lennon of the Fringe quartet, arrived in 1957 and blitzed the town. Cook hitched up with Alan Bennett, Jonathan Miller and Dudley Moore, and went Beyond the Edinburgh Fringe in 1960. British comedy was never the same after their foray; in their way, the Fringe four had as much impact on British society as The Beatles. Following Cook, Cambridge Footlights became the comedy equivalent of the Cavern, spewing out a series of household names: John Bird, Eleanor Bron, David Frost, John Cleese, Michael Palin, Eric Idle, Terry Jones, Clive James, Graham Chapman . . . Interestingly, both Nick Drake and his friend Robert Kirby auditioned for the club during their time at Cambridge, but neither was accepted.

Trevor Dann, who compiled the 1985 Nick Drake retrospective *Heaven In A Wild Flower* and is now in overall control of popular music coverage on BBC TV and Radio, was, in 1971, a student at Fitzwilliam College. Dann, who had bought *Five Leaves Left* as a teenager, was delighted to find himself reading history at Nick Drake's old Cambridge college, but the college buildings were far from homely: 'It's worth remembering that at the time Nick was there in the sixties, it was an even worse building than it is now. Only half of it was built, the bit by Huntingdon Road, everything the other side of the monstrous café block wasn't there. And also, the A14 wasn't a motorway, so all the lorries coming to the port used to come up Victoria Road, hang a right past the college, and the windows used to rattle something horrible. Every term I came back from holiday, I used to have to put Plasticine round the windows to stop them shuddering.

'I was just a lad who liked Nick Drake, who was at the same college. Then I met a bloke there called John Venning, who was a postgrad, and he had known Nick Drake. So I spent the odd evening in the college bar, trying to get him to reminisce. I suspect it was through him I found out that Nick had briefly had a college room. Somebody told me it was R24, so I managed to get myself into R24.'

Fitzwilliam College grew out of 'an institution which became the home of non-collegiate students in Cambridge who could not afford membership of an established college'. Its first buildings were occupied in 1963, but the buildings the college now occupies, designed by Denys Lasdun, architect of London's National Theatre, were inaugurated in 1966. Cambridge City Council's official guide describes Fitzwilliam College codedly as 'strikingly modern' and 'a riot of sculptural invention'.

When you read that Nick Drake studied at Cambridge, images spring to mind of punts gliding on the Cam and gowns flowing as cyclists scuttle across Jesus Green. The reality was, and is, somewhat different. Architecturally, Fitzwilliam has more in common with the boxy modern hotels which proliferate on industrial parks close to major motorway exits than with the traditional Cambridge colleges which grace the heart of the city.

Fitzwilliam College sits a good mile out of Cambridge, on the Huntingdon Road, its red-brick buildings and plain rectangular window-panes jarringly at odds with the public image of the city. Despite beautifully kept gardens and well-appointed lawns, Fitzwilliam looks less like a Cambridge college than a 1960s day-care centre. Victoria Lloyd (née Ormsby-Gore) remembered visiting Nick at Fitzwilliam when she spoke to Mick Brown: 'He was profoundly disappointed by it. He had this wonderful vision of going to Cambridge – the dreaming spires, the wonderful erudite people. We went up to visit and he was in this grim, redbrick building, sitting in this tiny motel-like bedroom. He was completely crushed. He just sat there saying "it's so awful".'

Strangely, though, when Simon Crocker visited he felt that, far from hating the modernity of Fitzwilliam, Nick was frustrated by the hidebound nature of the whole institution: 'I think for Nick Cambridge was a bit too . . . old-fashioned. I think he would have enjoyed one of the other universities better. I think he felt quite stifled. He didn't like the customs . . .'

Roger Brown, who went up to Fitzwilliam in October 1969, at the beginning of what should have been Nick's final year, wrote to me with his impressions of the place. Roger remembered Nick being spoken of fondly by contemporary musicians, including Fred Frith, who went on to join the band Henry Cow. More intriguingly, he wrote about the college as it was in Nick's time: 'In theory, a college such as Fitzwilliam with an active social life and back-up such as individual tutors, ought to offer an ideal environment for the transition from home and school to independent life as an adult. In practice however, many students were too young and not self-reliant enough. Nick Drake was not the only Fitzwilliam student to have difficulty in adjusting . . . It was not unusual for people to crack-up and spend time at the local mental hospital (Fulbourn, as I recall) . . . At the time, Fitzwilliam did not admit women, so the atmosphere was rather monkish and not helped by the emphasis on engineering, science, chemistry, law, rowing, rugby etc . . .'

So this was Nick Drake's Cambridge college: a suburban dormitory building, efficient and municipal, with little in the way of camaraderie, comfort or college spirit. The undergraduate rooms were cubicles, practical but cramped and impersonal; the whole place an outpost, far removed from the life of the city and the heart of the university.

Paul Wheeler met Nick and fellow-student Robert Kirby when he went up to Caius College in 1968: 'The way that Cambridge works is like a big club, and when I arrived at Caius, because I played music, they said: "Oh, you should meet this person", and Robert said: "Oh, you must meet Nick" . . . Caius was in the centre of town, and it had more of a traditional image of Cambridge. So I think this link between Caius and Nick is quite interesting, because in some ways he was on the border of a Cambridge life – he was living outside the town, and Fitzwilliam is quite a way out – whereas coming into Caius, which he did quite a lot because of Robert and me and quite a group of us . . . so in some ways there was more of a link between Nick and Caius than there was between him and Fitzwilliam.

'At Caius we had this dining club, which is very Cambridge, called The Loungers. And the only thing you had to do was "lounge by ye gate for one hour every day and observe what straunge creatures God hath made!" Every week or two we had a Loungers' Breakfast . . . and Nick was the "odd fellow" in this group, they had one or two people from other colleges . . . and that was the way we used to officially meet.'

Unlike Marlborough, on which he left a real and lasting impression, Fitzwilliam College has precious few memories of Nick Drake. He never completed his degree, quitting twelve months ahead of Finals, to journey down to London and seek a career in music. His departure, like his two-year residence, went largely unnoticed. Two years after Nick left Fitzwilliam, Trevor Dann went up and found that not a trace remained: 'The only person who knew about Nick Drake at Fitzwilliam was me, and I would tell people, and they'd go: "Who?" '

However, by 1994 the slow-burning flame of posthumous fame had begun to take hold. A notice appeared on the college notice board headed 'Calling All Guitarists'. A second-year student, Ewan C. Kerr, was organizing a guitar concert 'in recognition of the number of guitarists there are in college who never get around to playing in front of anyone'. The notice continued: 'You may or may not be aware that Fitz was home to a singer-songwriter legend (well I think so!) of the 60s called Nick Drake. The concert will be in memory of him (he died on November 25th 1974 – just 20 years ago last Thursday).'

Like most students at Fitzwilliam, Nick spent his first year living in, with 'bedders' to clean up his room and meals in hall on tap. But when he returned to Cambridge after the long vacation in autumn 1968, he moved into lodgings outside the college. It was during his second year, while he was living in rooms in Carlyle Road, that Paul Wheeler met him for the first time: 'It's just slightly outside the main university territory, Carlyle Road, just by this little bridge which leads on to Jesus Green, so that every time Nick came into town he would cross over the river, and I've always considered that "River Man" had to do with this . . .'

Much of Nick's time at Cambridge was spent visiting friends in other colleges – Brian Wells at Selwyn, Robert Kirby and Paul Wheeler at Caius; and they in their turn would visit him. One friend remembers Nick's room as 'very quiet and nice, books and records and dope', and Nick would often produce his guitar and play for them – songs which his friends would recognize on *Five Leaves Left* the following year.

Paul Wheeler: 'I remember Nick playing "Time Has Told Me" at

Cambridge. The first one that really struck me was "River Man" – that to me is the one that stands out. To be honest, I found a lot of his stuff a bit too . . . clean, too twee, whereas "River Man" had an extra dimension to it. I remember him playing those Jackson Frank songs, some standards of the time . . . but he'd certainly play something if he'd just written it. They weren't performances – Nick would play something, I'd play something, somebody else would play something. But what was so noticeable about Nick was that he was so . . . perfect! Other people would start and stop, tune up. He would never do that . . .'

Nick's mother, Molly, always regarded Brian Wells, who studied medicine at Selwyn College, as her son's best friend at Cambridge. Brian was an exact contemporary of Nick's at the university and provides a poignant picture of Nick during those two years. He remembers a college party where both he and Nick were struck by an outgoing girl who was dancing the night away. Nick was mesmerized, but Brian tired of the pursuit and returned to his rooms at Selwyn, only to be woken by Nick much, much later that night.

'I didn't get off with that girl,' Nick woke Brian to tell him. A less than sympathetic Wells watched from his bed as Nick drunkenly ambled around his room, finally selecting a massive medical textbook from the bookshelves. From somewhere else, Nick found a candle, which he lit and ceremoniously placed on the flat surface of the book, before proceeding off down the staircase.

'One of my fondest memories of Nick,' recalled Brian Wells thirty years later, 'was looking out of my window, and seeing him teetering off on his bicycle across the college, balancing that huge book on his handlebars. He was shielding the flame, and with the candle still flickering, he cycled off.'

'Cambridge was a very radical place,' Ian MacDonald recalls. 'I remember when we arrived in '68, meeting a friend who had been a year ahead of me at school, and when I arrived for my first term he recognized me and came up as the new intake were having their photograph taken, and he was laughing and said: "I thought we were weird when we arrived, but you lot look like the Mothers Of Invention." '

Ian went up to Cambridge in 1968 and met Nick Drake on various occasions: 'I wouldn't say I knew Nick at all, really. Though I was in the same places as him quite a few times . . . I actually spoke to him on only two or three occasions.' He went on to become Deputy Editor of the *New Musical Express* during the 1970s, and in 1994 his acclaimed Beatles book, *Revolution In The Head*, was published.

In the wake of The Beatles, Harold Wilson and gritty Northern cinema, classlessness was venerated, but it was still largely the children of the middle classes who made the trip to Oxbridge. Once there, though, the accents which had been so carefully and expensively chiselled in public schools and comfortable drawing rooms were swiftly flattened into *nouveau*-working-class tones. Clive James, who also studied at Cambridge, recalled the inverted snobbery of that period: 'There was a real pretension to inarticulacy, which I felt I couldn't share. There were an awful lot of university students running around in the sixties pretending they'd never been educated, a grotesque sound coming out of their mouth.'

In the late sixties, the connection between a hash reverie, psychedelic art and rock music was self-evident. Paul McCartney's admission in 1967 that he had taken acid sent shock waves across the nation; the Mick Jagger and Keith Richards bust that same year convinced everyone, particularly the readers of the *News Of The World* (then the world's best-selling newspaper), that all these pop stars were drug addicts.

Nick Drake was evidently no stranger to drugs by the time he arrived in Cambridge. There are accounts of him smoking dope during 1966, and strong indications from friends that he had tried LSD during the early part of 1967. In that, he was certainly not unique. A wave of drug-taking swept through the teenagers of Britain's middle classes during 1967. Most saw it as the beginning of a great odyssey, a trip to the centre of the psyche. Many made the journey, but some never came back.

Robert Kirby: 'There was always the undercurrent of the people who had gone, or wanted to go, a bit further, the acid side of it, I suppose . . . I'm not trying to ascribe the whole thing to drugs, but what I'm saying is that even then there were the people who put their toe in the water but didn't go the whole distance . . . You always got the impression that maybe Nick wanted more than just to put his toe in the water . . .'

The joy of long-playing records had much to do with the size and design of the twelve-inch sleeves, which were so convenient for rolling spliffs. Sleeves became iconic tokens: *Sgt Pepper* was the stained-glass window of 1967; Dylan's *John Wesley Harding* the maze of 1968 – turn the sleeve upside down and The Beatles and Lee Harvey Oswald appeared in the tree above Dylan's head. Tentative psychedelia was apparent on album sleeves by The Incredible String Band and Pink Floyd. The Small Faces' *Ogden's Nut Gone Flake* sleeve was as revolutionary as *Sgt Pepper*, but its circular sleeve made rolling up a nightmare.

The sleeves promised access to a closed world, and then there was the music those sleeves contained . . . Music was probably never more important than at that time, when pop was changing into rock and the single was being elbowed out by the LP. The liberating power of music was felt across the board, in folk, jazz, blues and rock 'n' roll. Clive James told me: 'I remember when "I Heard It Through The Grapevine" came out, and I spent the whole week listening to it in a pub in Cambridge on the jukebox.'

Iain Dunn, who was in his first year at Corpus Christi when, as a friend of Paul Wheeler's, he met Nick early in 1968, also remembers how important the music was: 'I saw an interview with Sting on the television recently, and he said something I thought was very true, which was that in those days everyone knew what number one was. These days nobody knows, because the whole thing is so fragmented. I think accessibility to material was much more difficult, so there was much more of a sense of belonging to a cult. So if you managed a trip up to London and got hold of a copy of, I don't know, Mississippi John Hurt, this was like gold dust. People would come round and it would be an event to listen to it . . . I remember hiring the cellar in my college because I'd somehow or other managed to get hold of a first copy of *Tommy*, and actually playing it like a concert.'

Ian MacDonald: 'Everyone took music much more seriously than we do these days. You'd gather together, sometimes people would be floating in and out of a particular room where people were smoking, they'd be playing records all day and people would come in and just sit, listening quite seriously all the way through The Beatles' *White Album*, and then drift off.

'A few years later, I remember – this was after I'd left Cambridge but was typical of the time – I met Mick Farren, who had just come fresh from an extraordinary twenty-four-hour bash at his flat in Notting Hill, where all the heads, Mick and Miles, had just decided that they were going to listen to everything that Dylan had released, including all the bootlegs, in chronological order, and nobody would leave until it was finished. I do remember when we all sat around reading aloud from *The Lord Of The Rings*. Incredibly embarrassing now, but there was that mad intensity.'

Sgt Pepper, 'A Whiter Shade Of Pale', 'All You Need Is Love', 'San

Francisco': dreamy and benign reflections of 1967's good vibrations. Iain Dunn remembers Cambridge reflecting the turbulence which was manifest throughout the world just a year later: 'We'd had the Summer of Love, and 1968 was the year of Revolution . . . So from it all being peace and love and freedom, the agenda for the next academic year, if you like, was revolution. The Garden House Riot, as it came to be called, was part of that, a protest against the Greek Colonels who had come to power by force during 1967. I can't remember who was in the hotel at the time, but it was something to do with protesting against the fascist junta . . . Coach-loads of people went up to the Grosvenor Square riot outside the American Embassy, protesting against Vietnam. So they were all highly political agendas. I think it was as much to do with being anti-Establishment as with being particularly committed to a cause. There were obviously those who were committed, but I think for most of us we were just happy to be rioting and rebelling.'

Throughout 1968 the world was rocked by dissent and chaos: in Vietnam, the Têt offensive severely shook American belief in a swift victory. Czechoslovakia briefly celebrated a liberating release from a stiflingly repressive government, before being crushed under the tracks of Russian tanks. Robert Kennedy was assassinated on the campaign trail. Martin Luther King was taken by a sniper's bullet in Memphis. Enoch Powell's 'rivers of blood' speech took racism on to the streets and into the headlines. In France, Japan, America, Britain, Poland, Spain, Italy and Mexico, students protested and rioted, shutting down university campuses and making their grievances spectacularly public.

Looking back on the period nearly thirty years after leaving Caius, Paul Wheeler was keen to put the period that he and Nick spent at Cambridge in the context of the times: 'The way that I recall the difference between 1967 and 1968 – '67 was the Summer of Love; '68 was much more political. In a sense '69 and '70 was the end of all that, more cynical, more depressed times . . . When I knew Nick, it was still in the flush of the optimistic times . . . My memories of Nick from that time are very funny, very humorous. He wasn't this grim, depressed . . . that came later. And also I would say that was the same for everybody, the turn of 1971/72 was a bad time for everybody. The depression was a sign of the times. Everybody felt down in '73, '74, because of the end of that era.'

The popular image of Nick Drake at Cambridge is of a tall, stooped figure, dressed in black, over-imbibing on hashish and

French Symbolist poetry. All very romantic, and romanticized. Paul Wheeler, who knew Nick as well as anyone at Cambridge, took issue with me over my account of a drive the two of them undertook to the East Anglian coast, about sixty miles from Cambridge. An earlier account by Arthur Lubow had Paul and Nick sitting in moonlit silence, listening to waves crashing on the Suffolk beach. 'There was something I wanted to say about Arthur Lubow,' Paul told me, 'something he got from me about going off to the coast . . . and I think in the article you wrote you have us coming back at dawn. It's all getting a bit romantic. I don't remember it as that. I do remember the occasion: I remember his driving off to the coast, and walking by the beach, but this idea of being an all-night thing I don't remember.'

The romanticization of Nick Drake has grown steadily in the years since his death, and appears unstoppable. Posthumously, Nick has been cast as a victim: of record company indifference, of a hostile society, of his own demons . . . But among those who knew him at Marlborough, Cambridge and while he was on Island Records, there is a feeling that he was not quite as disingenuous as he seemed; some suspect that even while still an apparently aimless student at Cambridge, he had an eye on future plans. Cambridge contemporary Iain Dunn certainly thinks he detected some deliberate image-making, despite the obvious shyness: 'He was very nice. Incredibly nice. But quite . . . I think "detached" is probably the word. Not remote . . . I wasn't quite sure if this was a conscious image that he was developing, or whether it was just the way he was. And I think in the end, I came to the conclusion that it was a bit of both. I think he quite liked the idea of there being an air of mystique about himself. But I think he was also genuinely, incredibly shy, and found himself to be quite remote from other people.'

Despite his closeness to Nick, Brian Wells also discerned a certain reserve, and an image-consciousness which is rarely acknowledged: 'My theory, and it is only a theory, my own impressions, I think he was always, not aloof . . . slightly detached from everybody, and I think most people felt this. I don't think Robert Kirby, or Paul Wheeler would ever think, Hi, Nick!, give him a hug . . . Nick was very conscious of his image . . . He was occasionally quite abrupt with people. You just got the feeling he was being rather dismissive of you.

'I think it was because he was feeling threatened by the closeness of a relationship. I'm a very open, huggy kind of person. I sometimes felt he thought I was a bit of a twit. It wasn't just my not being a musician, I wasn't kind of . . . cool. He was very aware of his cool. Actually, if you look at his photos, he was quite contrived in his appearance. He was always clean-shaven, with his long hair and his black jacket . . . He was very self-conscious and I think he was very sensitive. I also think he was quite precious . . .'

Ian MacDonald remembers Nick making a strong impression during those early days at Cambridge, not just as a result of his growing confidence on the guitar, but because of his height and physical presence: 'He was very slight physically, tall, slightly thin. He used to wear a loose, grey suit as I remember him. He looked . . . fragile, like something could happen to him. Yet he was observing at the same time; a very, very fine balance. An almost . . . translucent person.

'Byronic is going too far. Nick was too diffident to be Byron, he wasn't a wild man . . . He was someone rather fragile, but with a certain inner strength. But a lot of paradox: he was the kind of guy that women would want to mother. The impressiveness came through a kind of quiet power in those songs. Personally, he was quite a diffident person, he would mumble and there was that very faint half smile as he drew back from things.'

Nick's awareness of the way he looked and how he appeared to others also struck Iain Dunn: 'My most vivid memory of him around Cambridge was of this very tall, loping character with shoulder-length hair. But always very smart. I think he was very conscious of the way he looked. How he appeared to other people was all part of that . . . slight image-building thing that was going on. The velvet jacket, the Cuban-heel boots . . .'

The physical frailty, the lack of robustness which has become part of the myth of Nick in recent years, does not appear to have taken hold in Cambridge; the 'very well made, tall, strong' athlete of the Marlborough years was not yet erased. 'He never struck me as being unhealthy,' said Paul Wheeler. 'He always held himself very well, always looked healthy, so there was that – a word you always hear about Nick – elegance . . .'

Iain Dunn characterizes Cambridge in the late sixties as: 'Quite a lot of sex and drugs and rock 'n' roll. I don't remember doing a lot of work. Certainly if you were reading English, the idea of actually going to a seminar was thought to be quite bizarre. Not many people did. Not many people got up before midday.

'Nick was reading English, and I remember a friend of his was doing some big essay . . . a comparison between a seventeenth-century love lyric and the lyrics of Smokey Robinson. That was a fairly typical thing of the time. There were an awful lot of people reading English in those days who were asking the question: how come all literature stops with T.S. Eliot? You were desperately trying to incorporate into your English essay some kind of relationship with what was going on in the rest of your life, which was how exciting the new Beatles album was. And of course, as far as the Establishment was concerned, this was total anathema. Very few dons then had any conception of, or understanding, that this might be the way things were going.'

Before rock 'n' roll pulled on its pompous and ponderous seventies wardrobe, millions around the world were united by the sounds which came out of transistor radios and spinning black vinyl albums as the sixties wound down. Nick Drake was now fashioning his own material, but he remained immersed in the wonderful music which others were producing during 1967 and 1968. He loved the material of the new singer-songwriters like Tim Buckley, Leonard Cohen, Tim Hardin and Randy Newman, who were just beginning to make their mark. Ian MacDonald considered that, of all the people he met in Cambridge, 'Nick always seemed to be somebody who was passing through, right on the edge of things . . . only relating to people who spoke the same language, the same musical language.'

Other albums which found favour with Nick during 1968 included Love's *Forever Changes*, Van Morrison's *Astral Weeks* and, more surprisingly, the work of Fifth Dimension. To many who favoured more challenging bands like Traffic, Pink Floyd, Led Zeppelin, Santana and Cream, the chart-friendly, close-harmony group were anathema, but Nick recognized the high production values of the first three albums. He also admired two writers championed by the group: Jim Webb, who wrote their biggest hit, 'Up, Up & Away', and Laura Nyro, herself barely out of her teens. Nick was impressed enough by Fifth Dimension to recommend them to Robert Kirby: 'He told me to get the Fifth Dimension album *Magic Garden*, because of the use of rock and orchestra – same as *Pet Sounds*. He was the one who turned me on to the first Randy Newman album and Tim Buckley's *Goodbye And Hello* . . .'

Paul Wheeler: 'When I was at Caius there was a particular friend of ours who had an amazing record collection, from Bach to Motown. We spent a lot of time round there: he'd put on some Bach Suite, followed by jazz, Gregorian chants. And then put on Smokey

Robinson, Indian music . . . That blending together was very much a sign of the times, and I guess things like "Cello Song" reflect that . . .' One song he remembers Nick being particularly fond of was 'Song For Our Ancestors', from the second Steve Miller Band album, *Sailor*. An atmospheric piece, it begins with the sound of foghorns baying out, as a sepulchral organ plays beneath. As the guitars and drums brush in, it develops into an impressionistic wash, similar to those Pink Floyd were attempting at the time. An odd choice for someone whose perceived taste was for the precision-cut lyrics of literate singer-songwriters.

During their first term in Cambridge, Brian Wells met Nick in a pub called the Criterion: 'I went there because people who smoke dope went to the Criterion . . . I'd just come back from America, I'd been living there for a year, and I'd got a load of records – stuff like Sam & Dave which had been in the Soul Charts in America – that Nick hadn't heard. I'd got a few West Coast-type things, but I wasn't really into the West Coast stuff like Iron Butterfly . . .

'Nick was a very tall, very good-looking guy, who looked just like the guy on the cover of your book . . . We clicked, partly because we both smoked dope, and partly because I'd got this record collection. I was interested in music, and it became very clear early on that he was a guitar player who was in a league that was totally different to the one I was in . . . I'd come back to England, where there were these people who had been influenced by John Renbourn and Davy Graham . . . and Paul Wheeler was one of them, actually. Nick and Paul were both very good guitarists who were playing acoustic guitars with all sorts of bluesy, finger-picking styles . . . I was really quite awestruck by them both, actually.

'I had worked on a radio station in the States, so I was into American pop music rather than the underground; the hippie movement was wasted on me, I thought it was a load of old cobblers. But it did introduce me to people who smoked dope, which was what Nick and I had in common . . . I remember smoking dope and playing him things like Cannonball Adderley's "Mercy, Mercy", Sam & Dave, Aretha, "Never Loved A Man The Way I Loved You" . . . He was turning me on to things like Van Morrison's *Astral Weeks* and Donovan . . . He appreciated things like *The Notorious Byrd Brothers*.'

Besides listening voraciously, Nick was quietly, determinedly, working at his own songwriting, and trying the results out on friends, as Ian MacDonald discovered: 'I remember Nick playing

"River Man" and "Time Has Told Me" . . . on several occasions in various Cambridge college rooms . . . a very quiet, humble, kind man, who seemed to be viewing everything from a faintly puzzled, faintly amused distance. At the time, he was about to record *Five Leaves Left*, and we were all knocked out by the songs.'

Nick's Cambridge friends all share clear and fond memories of informal sessions when he played his own songs, and some remember occasions, often with Paul Wheeler on guitar, which were just jams, usually based around blues figures, with no discernible endings or beginnings. But although happy to get out his guitar and play for friends, Nick played precious few real concerts. Neither Iain Dunn nor Ian MacDonald recalls ever seeing Nick perform formally while at Cambridge, and Brian Wells agrees: 'I don't remember Nick doing gigs in Cambridge – only in our rooms. I would occasionally jam with him. I would struggle on, but he didn't think much of me as a musician, quite rightly. I think he and Paul Wheeler would do a fair bit together.

'In terms of gigging, that didn't really happen until after *Five Leaves Left*. We were aware that he had these mysterious friends, one of whom was Joe Boyd, and there was all this sort of stuff about "Well, I'm thinking of making a record . . ." I think some of us didn't quite believe it. It was a different life. He'd be in Cambridge, he'd smoke dope, he wouldn't do any work really, and we'd meet up and listen to music. Then he would go off to London, where he seemed to have a different life . . .'

Nick was listening to pretty much what everyone else of his age was hearing at the time, and when it came to guitarists his turntable tutors were as you would expect – Bert Jansch, John Renbourn, Davy Graham, John Martyn . . . Little of the electric flamboyance of Eric Clapton or Jimmy Page impinged upon his playing. Robert Kirby has clear memories of Nick playing in his rooms at Caius: 'He'd often come round and sit, not play his own stuff, but improvise blues. I mean, I love Jansch, Renbourn, Davy Graham . . . in the sixties we had the best of the world's acoustic guitarists . . . He was better than them at the blues. He could either do it in a complex sixties or seventies rock style, or he could make it sound like the original black Americans had done it before the war. He had studied it a lot, he really had. He used to talk about some quite esoteric forties and fifties players.'

Iain Dunn didn't foresee Nick's success, but sensed that he was working at honing his talent: 'I think in those days he did what

everyone did, which was play Bert Jansch at sixteen rpm, work out
what he was doing, and do it for themselves . . . He would turn up
and say: "I've got a new song" and you'd go: "Oh, what is it?" And
he'd play "Man In A Shed" or something . . . He was obviously a
very able guitarist . . . I do remember he had the most gorgeous voice,
just fantastic. It was so . . . sensitive, a slightly husky quality.'

May Balls – which actually take place during the first week of June –
are an Oxbridge tradition in which live music plays an important
part. In 1964 The Rolling Stones had to interrupt their debut
American tour to fly back and play an Oxford May Ball. The
incongruity is still striking, but it really did happen: on 10 June
1969 Nick Drake hunched over his guitar and sent out his wistful and
idiosyncratic songs to a braying, swaying, May Ball crowd.

John Mayall and the Liverpool Scene headlined the Caius May Ball
that year, together with Tuesday's Children, White Unicorn, Paul
Wheeler ('whose lyrical and humorous songs and guitar-playing have
been entertaining London and Cambridge audiences for several
years'), Fab Cab and The North-West London Contemporary Jazz
Five. As well as arranging for, and appearing with, Nick Drake,
Robert Kirby was also singing with The Gentle Power Of Song that
June night. There was also a Cambridge jazz group by the name of
Horn. Intriguingly, barely three years later, 'Horn' would appear as
the title of an instrumental piece on Nick's final album, *Pink Moon*.

The May Ball programme included the following profile: 'Nick
Drake's forthcoming LP, already hailed in the press as the record of
the year, was produced by Joe Boyd (producer of The Incredible
String Band and Fairport Convention). Robert Kirby arranged some
of the tracks on the album and his orchestra will be accompanying
Nick tonight.'

Robert remembers his performance with Nick at the Caius May
Ball: 'I wore evening dress, and the girls were at the ball anyway, and
they wore black, ankle-length dresses with white feather boas. They
were playing as a double quartet, an octet. There was a string-bass
player as well – his name was Colin Fleetcroft, and I've never seen
him since, but I'm sure he had an old tape recorder set up and
recorded it. I certainly scored for flutes. Nick was singing, and we
also interspersed it with the slow movement of Leopold Mozart's
Trumpet Concerto and the Albinoni Adagio & Fugue.

'It was in the Library. Nick did the four orchestrated songs, he did
a couple of songs without the strings, and after every third song we

stuck in these classical bits. Everyone talks about the sixties and flower power, but the May Ball was very much what it would have been like before the war. I think socially the big changes came in the seventies . . . when the educational establishment changed. In the sixties, the drug culture was there, but by and large, you still conformed, even if you didn't think you were at the time.'

When flautist and saxophonist Iain Cameron arrived in Cambridge the year after Nick, he soon became involved in the city's thriving undergraduate musical scene: 'I would go round to Paul Wheeler's room in New Court, and we'd blow. One afternoon I go round there, this would be April or May 1969, and . . . Nick is there playing songs – I definitely remember "River Man" – and just remember thinking what a dream of a song that was. How utterly stunning as a piece of music, partly because of the concentric guitar part in 5/4, the harmonies, very evocative, slightly mournful words. He also looked very impressive, like he looked on the records. A very beautiful person by any standards. Slightly reticent, slightly cool, insubstantial spirit . . .'

Cameron was co-opted into playing at the May Ball in the 'Kirby-led ensemble', and remembers the occasion in some detail: 'Nick was on about eleven o'clock . . . He was quite featured, he had his own space, a medium-sized room in Caius College devoted to Nick. It was reasonably well attended, an audience of thirty to fifty . . . It was quite ambitious, because of the Kirby arrangements . . . Nick was seated, playing guitar, there was a little woodwind section over to one side of the stage . . . a few strings, but I can't remember if there were girls . . . "Mayfair", "Time Of No Reply" I remember, stuff from *Five Leaves Left*. Now I would worry about whether we had a good PA, but I don't remember what the sound was like that night.'

Nick Drake performing while surrounded by girls in feather boas is an appealing and enduring image, and there is no doubt that it did happen. There is, however, a difference of recollection as to where and when. The striking tableau is generally attributed to the 1969 Caius May Ball, but others suggest that the boas in question appeared at another confirmed performance, which Nick gave at Cambridge's Pitt Club, in Jesus Lane.

Brian Wells remembers both performances but refuses to be drawn about feather boas: 'He did play at a May Ball; he also played at my ex-wife's twenty-first birthday party in the Pitt Club, with an orchestra, and I was at both of those gigs, because I did the sound PA. At the May Ball he was using the amplifier and speakers that we were using for our disco, and he came in . . . while I was in the middle of playing "Mony Mony" or something by Tommy James & The Shondells . . . saying: "You will make sure we've got the PA . . . ?" And I'm saying: "Hang on, hang on, let me just cue up this other record." And he was a bit concerned that I was a bit abrupt, and his comment was: "Oh, I can tell I've walked into a really busy situation . . ."

'The Pitt Club with the orchestra was a bit scratchy . . . Robert Kirby had a string quartet with him as well . . . They definitely played "Time Of No Reply" – I was always surprised that wasn't on *Five Leaves Left*, because it was something he played quite a lot. He played most of the *Five Leaves Left* stuff.'

The now familiar picture of a reserved and image-conscious young man, preoccupied with his music, seems at odds with Nick's apparent enjoyment of playing for his friends, pints of beer at the Criterion and college parties. Nick enjoyed the conviviality of Cambridge. It was an easy place to get seduced by, and during his two years there Nick embraced university life. There were plenty of spontaneous drives out of town too, when friends like Robert Kirby and Paul Wheeler piled into Nick's Vauxhall Viva, with Nick heading for the Suffolk coast or local points of interest.

Robert Kirby confirmed this light-hearted, almost fun-loving, side to Nick: 'He liked to go to parties. He came out to a party at my brother's in Hertfordshire, played the guitar there quite happily. He liked a drink, he talked . . . I can remember punting, swimming. Getting in the car and just looning off on the spur of the moment. Talking about anything at all. He had been a sportsman, a very good athlete. I can remember him trying to chuck me in the river, me trying to chuck him in the river. However, he did, from the very first time I met him, have this incredible presence. He was tall, very good-looking. He was imposing just when he came in the room. Without speaking, he would impose his presence on you unintentionally. All women liked him. I remember all my girlfriends fancied him.'

One of the theories frequently put forward to try to explain Nick's later depression and decline is that he was gay and unhappy about it. Nick was undoubtedly attractive to women, and Richard Charkin acknowledges that he didn't seem very responsive to this interest, but he doesn't believe that Nick was homosexual. Like so many others I have spoken to, he felt that over the course of all the time they spent together, he would have sensed such an instinct, even if repressed: 'We used to go down to the Criterion . . . Girls used to really love him, and he never did a bloody thing, he never lifted a finger . . .

People have said he was gay, he was pretty, but I think, together for a month in Morocco, and two years at Cambridge . . .'

For all his conviviality, there was always a more serious side to Nick's nature; but as Robert Kirby explained, that wasn't unique to his friend. Cambridge did have that effect on people: 'There certainly was a dark side to Nick, right from the start . . . I remember the first time I heard "Three Hours" – at Madingley, the American cemetery – we'd gone out there one night, and it was very scary, just to hear him play that there. I'm not saying that dark side was all based on drugs, or him reading *The Myth Of Sisyphus* . . . I think Nick did look into these things like Wittgenstein, Camus, structuralism . . . That sort of blank, negative, nihilist side of life . . . but he wasn't unique in that. Walking around Cambridge in those days, there were fifty people worse than Nick that you would pass on the pavement every hour . . .'

Studies did not worry Nick unduly at Cambridge, but apart from participating in the wide-ranging social scene, it was at Cambridge that he really began to hone his guitar style and songwriting. In the university's green pastures, between 1967 and 1969, Nick Drake slipped quietly from shy schoolboy to introspective young man with a clearly defined picture of his future.

Robert Kirby was at Caius on a music scholarship when he first met Nick Drake during their second term at Cambridge in early 1968. Kirby was already involved with The Gentle Power Of Song, a close-harmony singing group at the university, who had landed a recording deal with Polydor and released a couple of singles. In February of that year Nick had played a gig at London's Roundhouse, as a result of which Ashley Hutchings of Fairport Convention had alerted Joe Boyd to the singer-songwriter's abilities. Somehow Nick had learned of Robert Kirby's musical pedigree and, during the spring term of 1968, approached him about possibly arranging songs for the album which would become Nick's debut recording.

'It was during the spring term, March or April 1968, that Nick first approached me,' Robert told me. 'When I first met him, he was importing those psychedelic posters from LA, and he was selling those as a sideline . . . Nick came round to my room in Tree Court at Caius and said he'd got a recording deal and knew that I'd done an album for Polydor . . . He had his guitar with him and he played me "Day Is Done", "Way To Blue", "I Was Made To Love Magic" and "Time Of No Reply". The version of that he played me was much faster than the one which was later released. We did an arrangement of that, which was one of the first four I did.'

By the end of his first year at Cambridge Nick Drake already had his sights set on a career as an Island Records recording artist. During his second year he worked hard polishing his own songs and his skills as a guitarist. In the light of this chronology those intimate sessions trying out new material in studies and bedsits around Cambridge begin to take on the air of workshop performances or warm-up gigs. It has become part of the myth that Nick stumbled into the music business unwittingly, that the 'success' thrust upon him by others damaged him irreparably, but the evidence contradicts this view. Nick worked hard at his music, and cared too deeply about it to let it go to waste.

Brian Wells first met Nick in October 1967: 'He probably hadn't met Joe Boyd by that time, so it's interesting, because he had all this network going on in London, and one got the sense that he had some sort of deal going . . . I think different folk were in different compartments. A bunch of people at the funeral met up for the first time, and were all from different walks of life . . . Occasionally he and I would get together in London during holiday time. It was actually a bit awkward . . . I felt slightly out of my depth in London. He clearly had all these slightly special people, like the Ormsby-Gores, and names like Eric Clapton got mentioned, and I felt slightly star-struck, hanging around with this guy whose guitar-playing I loved, who by then had started to record.'

Nick's parents, though always supportive of his music, were troubled when he announced that he wouldn't be returning to Cambridge for his final year. Molly's voice is sad and slightly baffled in the recorded interview: 'I don't know if his only ambition was to be a musician. He read English at Cambridge, he was very interested in literature, he felt all the time that he was torn between the two things, and finally he gave up. He left Cambridge before taking his degree, which to us seemed a terrible thing; he had passed the first part of his degree, and he was within nine months of the finals. We all said this is the most terrible thing to do, as any parent would, and Rodney said to him at least if you get your degree you'll have a safety net, and Nick said: "The last thing in life I want is a safety net!"'

'He was confident about the music,' Rodney Drake said. 'He made his first album while he was still at Cambridge. He was quite convinced that was what he wanted to do. I have said before that I don't think we realized how good his music was – but he did. That first record, *Five Leaves Left*, was acclaimed by the critics, but it never sold in quantities. We thought it was a great mistake that he left Cambridge, but I don't think now, looking back, that it was. It might have been better if he'd left earlier, because he had this music in him.'

Molly added: 'I think he felt, having brought out *Five Leaves Left,* that if he went slogging on at Cambridge for another nine months, he would just miss the peak. Miss his chance. Miss his foothold in the world.'

The sessions for *Five Leaves Left* began at Sound Techniques studios in London, in July 1968, and continued intermittently for the best part of a year. Nick was barely twenty-one years old, but with the completion of the album his future was decided. In the summer of 1969 he left Fitzwilliam College. For Nick, a contract with Island Records was justification enough for quitting Cambridge. But the real vindication of his decision to manage without a safety net lay pressed in the vinyl of his first album, *Five Leaves Left*, which Island Records released on 1 September 1969.

As he left Cambridge behind him, Nick's only qualifications were those he carried with him from Marlborough. Intriguingly, in his university recommendation of October 1966, Nick's housemaster, Dennis Silk, had written presciently of his pupil: 'He himself loves music and plays several wind instruments and would, I think, secretly like to be good enough to make his living in music.'

BOOK II:
DURING

6

'I saw Nick at the Roundhouse,' Ashley Hutchings recalls. 'He was on a bill, a charity gig, with a friend, and I was playing with Fairport. I was in the audience wandering around before going on, and my eyes went to the stage . . . The thing that struck me first of all was his demeanour and his charisma. I didn't take the songs in. He sang well, he played well enough, the songs were interesting. But it was Nick the person; Nick the figure on-stage which really registered. That is what made a really strong impression on me.'

Just three years older than Nick Drake, bass player Ashley Hutchings had founded Fairport Convention in 1967. He would guide the band through their classic years, effectively inventing English folk-rock with Fairport's seminal 1969 *Liege & Lief* album, but soon afterwards he left. He went on to pursue his own vision of indigenous English folk music, played on electric instruments, with Steeleye Span and The Albion Band, with whom he still performs.

Ashley struggles to define exactly what struck him about that first performance: 'It was a unique impact . . . because in no other case did I then go away and recommend an artist to a manager. I mean, instantly I went away to Joe and related that I'd seen Nick, been very impressed with him . . . To such an extent that I can't remember anything about who played with him. I have been asked over and over who was with him – was it a guitarist, a bassist? But it was Nick I focused on. I went up to him after he came offstage and said how much I had enjoyed it, and did he have any plans? He said no, he was casting around. I said, well, I'm with Fairport Convention, we're signed to Joe Boyd, and may I mention you to him? Or words to that effect. I recall him writing something down, a contact address or something . . . I definitely got a contact off him that night, otherwise he would just have vanished off into the underground of 1968.'

In later years, when Nick's reluctance to perform to promote his records became legendary, it seemed ironic – almost incredible – that it was his stage presence which first alerted Ashley to his potential. Looking back nearly thirty years to that gig, Ashley tries to explain precisely what impressed him so forcefully about Nick's performance: 'I remember this very good-looking boy, who held himself very well on-stage, and I just thought, here's someone who's really got something. It contrasted so nicely with what was going on at the time – there was a lot of extravagance at that time. And he stood very still, and he performed very simply.'

David Wright, Nick's schoolfriend from Marlborough, was also at the Roundhouse in 1968, but his memories of that crucial gig are rather different: 'Somebody said: "Nick's playing at the Roundhouse, why don't we go?" . . . I have a vague recollection that as Nick came out, he was out of his head, capable of playing the guitar, but pretty smashed. He said what a big night it was because he was being watched by record company people, but it was obvious we weren't getting through, it was all "Oh hi, man . . ." Country Joe & The Fish were definitely on, who were sensational.'

The precise date of the Roundhouse appearance which sparked Ashley's interest is elusive and likely to remain so. Over the years, it has even been suggested that Ashley's memory is at fault, and that he first saw Nick perform at Cambridge. Robert Kirby, who was more involved in Nick's early Cambridge performances than anyone, thinks Cambridge a less likely venue: 'I don't know about the Roundhouse gig, but I don't know where Ashley would have seen Nick perform at Cambridge . . . And Nick was down in London a lot. I would tend to go with what Ashley said.'

Journalist Pete Frame has a dim memory of seeing Country Joe wandering through the crowd at the Roundhouse, incongruously dressed in a sports jacket. But the Roundhouse was a focal point of the London underground scene, and gigs were held there frequently. Along with The Doors and Jefferson Airplane, Country Joe & The Fish were among the leading West Coast outfits, and one of the first to make the trip to Europe. The band's UK debut at the North

London venue in February 1968 seems on balance the likeliest occasion for Ashley's discovery of Nick Drake.

On Ashley's recommendation, Nick supplied a tape of four of his own songs to Fairport's manager, a man whose name would come to be inextricably linked with that of Nick Drake. Joe Boyd was only twenty-six, but had already carved himself a considerable niche in British rock music by the time he first heard the name of Nick Drake. For his part, Nick was already familiar with Boyd's name as producer of albums by John Martyn and The Incredible String Band.

Born in Boston, USA, in 1942, Boyd was a fresh-faced music veteran. A former room-mate of Tom Rush and teenage friend of Geoff Muldaur (and later producer of Muldaur's ex-wife Maria's 'Midnight At The Oasis'), Boyd first came to London in 1964, tour-managing The Muddy Waters Blues & Gospel revue. He was production manager at the 1965 Newport Folk Festival, best remembered for providing the platform for Bob Dylan's controversial first electric performance. Dylan's pick-up band that July evening were plucked from The Paul Butterfield Blues Band, whom Boyd had encountered earlier in Chicago. Impressed with Butterfield's musicians, Boyd recommended them to George Wein at Elektra Records. Wein was suitably grateful and 'as kind of a reward' let Boyd run Elektra's London office. Boyd arrived in London in November 1965 and within weeks London began to swing to the boom of the beat groups, and gentlemen's hair began to edge over their ears. It was a time to be young.

Originally Boyd's brief was to market the Elektra label in Europe by helping promote acts like Tom Paxton and Judy Collins, but overwhelmed by the wealth of indigenous talent London was producing, the young American began erring more towards A&R. Within a year of arriving in London, he was recommending to Elektra in New York that they sign new bands like Cream and The Move, but the label passed on both. One of the first acts Elektra did allow Boyd to sign was a group called The Powerhouse, a studio-only, blues-based supergroup featuring Eric Clapton, Steve Winwood, Paul Jones and Jack Bruce, who recorded briefly and anonymously for the label. The London underground scene burgeoned and Joe Boyd was the man with his finger on its pulse.

Throughout 1966 Boyd flitted around the happening hot spots of the capital. He co-founded the Notting Hill Free School, which led to his seeking a venue for charity gigs, which led in turn to the unveiling

of the UFO Club. By 1967 Boyd had overseen the first recording
sessions of two hotly tipped bands: Pink Floyd and Soft Machine, as
well as producing the Floyd's debut single, 'Arnold Layne'. But
Elektra passed on the Floyd, as had Chris Blackwell's fledgeling
Island Records, and EMI insisted on using a staff producer for the
band's first album. Frustrated by corporate obduracy, Boyd decided
to go his own way.

Witchseason was initially set up late in 1966 as a production
company to oversee Pink Floyd, but when the Floyd connection was
severed early in 1967, Boyd kept the name, which was inspired by a
recent Donovan hit, 'Season Of The Witch'. Based in Charlotte
Street (coincidentally crossing Donovan's 'Sunny Goodge Street'),
Witchseason was unique at the time in offering its artists the
complete package: management, concert promotion and record
production.

Anthea Joseph worked alongside Joe Boyd at Witchseason. Her
background was very much on the folk side of the London music
scene – at one point she was running seven folk clubs in the capital
every week. Such was Anthea's reputation on the London folk scene
that when Bob Dylan arrived in London for his first visit in 1962, he
had been given two names to contact: *Melody Maker*'s venerable jazz
and blues master, Max Jones, and Anthea Joseph. Anthea recalled
those days at 36 Charlotte Street: 'Hardly spacious accommodation.
It was one of those Georgian houses, you went up a rickety staircase,
you came to our floor. Joe had an office . . . I had an office, then we
had a sort of open-space bit which people congregated in . . . There
was very little furniture. And everything came off the back of a lorry
. . . Very few chairs, so people spent a great deal of time sitting on the
floor . . . We had a publishing company and then there was the
record company, so we were Witchseason/Warlock. Warlock was the
publishing company and that upset The Incredible String Band no end
– and Nick, I might add. I thought he'd find it funny, but he didn't . . .'
Boyd had signed The Incredible String Band to Elektra, where he
produced their breakthrough albums: *The 5000 Spirits* . . . and *The
Hangman's Beautiful Daughter*. Otherwise, at the time he first heard
the name of Nick Drake, Witchseason's roster comprised Fairport
Convention and John and Beverley Martyn. The first time Boyd
remembers meeting Nick Drake was when Nick came into the
Witchseason offices to deliver a reel-to-reel tape he had recorded
in Tanworth during the Christmas vacation after his first term at
Cambridge. There was something intriguing and quietly compelling

about the songs on that tape, and to his eternal credit, Boyd recognized their quality straight away.

In a radio interview in 1986 he spoke of hearing Nick Drake for the first time: 'The first time I heard the songs I immediately knew I wanted to make a record with him. The songs were just so much better than the things that I was hearing at that time. I think on that demo tape was "Time Of No Reply", "I Was Made To Love Magic", "Time Has Told Me" and one other track that ended up on *Five Leaves Left* [probably "River Man"] . . . and I just went home and played that tape over and over again.'

Fairport Convention's first album had appeared on Polydor, but by 1968 the Witchseason acts had found a new home – at Basing Street, London W11 – with a company busy establishing itself as the British music scene's leading independent label. Island Records was the brainchild of Chris Blackwell, who was born in London in 1937 but had spent an idyllic childhood growing up on the West Indian island of Jamaica. He was sent to public school in Britain, but was expelled from Harrow aged seventeen, and on returning to Jamaica, served as aide-de-camp to the island's Governor-General, Sir Hugh Foot.

While living in Jamaica, Blackwell found work at various times as a water-skiing instructor, real-estate salesman, and early in 1961, location manager for a little film about a secret service agent, based on a novel written by a close friend of his mother's. The film was called *Dr No*; the friend was Ian Fleming.

In 1959, as a teenager, Blackwell had spent a formative six months in New York, where he was mightily impressed by the enthusiasm and musical policy of the nascent Atlantic Records. On his return to Jamaica, he launched Island Records, and by 1960, had his first Jamaican number one: 'Little Sheila' by Laurel Aitken. Within two years Island Records had released two LPs and twenty-six singles. By 1962 Island's Jamaican records were actually selling better in England, especially in the West Indian immigrant communities around London, Bristol and Birmingham. So on 8 May of that year Chris Blackwell boldly launched Island Records in the UK. The operation was run from his front room, with Blackwell delivering the product from the back seat of his Mini-Cooper. In 1989 he would sell Island Records to the Polygram group for an estimated £200,000,000.

In March 1963 Blackwell rented Island Records' first premises, at 108 Cambridge Road, London NW6. Initially, sales were all to the Jamaican community, but ska and bluebeat were soon taken up by the Mods, who were busy roaring round the capital on their scooters. The labels on those early Island records were designed by a young advertising agency, Saatchi & Saatchi. Blackwell subsidized his quality Jamaican releases (including the 1963 debut single from one 'Robert Marley') with parallel product, including two albums of bawdy rugby songs and the risqué *Nights Of Love In Lesbos*!

Blackwell's first hit came in March 1964, with 'My Boy Lollipop', by Jamaican teenager Millie, who later became one of only two acts to cover a Nick Drake song during his lifetime. Accompanying Millie to a TV appearance on *Thank Your Lucky Stars*, which was recorded at the ATV Studios in Birmingham, Blackwell was advised to check out an R&B quartet at a tiny club in the city. Hearing a fifteen-year-old Stevie Winwood belt out Ray Charles numbers in front of The Spencer Davis Group, he knew immediately that he was in at the beginning of something. But he also recognized that the potential of The Spencer Davis Group was too big for Island at the time, and though he went on to manage and produce the group, their records were licensed – as was the Millie record – through Fontana.

A run of hits throughout 1965 and 1966 confirmed Blackwell's instincts about the commercial potential of The Spencer Davis Group and the teenage Stevie Winwood. They became the first white British act to be signed by Blackwell, and the signpost to the future of Island Records. By the end of 1966 the band were releasing harder, more pounding material such as 'I'm A Man' and 'Gimme Some Lovin'', but eighteen-year-old Winwood was tiring of the pop restrictions of The Spencer Davis Group.

There was a definite schism between the commercial pop groups and the underground bands in the late sixties. Bands like Fairport Convention, Pink Floyd and Jethro Tull, who had emerged blinking from the underground and into the charts, would appear, faintly embarrassed, on *Top Of The Pops* to promote a single which had flukishly emerged as a chart contender. But the distinction between serious bands and pure pop groups like Marmalade, Dave Dee, Dozy, Beaky, Mick & Tich and The Tremeloes, was carefully maintained.

Within the first months of 1967 Winwood shook off his pop shackles and formed Traffic. Blackwell may have been concerned at the cost of Traffic's debut album (a then staggering £5000), but the group were soon established as the first major Island act. As the sixties upped the ante, Island began its first golden age.

Following the floodgates opened by The Beatles' *Sgt Pepper* album in June 1967, Blackwell was quick to appreciate how potent that new music could be. The other major labels soon jumped on the Progressive bandwagon, giving house room to underground bands on such labels as Harvest, Deram, Vertigo and Dawn. Island kept the higher ground.

David Betteridge was effectively Blackwell's deputy at Island Records during the years that Nick was there. Appointed Managing Director of the label in 1968, it was he who handled the day-to-day running of the company during its glory years. Recognizing his MD's sound commercial leanings, Blackwell allowed him his head when signing new acts. 'I tried to sign Queen . . . Procol Harum, we all loved "A Whiter Shade Of Pale",' Betteridge recalls, 'but they were wrapped up with a publishing house and we couldn't get them. I can remember Chris and myself sitting down with Peter Grant trying to do a deal to sign Led Zeppelin, but we just didn't have the money. A hundred thousand dollars, worldwide, including recording costs, excluding America.'

By September 1969, when Island released Nick Drake's *Five Leaves Left*, the label already boasted Jethro Tull, Spooky Tooth, Fairport Convention and Free; waiting in the wings were Mott The Hoople and King Crimson. There was undeniably something special about Island Records during those heady years. Inextricably linked to the most innovative and exciting noises emerging from the underground, Island seemed somehow to stand outside the mainstream. If you bought a record released on Island, you knew you were in safe hands. You might not understand the album and be baffled by the oblique-ness, but once that little pink 'i' began revolving, you could be sure you were in good company.

Another hallmark of good quality was the tiny image of a flying witch, which announced that the record now playing was a product of Joe Boyd's Witchseason company. Throughout 1968 Boyd's acts criss-crossed the country: The Incredible String Band, enchanting and irritating in equal measure; Fairport Convention, hauling up and down the pre-motorway roads, swerving from university campus to campus. But Boyd was keeping his ears open for something fresh, and Ashley Hutchings was able to provide that freshness.

Anthea Joseph: 'There were the Incredibles, John and Beverley [Martyn], Fairport, Dudu Pukwana . . . and Nico ("Get me a tele-vision show." "Where are you, Nico?" "I'm in a telephone box on Tottenham Court Road." "How long are you in town for?" "I leave tomorrow to see my friend.") . . . All sorts of odds and sods used to pass through there, but those were the core – Fairport and The String Band were really the serious ones, and of course Nick.'

Struck by the sounds he had heard on the reel-to-reel four-track tape, Joe Boyd signed Nick to Witchseason in 1968. Witchseason offered a unique three-tiered package to its act: management came through Boyd, as did the company's record production, with Boyd as producer and John Wood as regular engineer. The company also offered music publishing through its Warlock Music arm, with offices in Oxford Street. Boyd even had a finger in the visuals – Osiris Visions, who produced a lot of material for the Island acts of the day, were linked to him.

The timing proved fortunate. In 1968, the year that Nick Drake signed his first professional contract, UK sales of long-playing records overtook singles for the first time. It was a sea change which would bring real benefits to artists like him. In 1968 the margin was only slight – 49,184,000 LPs to 49,161,000 singles – but it was sufficient to make the music industry far more inclined towards album-oriented acts. That Nick was perceived in this way is confirmed by the fact that during his career he never released a single.

Anthea Joseph recalled Nick's earliest days at Witchseason: 'I remember him arriving: this tall, thin, very beautiful young man . . . who didn't speak. He could just about say hello to you, once he'd decided that you were a human being. And he wrote these extraordinary songs. He'd come in and he'd sit, just sit, doing nothing, reading the paper, watching the world go by.

'Nick was signed to Witchseason . . . We had our own label, but Joe, as ever, was running out of money, and he and Chris Blackwell got together – like-minded persons, very similar sorts of people – and Chris, who was making it relatively big in this country at the time, suggested that he take over the Witchseason label. Joe said that he could do that, provided he had the Witchseason logo on the disc. So it was Witchseason, although Island controlled the work, and Joe remained the boss man as far as Witchseason was concerned. And it worked very well.

'They were all on a stipend . . . It must have been something like £15 or £20 per week. It was a lot at the time; it was enough to live on without starving to death and you could pay your rent.'

Nick had written the ten songs which constituted his debut album over the preceding eighteen months. Friends from Marlborough recall hearing songs which appeared on *Five Leaves Left* for the first time in

Aix during early 1967, and Cambridge contemporaries heard the
same songs played in college rooms during Nick's time at university.

The one weakness of Nick as a writer, the fundamental flaw, is the
adolescent obsession with loneliness and the inability to communicate, which betrays his extreme youth when he wrote the songs. He
wrote songs such as 'Time Of No Reply' and 'I Was Made To Love
Magic' at an age when most people feel that no one understands them
and that really meaningful communication is impossible. It is a
landscape Bob Dylan recognized on 'A Hard Rain's A-Gonna
Fall': 'where black is the colour and none is the number'; a place
the majority of us visit, but soon leave. For Nick, though, it became
home, and he stayed there far too long.

Paul Simon flitted through the streets of alienation on 'The Sounds
Of Silence' and noticed flashing neon illuminating vast crowds,
drawn together by their very inability to communicate; but later
he discovered the restorative powers of life and love, music and hope.
Nick Drake never had time to develop and grow as a writer, or as a
person. The appeal of his work comes from the universality and
purity of his themes: lack of understanding, lack of affection and lack
of communication; but a deeper understanding of the rich complex-
ities of human experience takes years. Age might have consoled him
and filled him with wonder and wisdom, had he had time. But we can
only imagine how he would have developed as a songwriter, and
perhaps that is the greatest loss of all.

Anthea Joseph had already witnessed first-hand Dylan's impact on
the contemporary music scene when she began working closely
alongside Nick, so her observations of Nick's writing are particularly pertinent: 'Nick never made the connection that I'd known
Dylan. Everything was interconnected. The only thing, I suppose in
retrospect, is that what Bob did was to liberate people in words. I
mean, he wrote these extraordinary songs . . . We'd all grown up on
Bill Haley and stuff . . . but this small little Jewish miracle turns up
and he had a tremendous impact on everyone, even The Beatles. They
would *never* have written the later stuff without that influence.
They'd have just mooned and Juned for ever, and they'd have made
lots of money, but they would never have written some of the songs.

'Bob was like a great big buffalo, with horns pointing . . . just
absolutely blitzing everything. I mean, it was amazing. He had an
enormous effect on Nick. I mean, that's why Nick wrote the way he
did . . . I'm not sure about how good those songs really are. He was
extraordinary and he was unique. But he was not, I think, on a par

with the Dylans, or even the Paul Simons of this world . . . Or the Richard Thompsons, because when he started seriously writing songs, and Joe acquired him, it was too late, the damage was done. The growth wasn't there – the intellectual growth in song-writing terms. It would have been very interesting to know what would have happened if he hadn't become so ill and been so damaged. Where he would have gone, because the brain was there.'

By the time Nick Drake went into Chelsea's Sound Techniques studios with Joe Boyd to record *Five Leaves Left*, the songs were largely written and polished – the challenge would be getting the arrangements right. This was Nick's first album, but even as a student he'd had a very clear idea of how he wanted it to sound. Nick's mother had observed that from an early age he was 'an absolute perfectionist'; others were about to discover the same thing.

Joe Boyd: 'I probably enjoyed making those records as much as anything I've ever done, the material was so rich that it lent itself to contributions, which in a way is more fun for a producer. It feeds your ego, I suppose. The Fairport would arrive as a ready-made band, with arrangements that they'd already worked out live, and you are basically recording something that exists. With Nick, there was the opportunity to be creative, and the wonderful thing about his music was that when you did bring in a John Cale, or a Richard Thompson . . . that was incredibly exciting and fulfilling to hear what happens when really good musicians . . . would begin to play and hear what was going on. People had incredible respect for him.'

It was either Peter Asher – Head of A&R at The Beatles' Apple label, or Tony Cox – an arranger with connections at Island (not Terry Cox of Pentangle, as has been suggested) – who recommended that Boyd use Richard Hewson to do the arrangements for *Five Leaves Left*. As house arranger at Apple, Hewson worked with The Beatles on 'The Long And Winding Road' and on Mary Hopkin's worldwide smash 'Those Were The Days', and had successfully arranged the strings on James Taylor's eponymous debut album.

Despite the impressive credentials, Nick did not consider Hewson's arrangements suitable for his album, and instead called in the services of his colleague and friend from Cambridge, Robert Kirby, who explains: 'I arranged "Way To Blue", "Day Is Done", "Thoughts Of Mary Jane" and "Fruit Tree" at Sound Techniques. We were both nineteen. Those four tracks with the string quartet, we did in one three-hour session. We did them live with Nick; nothing was over-dubbed. So Nick was playing guitar, and we were doing the quartet and the string bass with him. He would play his part in exactly the correct tempo each time there was a take. Most of the time was spent getting a decent string sound.'

In an interview with *Musin' Music* Boyd recalled Nick's disappointment that Hewson's arrangements did not match the sounds inside his mind: 'Nick didn't like them and I agreed, they were a bit corny, and when we were trying to think what to do, Nick kind of said rather timidly, "Well, I have this friend from Cambridge who might be quite good," and I said "Oh sure, has he ever done anything, has he ever done any work?" and he said "No, but I think he'd be quite good." And there was something in the way Nick said it . . . Nick was very, very definite when he knew he was on firm ground and you could tell that it was a firm idea that he had, and I said "Let's give it a try." '

A meeting between Nick, Robert Kirby, Joe Boyd and John Wood did little to allay the fears, but once Kirby's arrangements were heard on the first run-through in the studio, Boyd and Wood were convinced. It must have been intimidating as a newcomer to be working with a fifteen-piece string section, but Kirby was unfazed, and his arrangements remain an integral part of the distinctive sound of Nick's debut album.

Harry Robinson arranged 'River Man'. A venerable Scottish band leader, Robinson was also the Lord Rockingham whose XI had been one of British rock 'n' roll's greatest novelty outfits. Robinson's career has spanned the whole history of British rock 'n' roll, from arranger on The Allisons' 1961 'Are You Sure', through work with Sandy Denny and Nick Drake, right up to Everything But The Girl.

Double-bassist Danny Thompson recalls how the latest match was made: 'Ben [Watt] went and dug Harry Robinson out for the last Everything But The Girl album. They kept saying: "Where is he now?" and I said, well, he doesn't want to do anything . . . So they found where he was, and he said: "Oh no, I haven't been asked to do anything for years, oh no." So they went to his house and played him the stuff of Sandy's and Nick's. He said: "Oh, I'd forgotten all this." It stirred him up, so he did some arrangements for their *Amplified Heart* album. That's a good thing that came from what he did with Nick Drake . . .'

Talking on Swedish radio in the only full interview about Nick he had given before this book, Robert Kirby remembered the circumstances of Nick's recording debut: 'I found him very easy to work with; he gave me quite a free hand. He gave me a song like, say, "Fruit Tree", on the first LP. He came round one day, played it, and I taped it on to my tape recorder. He said that he possibly heard oboes on it, and strings, and that was about it. I used to then sit with him and go through exactly how he played his chords, because he always detuned his guitar. He used strange tunings, not proper guitar tunings, and not the ones like people use in D tunings. He had very complicated tunings. Very complicated. Sometimes a low string would be higher than the string above. And so it would be very important for me to write down exactly how he played each chord, and every bar. And I would do that with him; that sometimes annoyed him, I think, because it took a long time. But I had to do it. And then he'd go away and leave me to do the arrangement how I wanted it. And he was very easy to work with.'

For *Five Leaves Left*, Kirby worked with fifteen classical musicians, including principal violinist David McCallum – father of the actor – and the man who taught Jimmy Page how to apply a violin bow to his electric guitar when they were playing on a session together before the formation of Led Zeppelin. Kirby's arrangements – their effectiveness often due to his restraint – are heard at their best on 'Way To Blue', where Nick puts his guitar to one side and is only accompanied by Kirby's pointed and supportive orchestration. The effect is of a boat gently bobbing on a sea of strings. The intimacy and impact of *Five Leaves Left* is further enhanced by the assured production of Joe Boyd and John Wood.

The sound which Nick wanted for his record was directly inspired by the debut album of the young Californian singer-songwriter Randy Newman, which had made a strong impact on Nick when he heard it earlier in 1968. Played alongside *Five Leaves Left*, *Randy Newman* has striking similarities, most obviously the lush orchestrations which punctuate the songs – particularly the opening 'Love Story' and the spellbinding 'I Think It's Going To Rain Today'. Newman's arrangements almost masked his unremarkable voice and one-dimensional songs, and his background in film music was evident, notably on 'Cowboy'. But it was the orchestral accompaniment, massed and used as an instrument, that give the record its real impact and made such an effect on Nick.

Paul Wheeler: 'When that first Randy Newman album came out it didn't sell at all, and the record company gave copies away . . . they said it's such a good record, they gave it away. That sort of thing Nick picked up on. I remember the picture on the sleeve, of Randy Newman, totally isolated . . .'

The musicians on *Five Leaves Left* were familiar names from the folk-rock fraternity of the time – Fairport Convention's Richard Thompson played on one track, and cellist Clare Lowther had worked with The Strawbs. Danny Thompson, besides playing double bass with Pentangle, was a regular first call for many of Boyd's Witchseason acts, and by the time he came to contribute to *Five Leaves Left* he had already played on albums by John Martyn and The Incredible String Band.

The sessions for *Five Leaves Left* began in July 1968, but the album's release was delayed for a year, partly because the studio was coping with the installation of its first eight-track equipment, but also because of the way that Nick was coaxed into recording by his producer. 'The way that I worked with Nick was very different from the way I worked with the other artists,' Boyd recalled in a *Musin' Music* interview. 'We worked . . . together slowly. There was no self-contained group around Nick. With the other groups or artists we tended to go in, do a record in a concentrated period of time. With Nick, we just went in, did a couple of tracks, listened to them, thought about it, thought what we wanted to do with them, worked on them a bit, put down a few more tracks, wait a month, wait six weeks, think about it some more, perhaps work with an arranger . . . It was very different, and it was very reflective.'

Nick Drake's painstaking approach to his craft was apparent from the moment he first entered the studio to make his debut album. He was barely twenty, and still a student splitting his life between the serenity of his home in Tanworth and the more hectic allure of Cambridge, but while he may have been soft-spoken and painfully shy, there was also a determination, an intensity in Nick, which was almost intimidating in one so young.

Danny Thompson doesn't remember much discussion with Nick about music during the sessions: 'I got played the stuff, and I played it. He was surrounded by strings and all kinds of musicians – half the LSO was there . . . I was left to get on and do what I do, which was pleasurable for me. The communication was through Joe. Joe is this great catalyst . . . he used to conjure up nice mixtures, put them in the pot. There were deadly serious straight musicians . . . some people assume it was just me and Nick in there, having a fag and talking about crumpet and playing, but it wasn't at all. He was in one corner of the studio not even playing – his tracks were already down. He was watching as I played, he had a grin on his face. They were my bass lines. There was nothing written for me. There was that instant rapport that a musician has with another musician who realizes that that's what he wants . . . There were times there was just the two of us working out things and times when they had all these strings in . . . But even when there was just the two of us, he wasn't "did you hear the one about the Irishman . . . ?" '

The delay between the recording and release of his debut album had in part to do with Nick's determination that the record should sound as perfect on vinyl as it did in his head. There was also the fact that he was still ostensibly studying at Cambridge, some sixty miles away. Anthea Joseph witnessed this painfully slow gestation at close quarters: 'I spent an awful lot of time at Sound Techniques, Old Church Street, Chelsea . . . The first album took ages. Ages. It went on for months . . . What I always felt was that Nick would sort of pack up mentally, so you had to stop. There was no point in trying to push it, because you weren't going to get any further. Joe was wonderful with him: "Put him in a cab, take him home." But he was determined to get that record out of him if it was the last thing he did. And he did it, but again giving space – always the space. He was like that with all of the albums – sometimes more than he should have been.'

Boyd, in an unsourced interview, remembered the sessions for Nick's debut album: 'Making Nick Drake's *Five Leaves Left* was one of the most enjoyable studio experiences for me. ['Three Hours'] "cooks" more than almost any other, because of the rhythm section of Danny Thompson and Rocki Dzidzornu from Ghana. The title reflects, I assume, the time it took in those days to get from London to Cambridge, where Nick had been going to university. It shows off his startling guitar technique, he had listened to some of Robin Williamson's colleagues, like Bert Jansch, John Martyn and Davy Graham, but he had his own style with complex tunings which have often mystified imitators. His photographic image shows a delicate and shy person, which is true in a way, but his hands and fingers were very large and incredibly strong. People often talk about his voice, his melodies and his lyrics, but it was the cleanliness and strength of his guitar playing that served as the spine of most tracks and made everything work.'

The story behind the title of Nick Drake's debut album is as well known to fans as the album itself: it was the caution found toward the end of every packet of Rizla cigarette papers. A reminder that there weren't many opportunities left. 'All smokers will recognise the meaning of the title,' began *Melody Maker*'s single-paragraph review, which went on to call Drake's debut 'interesting'. Robert Kirby is sure that Nick intended the reference as 'an in-joke' – by the time of its release, everyone who knew, knew just what Rizla papers were being wrapped around. In the short life and work of Nick Drake, omens and portents abound; and the title *Five Leaves Left* took on even greater significance, when, just five years after its release, he was dead.

In 1996 Alex Skorecki was kind enough to send me a copy of a short story written around the turn of the century by the American writer O. Henry which he thought of interest. 'The Last Leaf' concerns a young painter, dying of pneumonia in her Greenwich Village garret. The doctor senses she has already given up on life: 'She has one chance in – let us say, ten . . . and that chance is for her to want to live.' But what keeps her attention, and keeps her alive, is the ivy growing in the yard outside:

'They're falling faster now. Three days ago there were almost a hundred. It made my head ache to count them. But now it's easy. There goes another one. There are only five left now.'

'Five what, dear? . . .'

'Leaves. On the ivy vine. When the last one falls I must go too.'

Given that Nick was reading English at Cambridge while recording his first album, it is quite possible that he had read the O. Henry story. In which case he would have known that Henry's story had a hopeful ending – the artist's life saved by the love of her friend and an old man's sacrifice.

Whether it wears myriad influences on its sleeve (the first efforts of Bob Dylan and The Rolling Stones); distils a stage act on disc (as with The Beatles and Paul Simon); explodes with the never-get-a-second-chance frenzy (Bruce Springsteen); or opts for 'Let's put all the singles on' calculation (The Sex Pistols and Oasis), a debut album is always a statement of intent.

Five Leaves Left is an astonishingly mature and assured debut. From the cover in, it speaks volumes of its author: the elegant, enigmatic figure, shot three-quarters on, looking out of a window, half smiling at some half-forgotten joke. A wistful, autumnal mood is evoked by songs such as 'Day Is Done', 'Time Has Told Me' and 'Cello Song'. The titles suggesting isolation and painful self-awareness, like the songs from a room which Leonard Cohen was so visibly and tortuously producing. The world of Nick Drake, on the evidence of this album, was a vacuum, where the only way was to blue.

From its Rizla-inspired title to a song like 'The Thoughts Of Mary Jane' ('Mary Jane' being a euphemism for marijuana), the record was a dope-smoker's delight. The sense of world-weariness, the shifting, loose atmosphere which pervades the record, is redolent of the late sixties. Much of the atmosphere comes from the husky timbre of Nick's singing, the sound of his voice, as if he had just inhaled and was slowly letting the smoke out.

Much of the record's appeal came from Nick's voice, but also from the dexterity of his playing, which manages to be noticeable without ever appearing intrusive. The album does have flaws, particularly the inconsequential 'Man In A Shed'; and perhaps the arrangements are a tad lush. But play *Five Leaves Left* back to back with any other record from the same year and you are struck at once by the quality and timelessness of Nick Drake's debut.

Lyrically, the songs on *Five Leaves Left* are largely unremarkable. Nick tended to use lyrics as part of the pattern, an integral mix with his guitar, voice and arrangement. The words of 'Fruit Tree' are eerily prescient: a song which recognizes the frailty of fame, and that the only real fame is posthumous. Otherwise, the lyrics, taken in isolation, would not have seemed out of place in Marlborough's school magazine. Lost love, a sky-bound princess, unrealized love, inability to communicate, unrequited love – all revealed a tendency to idealize, because little of what Nick wrote at that time came from experience of the world outside himself.

On 'Day Is Done' there is an image of a tennis court which could have come from Antonioni's contemporaneous exposition, *Blow-Up*. The image of a rose without a thorn, which appears in 'Time Has Told Me', was made popular by Leonard McNally's eighteenth-century poem 'The Lass Of Richmond Hill'. The language on *Five Leaves Left* is ornate, self-conscious even, as you might expect from someone who was still nominally studying for an English degree.

It is only when Nick's voice carries the words to meet his masterly music, and the Boyd/Wood alchemy comes into play, that the magic is made – sublimely well on songs such as 'River Man', 'Cello Song' and 'Three Hours'. The rolling guitar which ushers in 'Cello Song' is fluid and quite distinctive, Clare Lowther's bowed cello and Rocki Dzidzornu's congas lend an exotic colouring; but always, the glue that binds the song is Nick's playing: the rolling, relentless guitar which never rests.

'River Man' is enriched by Harry Robinson's lavish string arrangement, which kicks in just as Nick reaches the first refrain. 'River Man' is the song Nick's Cambridge contemporaries recall him performing most often in various college rooms, and knowing that adds to the song's identification with the city. When Nick sings about shows which last all night during summertime, you can picture May Balls during the early summer days after exams have finished, played out along the silver spine of the River Cam which flows through the city.

'Three Hours', one of the album's most beguiling tracks, is the only song we know to be directly inspired by someone Nick knew. Jeremy Mason, Nick's old friend from Marlborough, accompanied him on that pivotal trip to Aix in 1967, but hadn't seen him for some time after that: 'I bumped into a chap called Robert Kirby, at the George in Bishop's Stortford. We were talking about Nick, and he said: "Oh, so you're Jeremy Mason . . . Nick wrote a song about you on this LP we've just been doing; it's called "Three Hours"' '. This would have been 1969.

'When I asked Nick whether this tune was about me, he said yes. I said: "Well, what does it mean?" He said: "Well, if you don't know it doesn't matter . . . it's the way I perceived your situation at that time." And believe me, I've listened to it a thousand times . . . Three hours from sundown, Jeremy flies . . .'

Despite the mention of London in the second verse, 'Three Hours' has echoes of Aix, a city dating back to Roman times, and nearby, cave paintings reaching back even further. Joe Boyd assumed that the title alluded to the time it took Nick to travel to London from Cambridge, but since we now know that the song was about Jeremy Mason, it seems possible that it refers to the time it took to get from Marlborough to London.

Five Leaves Left is an impressive debut; there is real audacity on 'Way To Blue' and 'Fruit Tree', where Nick sings simply against an orchestral backing, the rock 'n' roll reliability of bass, drums and guitar removed. What mars the album is an apparent straining for diversity, obscurity and eclecticism, as on the unsuccessful jazz meanderings of 'Saturday Sun' and the juvenile narrative of 'Man In A Shed' – a facile rewrite of The Beatles' 'Fixing A Hole'. As with the films of James Dean, because Nick left such a small body of work, too much is often vested in those few precious discs. *Five Leaves Left* was indeed a remarkable debut, but its real significance at the time was as a signpost to what could be, rather than what was.

Robert Kirby came down from Cambridge soon after Nick, with his life clearly mapped out. Proud as he was of his work on *Five Leaves Left*, he had seen it simply as a diversion, a distraction from his intended path: 'The first album got a lot of critical acclaim, a lot of acclaim from musicians, peer group, which was almost worse . . . I had decided that I'd be quite happy teaching music at a public school – doing the choir, a bit of Gilbert and Sullivan. But when I got the cheque for doing Nick's stuff . . .

'Joe got me some work, then I did *Zero She Flies* for Al Stewart. When I saw what the offers were I thought, there's a career here as arranger. It all came in very quickly . . . I worked with Ralph McTell on his first two albums, Tim Hart and Maddy Prior, Keith Christmas, Shelagh McDonald, Andy Roberts . . . Dave Cousins' solo album *Two Weeks Last Summer*. It seemed a positive thing to do, to get on with a career as an orchestrator.

'I certainly think a factor in his leaving Cambridge, was that Nick had been told by people he admired that there was an obvious career carved out for him. To promote the first album, to be available . . .'

7

The first the world at large knew of Nick Drake came with the release of *Five Leaves Left* in September 1969. Nick's debut was squeezed in between ILPS 9104, Free's second album, *Free*, and ILPS 9106, the Joe Boyd-produced, Dr Strangely Strange album *Kip Of The Serenes*.

Initial printings of the album sleeve switched around the running order – in those days there were two sides to an album – and Side One closed with 'Way To Blue' and 'Day Is Done', but the order was transposed on the sleeve. Also on that first run of albums, the lyrics of 'Three Hours' are inexplicably printed as 'Sundown'. A mint-condition, pink-label copy of the album from 1969 would now be worth £30.

Island Records' inaugural press release which introduced Nick Drake to the world, ran in part:

'NICK DRAKE is tall and lean. He lives "somewhere in Cambridge", somewhere close to the University (where he is reading English) because he hates wasting time travelling, does not have a telephone – more for reasons of finance than any anti-social feelings and tends to disappear for three or four days at a time, when he is "writing", but above all . . . he makes music!

'As a child, NICK took classical piano lessons and later progressed to guitar and a love of the blues. But by his early teens was involving himself in writing music and lyrics. He developed a real talent for composing beautiful melodies and writing fine lyrics which coupled with his raw and often plaintive voice caught the attention of Tyger Hutchings of Fairport Convention one evening when they were on the same bill.

'At his recommendation Fairport's Manager and Producer Joe Boyd went to see NICK . . . and so started the chain of events which led to the production of FIVE LEAVES LEFT – ILPS 9105 – a unique album, fresh and original, the first of many LPs . . . from NICK DRAKE.'

Vivien Holgate's piece was pretty standard press fodder for the time – trying to whip up a bit of interest in an act that nobody knew about, or wanted to. Not when there was a chance to see Led Zeppelin at Surrey University for 7/6d on the door, or listen to new albums from The Band, Pink Floyd or Bob Dylan. The only ace in the hole was that air of tantalizing mystery.

Nick's introduction to the media was calculated to make him appear more mysterious and abstract than the shy, but certain twenty-year-old he actually was. The vagueness about his location ('somewhere in Cambridge') and that eschewal of material possessions ('he does not have a telephone'), the concentration on his purity of intention, valuing music above all else, all helped to flesh out the picture of a singer-songwriter eager for recognition.

Highlighting Nick's 'love of the blues' was a sign of the times. At the time, white-boy blues was all the rage: Cream had split in 1968, but John Mayall was still providing a finishing school for the next wave of Guitar Gods – Mick Taylor had replaced Brian Jones in The Stones; Peter Green's Fleetwood Mac were making headway, while Eric Clapton had gone on to join Stevie Winwood in the much hyped, short-lived supergroup Blind Faith. All offered highly visible platforms for extended workouts on the guitar. It was the era of the Guitar Hero, and blues was the currency.

Of all the blues giants, none towered taller over the landscape of the 1960s than the late Robert Johnson. It may seem disingenuous to suggest a connection between the haunted bluesman of the Mississippi Delta, who sold his soul to the Devil at a midnight crossroads in return for playing the guitar like no one else, and died poisoned by a lover's jealous husband, and the public-school-educated, well-spoken scion of an upper-middle-class English family. But as time went on, the lives of the two men, superficially so different, appeared to be haunted by the same demons.

Nick Drake's fondness for the blues is well documented and like many middle-class white kids of his time, he was fascinated by the lives of the poor black bluesmen. That fondness may well have shaped the title of the fourth track on *Five Leaves Left* – 'Way To

Blue'. After Nick's death, his friend Robert Kirby said that one of his
regrets was that he would never now get to hear Nick play the blues
again.

The first time you hear it, there is something enticing about Nick's
voice – frail and wistful, it cannot help but call you in. There is a
cobweb fragility, but it is the voice of a friend, a friend you haven't
seen for a long while, and who you're not sure you'll be seeing again.

There is an intimacy to Nick's singing which makes it the perfect
voice for headphone communication. Not these modern, flimsy
cotton-bud earpieces which make you go Walkman crazy on the
Underground, but good, old-fashioned headphones – big, bulky cans
which wrap around your ears, insulating you from the world and
making you look like a Second World War bomber pilot. While the
music coils around your head in the otherwise silent dark.

Paul Wheeler remembers Nick being intrigued by headphones
when they first became fashionable: 'He was fascinated by the idea
that he could sit in the car with headphones on . . . Maybe he foresaw
the kind of insular world, a Walkman world . . .'

Despite his avowed fondness for American blues, what registers
first is the innate Englishness of his beautifully enunciated singing
voice. From the birth of rock 'n' roll, British singers have strained for
a mid-Atlantic sound in their singing voices, attempting to ape the
Bronx authenticity of Dion, the Texas hiccuping of Buddy Holly or
the Deep South snarl 'n' sneer of Elvis. But Nick makes no concession
to the prevalent American sound.

Even though The Beatles' early repertoire was 100 per cent
American-influenced, part of their appeal was that they didn't try
to sound like Elvis, or like the Queen. By the time Nick came to
record, there was certainly no shame in sounding English, but few
singers in rock history have sounded quite as English as Nick –
certainly not so politely upper-middle-class English. Later, Ian Dury,
Paul Weller and John Lydon would be lauded for their refusal to
adopt American vocal mannerisms, but that was largely a result of
Punk's veneration of working-class culture and attitudes.

Nick Drake's singing voice is more Noël Coward than Robert Plant.
The only other singer I have heard who sounds remotely like Nick Drake
is Peter Skellern. The Bury-born Skellern was a year older than Nick,
and his singing voice contains a hint of the North, rather than Nick's
public-school received pronunciation, but there is the same vocal
huskiness and precise Englishness in both men's singing styles.

With origins knee-deep in American music, it was not until the 1970s that British rock stars felt confident enough to display their own natural voices: Pink Floyd's Dave Gilmour and Kevin Ayers came from the same social class as Nick Drake, and kept the voices they were bred with. The Floyd's Syd Barrett also refused to sacrifice his natural voice when recording. But unashamed posh pronunciation in pop didn't arrive until the year of Nick's last album, when Roxy Music made their debut – also on Island – and the rock world marvelled at Bryan Ferry's mannered tones.

Nick's labelmate John Martyn considers this unashamed English-ness an important part of Nick's enduring appeal. Interviewed on Radio 1 a decade after Nick died, Martyn said: 'The thing that set him apart . . . is his implicit, innate Britishness. Whilst everyone else on the Island roster . . . including myself, were having flirtations with American-based sounds – in the same way that Elton John was with his very first record . . . the whole idea was to try and sound like The Band if you could . . . He was just very quietly going his own way and producing very . . . British sounds.'

In the gentle and perfectly modulated vocal stylings of Nick Drake are all the years spent at Marlborough and Cambridge. There are no dropped aitches or final Gs. The sound of Nick Drake singing is almost aristocratic in style. But unique as the voice was, ultimately it was the songs he sang and the way those songs were set that marked him out.

On its release, *Five Leaves Left* received the sort of quiet, respectful admiration that the bulk of Island releases were accorded – though the words 'Witchseason' and 'Joe Boyd' undoubtedly lent some extra credence to the debut of this young unknown. *Five Leaves Left* was released on 1 September 1969, but the appearance of a trade ad and review two months before, suggest that the record was originally slated for a summer release.

Melody Maker of 5 July 1969 featured an advertisement for Fairport Convention's third album, *Unhalfbricking*. This was the band's second LP for Island ('it may even be better than the first'), and the record company ad also found space to mention the debut releases of Dr Strangely Strange and Nick Drake: 'All the LPs were produced by Witchseason – that means Joe Boyd and the artistes concerned . . . There's nothing unusual about the fact that Nick Drake writes his own songs and plays good guitar – you've heard that before about hundreds of new artistes. Listen to the record because of the great playing by Danny Thompson, Paul Harris and Richard Thompson and the amazing string arrangements – then you'll find out about the singer and his songs.'

The same issue of *Melody Maker* carried an advertisement for the first Rolling Stones single since the death of Brian Jones, the swaggering 'Honky Tonk Women'; there was also a full-page ad for 'Give Peace A Chance' – a picture of a telephone directory with the tag-line 'You are the Plastic Ono Band'. The letters page featured one B. Odwyn, claiming that Led Zeppelin 'must be the most over-rated group in Britain'. The Liverpool Scene were looking for a new drummer: 'We don't want anyone who doesn't play with feeling.' In the Folk Forum column, Nick Drake was conspicuous by his absence, but The Strawbs were at the White Bear, Hounslow, Ron Geesin was at Cousins and Al Stewart at the Hanging Lamp, Richmond.

Five Leaves Left was reviewed as you would expect, in the *New Musical Express* and *Melody Maker*, the two most important weekly pop-music papers. The *Melody Maker* review, dated 26 July 1969, which ran to fewer than fifty words, makes for interesting reading in these days of ponderous, full-page expositions: 'All smokers will recognise the meaning of the title – it refers to the five leaves left near the end of a packet of cigarette papers. It sounds poetic and so does composer, singer and guitarist Nick Drake. His debut album for Island is interesting.'

Five Leaves Left was the last review on half a page that week, and was preceded by The Third Ear Band – 'a demanding mixture of Eastern and European influences'. Other reviews that week included Fairport's *Unhalfbricking* ('Fairport maintain a gentle, tasteful approach and should they ever seem too steeped in sadness, humour bubbles through'); The Paupers' *Ellis Island*; Mighty Sparrow & Byron Lee's *Sparrow Meets The Dragon*; Nova's *Local Nova*; Murray Roman's *Blind Man's Movie*; The Unauthorised Version's *Hey Jude*; Burt Bacharach's *Make It Easy On Yourself*; and soundtrack albums of *The Italian Job* and *Monte Carlo Or Bust*.

The *NME* review of *Five Leaves Left*, by one G.C., appeared in the issue dated 4 October 1969: 'Nick Drake is a new name to me, and probably to you. From an accompanying biography I read that he is at Cambridge reading English, was "discovered" by Fairport Convention when they played on the same bill and spent some time travelling in Europe, a trip which has greatly benefited his songwriting. I'm sorry I can't be more enthusiastic, because he obviously has a not inconsiderable amount of talent, but there is not nearly enough variety on this debut LP to make it entertaining.

'His voice reminds me very much of Peter Sarstedt, but his songs lack Sarstedt's penetration and arresting quality. Exceptions are "Mary Jane", a fragile little love song, and "Saturday Sun", a reflective number on which the singer also plays a very attractive piano.'

For folk-related, Witchseason-style acts, the pages of *Melody Maker* were the natural habitat and crucial platform. The paper's August round-up of LP releases found Jethro Tull's second album, *This Was*, voted Pop LP of the Month. Other selected titles were Fairport's *Unhalfbricking*, Julie Driscoll & The Brian Auger Trinity's *Street Noise*, Yes's eponymous debut, Dionne Warwick's *Soulful*, Clouds' *The Clouds Scrapbook*, Tim Buckley's *Happy Sad* ('needs a lot of listening') and Dr Strangely Strange's *Kip Of The Serenes* ('creeping ennui sets in with numbing effect'). Squeezed between Lonnie Donegan's *Lonnie Rides Again* and Betty Everett's *There'll Come A Time* was *Five Leaves Left* ('interesting debut album from composer-singer-guitarist Drake').

The pop landscape of 1969 was dominated by new acts like Led Zeppelin ('the new Cream'), The Doors – Jim Morrison's shaving off his beard was worth a mention in the *MM* – as was one Paul Monday, who bore an eerie resemblance to Gary Glitter, with his new single, 'Here Comes The Sun'. Besides Nick Drake, the year saw debut albums from Led Zeppelin, Crosby, Stills & Nash, Blind Faith, King Crimson and Noel Redding's Fat Mattress. But the old guard were still of interest: 'Will you be on the Isle of Wight on August 31?' an *MM* ad asked. 'Bob Dylan will!' Advance sales of 50,000 were announced for the new Beatles album, *Abbey Road*. 'Presley Says "I'm Coming To Britain"!' ran one headline, while The Rolling Stones went the other way, announcing an American tour which would conclude with a free concert somewhere in California.

It was the year of Woodstock. A time for forging a new nation, united by peace and love and rock 'n' roll, and led from the front by Dylan and The Beatles, Donovan and The Stones – the shamans who had all the answers. Amid the frenzy of tribal gatherings, love-ins and days of stardust, there wasn't much room for newcomer Nick Drake.

The impact of the prestigious *Melody Maker* readers' poll was substantial, alerting the world to the names to watch. The final poll of the sixties was dominated by names which had already mapped out the pop landscape of the decade – Dylan, Beatles and Stones. In the 'Brightest Hope' category, Blind Faith, Creedence Clearwater Revival and Led Zeppelin were the new names which attracted readers' votes. Nick Drake received no mention.

The pre-publicity had not even reached some of those closest to Nick, as his sister Gabrielle admitted: 'I had begun acting professionally, odd bits of television, and had a flat in Battersea. Nick was working with Joe Boyd, and looking for somewhere to live. He was never very good at integrating people from the different portions of his life. I knew he was recording but I didn't know how far it had got. By this time, he had become much more introverted. He suddenly came into my room one day, said: "Here you are", and threw down this record, which was *Five Leaves Left*. I couldn't believe it. There it was, a record, with my brother's picture on the front.'

Simon Crocker knew Nick well at Marlborough and had visited him in Cambridge: 'For us, someone we knew, making a record. And then I guess he left Cambridge, and I didn't hear anything at all, he kind of dropped out, and obviously what he was doing was recording his album, because the next thing was I was walking past a record shop one day and suddenly there was this album of Nick Drake. I remember ringing everyone I knew who knew Nick, saying: "He's got a record out, and it's on Island!" We were all terribly proud of him. And then played it, and it was so good, so we were doubly chuffed.'

Iain Dunn, who had heard Nick's songs evolve in various rooms around Cambridge, was surprised at what he heard on *Five Leaves Left* when it was finally released: 'I remember being disappointed – I think it was probably part of the culture rather than the quality of the album – but it felt over-produced, which actually now it doesn't at all . . . It didn't feel like the same person who'd been sitting in the room playing songs. Inevitably you thought there were better songs that should have gone in . . . there was that difference between "it's official", and a rather attractive unofficial side of it.'

Iain Cameron also remembers reservations: 'The inside feeling among the cognoscenti was that the arrangements, the production, are not 100 per cent sympathetic to the spirit of the songs – of the performance as we knew and loved them. There was a feeling that it was slightly overdone, hasn't quite got the delicacy required, except, I must say, the Richard Thompson . . . there you have two masters complementing each other, it is a textbook account of how to sensitively accompany a good song and add something to it.'

In the summer of 1969, having learnt that he was to be enshrined on the second track of *Five Leaves Left*, Jeremy Mason rang Nick, whom he had not seen since Aix, and arranged to meet up in London. The meeting was only a few weeks before *Five Leaves Left* was released, but Jeremy remembers that Nick was not yet happy with the way it was sounding: 'He was speculating whether he needed another instrument to make his music "more interesting". He was talking about learning the sitar, or something more exotic.'

By the time Simon Crocker bumped into him on the street in London, about a month after the album came out, Nick had a whole new set of worries: 'The only thing I remember him saying was they wanted him to play live. They wanted him to go and do concerts, and he was kind of nervous of doing them on his own.'

Island Records were happy enough with *Five Leaves Left*, the album coming in at between £3000 and £4000, so even if it didn't sell, the outlay had been minimal. David Betteridge recognized that there was a real problem getting new acts noticed: 'Nick was definitely one of those artists where, in retrospect, this was a worthy talent. But there was so much talent about then . . . so many things happening . . . that artists weren't being picked up or weren't being promoted properly . . . Nick's albums were well received inside Island, but there were certainly the questions: "Where's the single?" and "Is he on the road?" And if you can't answer those two questions . . .'

In the absence of a single, and with Nick reluctant to undertake gigs to promote the album on his own, sales levelled off in the low thousands. By the time of its release, Pete Frame had founded *Zig Zag* magazine, the first English publication to take rock 'n' roll seriously. Like *Rolling Stone* had been doing in America since 1967, Frame set out to try and make sense of the burgeoning rock culture: 'I'm not surprised Nick's records only sold 5000 – that's all a New Riders Of The Purple Sage album would have done. But the Underground was very small. A lot of the hippies didn't have any money, and if they did they'd spend it on dope. I remember seeing a memo from the bloke who set up Dawn – Pye's "Underground" label – explaining to Louis Benjamin, who ran Pye, what the Underground was: "Hippies are obliged to smoke dope and listen to these kinds of records and Pye are not filling this niche in the market."'

Low sales have been cited as a reason for Nick's growing depression, but they were not uncommonly low for a debut album from an unknown singer-songwriter. The previous year, Ralph McTell's debut, *Eight Frames A Second*, sold barely 3000 copies. To try to boost sales of *Five Leaves Left*, Nick did, reluctantly and sporadically, go out to try his hand at promoting the album, but the gigs were fragmentary and disappointing.

Folk singer Bridget St John, who was just beginning her career, was working the same circuit as Nick and remembers him as a kindred spirit: 'We write differently, but in some ways from a similar sensibility. The gigs I did with him were mostly at Les Cousins, on Greek Street in Soho, from 1969 onwards. I have a picture of the two of us one summer evening, sitting quietly on the steps outside a pub a little north of Cousins on the opposite side of the street. We never talked a lot but this night was probably a little different – or it wouldn't have stayed with me. My feeling is that mostly we understood each other without the need to say much. Both shy and best able to say things through songs rather than conversations.'

8

The end of the first year of the new decade lay bitten and spat out, like an old cigar. All the conflicts and confusion, all the tension and buoyancy which the sixties had raised, remained unresolved at the end of 1970.

The Beatles had been the fairy tale which obsessed the sixties, but the new decade did not bring a happy-ever-after ending, just a bitter, protracted and very public break-up. The deaths of Jimi Hendrix and Janis Joplin within weeks of each other in the new decade's opening year also seemed to presage pessimism, rather than an overspill of sixties optimism.

Anthea Joseph's working days were spent around the Charlotte Street offices of Witchseason: 'I was the in-house nanny. My job was looking after Fairport particularly, but if they were off somewhere, and I was in London, I was given someone like Nick to nanny. He needed more nannying than most, because he *loathed* live performing – he was difficult enough in the studio, where he hadn't got an audience, but Joe had endless patience with the most difficult people – Nick in particular. So he was given space to do what he wanted, when he wanted to do it. When he was in the right frame of mind . . .'

Boyd's idea of a Witchseason family was partly altruistic, in keeping with the communal vibe of the times, but it was also economic. Offering management and agency representation, Witchseason could cut costs by having artists help each other out on record. Late in 1969, Fairport Convention had moved to a converted pub called the Angel, in the village of Little Hadham, near Bishop's

Stortford. A few months later Nick paid a visit to the Angel to rehearse with Fairport guitarist Richard Thompson, bassist Dave Pegg and drummer Dave Mattacks, who would accompany him on his next album.

Dave Pegg: 'It was sometime during early 1970. It was actually very good fun, because we had a rehearsal room there, which was very rarely used . . . Nick came down for about three or four days . . . He was so introverted, you could never tell if he liked stuff or not, but we got an awful lot done in that time. It was just running through arrangements for *Bryter Layter*. He had all the songs, and fairly positive ideas about how he wanted them done. His songs were fairly guitar-based, and he was a great guitarist. That was enough, really, on a lot of those things – they were so complete with what he did, and it was early days, we were only learning rhythm-section things.'

In London, Robert Kirby was aware that Nick lived in a succession of different places: 'I remember Nick in a flat down in Earls Court that someone had lent him. There was a monkey that used to sit on the record player going round . . . That was one of his bolt-holes. Nick used to have a lot . . . Certainly he was in Haverstock Hill while we were recording *Bryter Layter*. His was the back room on the ground floor overlooking the garden on the corner . . . french windows opening out . . . Very imposing, large, Gothic house which has been demolished . . . Bare floorboards from what I remember; a record player, a few books, a guitar, a single bed, posters on the wall. He got more minimalist as time went on.'

It was in this big, rambling, Victorian house near Chalk Farm Tube, in his ground-floor room, sparsely furnished, that Nick wrote the songs which would form his second album, *Bryter Layter*.

Haverstock Hill winds up into Hampstead village. To the north, beyond the tall, looming, Victorian properties, lies Hampstead Heath. It is one of the most appealing addresses in London: Martin Carthy had lived there in the early sixties as he began making his mark on the London folk scene – Anthea Joseph remembers Carthy and his wife and a young Bob Dylan chopping up a piano for firewood during the bitter winter of 1962. Richard and Linda Thompson occupied a property just off Haverstock Hill in the seventies, and The Strawbs' song 'Pieces Of 79 & 15' referred to properties the band once occupied in Haverstock Hill.

Brian Wells remembers how Nick continued to compartmentalize his life even when he was living full time in London: 'He had all these mysterious friends in London, and he would keep all his friends in different compartments, and would kind of allude to "Well, I've got these friends in London". They were rather special people . . . He would say, I'm doing a record, doing these sessions, but I never met John Wood. I never met Joe Boyd. I never met any of these people. They were names that Nick would occasionally allude to. I guess he was quite good at keeping people at a distance. In Cambridge I felt he and I were buddies, and then subsequently when he was living in Haverstock Hill, I would go and see him, and by then he'd become odd . . . I think *Bryter Layter* was being recorded around then. I remember being in a room with Nick with Robert Kirby, and Nick was playing Robert some of the songs, some of the tracks that needed to have arrangements on them.'

Nick's Hampstead period boasts all the hallmarks of poetic bohemianism: the artist, alone and suffering for his art (Arthur Lubow had the Hampstead room 'so cold that he took the mattress off the bed, dragged it near the gas fire, and piled up blankets for warmth'). But Molly Drake felt that it was while he was in his bedsit in Haverstock Hill that 'the shadows closed in' around her son. It seems that at some point, bohemian isolation gave way to lonely depression.

Anthea Joseph, who spent many hours sequestered with Nick – at Witchseason, backstage at concerts or in radio studios – concluded that he was paranoid: 'He wouldn't let you in . . . I felt he was really terrified of the human race. Everything was a nightmare. But he wasn't nasty, not at all. He'd just go and sit in the corner. He wouldn't throw paddies and jump up and down. He'd just say: "I'm going", and then you'd have to persuade him to come back. He really was frightened. It was difficult, because it's so hard to deal with people like that, because you can't talk to them. Because they won't talk. Richard, Sandy, John Martyn, were all extremely serious – and in their individual ways were equally difficult to deal with. But you could talk to them, which was the difference . . . I don't remember any "ordinary" conversations with Nick. Never, not one. That's what was so weird, because mostly with almost anybody that you see on a weekly basis, some sort of conversation developed, even if it's only "Where's my beer?" "Can't I have some more money?" Never even that. He'd just come in, and *be* there, but wouldn't talk.'

Nick ventured out sporadically to gig, and fairly frequently to Chelsea – where the Sound Techniques studios were located, close by the Thames – to begin recording his second album for Island. The recording of *Bryter Layter* spread over nine months during 1970, and one reason suggested for the delay was Nick's unhappiness with the sound of the violins which featured on many of the tracks. Robert Kirby was again called in to arrange Nick's music, with Joe Boyd producing, and John Wood engineering the album.

Robert Kirby: 'Joe's strength was that he was good at getting a team together who could work together properly . . . John Wood did fashion the sound, but in the first place, it was Joe who put the team together to get that sound. I think they made a very good pair.'

Joe Boyd: '*Bryter Layter* is certainly the record I felt most completely satisfied with. The one record I can listen to with unalloyed pleasure, and not think for a minute, oh, I wished I'd mixed that differently. We certainly put an awful lot into it. John Wood loved Nick, and I think took tremendous care, which you can hear in the way it stands up. I think the sound he got on Nick's voice, the sound on the acoustic instruments, is just very, very good. We did have that feeling of real pleasure and excitement about the record. We remixed it endlessly . . . Whenever I'm stuck in a studio and I can't face listening to a song again, I say: "Remember *Bryter Layter* . . . and remember how rewarding it is to listen to now." It was only eight-track, but there were so many layers and different ways of approaching it.'

American drummer Mike Kowalski was another musician who worked on *Bryter Layter*: 'Nick was shy, but he obviously knew his stuff. As a guitarist, I'm sure he knew Django Reinhardt and Joe Pass, his jazz playing was strong and rootsy. The drummer's booth at Sound Techniques was tiny, but it was a big, comfortable studio. Joe Boyd hardly said a word. Nick was very much in control. He did all the communicating. He was very demonstrative. He'd demonstrate just what he wanted in the studio, improvise, and let you groove with it. I remember there were quite a few takes. He wouldn't let the improvisation get out of hand. He would recognize certain accents, he would hear you playing embellishments and ask you to accentuate that. "At The Chime Of A City Clock" was like that. "One Of These Things First" I remember as being a special track. Nick had this weird-looking old box, an acoustic guitar which was amplified. There wasn't anything he couldn't play: jazz, waltz, 5/4. Ed Carter played my 1954 Fender Precision bass on "One Of These Things First".

'I got on fine with Nick. He was shy, but he came down to stay with my wife and daughter and I one weekend at Chilham. We had a beautiful old cottage in the village, and Nick came down. Maybe because I was American we could communicate. He talked about music, we were both young . . . We were kids, you don't think about what's going to happen. We were young, with hair down to our waist, smoking dope.'

Dave Pegg, who played bass on most of the tracks on *Bryter Layter* remembers Boyd playing a more influential role during the sessions: 'It was a very exciting record for me to be involved in . . . you got things like a brass section, people like Ray Warleigh there. There were some really interesting players on some of that stuff. Most of it was done live, and it was done fairly quickly. You'd have the benefit of the arrangements that Robert Kirby did – he was a fantastic arranger, who had a really original approach . . . It was a noticeable development from learning the stuff at the Angel, which was all very skeletal.

'Joe was more or less in charge of it in the studio. It was very much Joe and John Wood and Robert Kirby. It was actually a very fun thing to do. All those *Bryter Layter* tracks. You got a real buzz off what was happening, which is not always the way with recording. Moments of great joy in the studio very rarely happen . . . Nick's was one of the most memorable and enjoyable weeks I've ever spent in there. I still play that record all the time . . . it's one of the few records I've been involved with that I do play, all the time. And that isn't just hindsight, before I had it on CD, I went through the vinyl copies.'

Bryter Layter was released on 1 November 1970. As ILPS 9134, it was one of the last Island albums to be released with the familiar pink label. It was sandwiched between John and Beverley Martyn's *Road To Ruin* (ILPS 9133) and Cat Stevens' *Tea For The Tillerman* (ILPS 9135).

Even before joining Island, and becoming Nick's press officer, David Sandison was aware of the label's cachet: 'Island was one of those labels that if you leafed through the album racks, you stopped. It was like Elektra, like Atlantic . . . Nick's initial sales I'm sure were to do with that thing about Island. I can remember buying Island albums even though I didn't know the act – they just looked interesting . . . But obviously the hard-core folk lot would have known about Nick via the Fairport connection and Witchseason. He had done some gigs, and word might have spread, which would account for a few hundred sales.'

In 1970 Martin Satterthwaite also joined Island, to work in the promotion department: 'Island was very strong in the early seventies: they had the folkie stuff, with Nick, Richard and Linda, Sandy; the reggae side, which had grown out of ska and bluebeat; the rock side with Free; and then there was the pop side with Sparks and Roxy Music. At that time Island had the same sort of impact as Motown a few years earlier: if a record came out on Motown, you went out and bought it, you didn't even bother to listen to it, you just trusted them.'

Although he only released three albums on Island during his lifetime, Nick is irrevocably associated with the label, and appeared on a number of other Island albums. It was actually these other releases which helped Nick reach the biggest audience during his lifetime. CBS had pioneered the budget sampler album in 1968 with *The Rock Machine Turns You On*, but Island were swift to follow in May 1969 with the enticing twelve-track *You Can All Join In*. As many of the artists as could be assembled, gathered shivering, at seven o'clock one cold winter morning in Hyde Park, for the cover shot. Nick has been rumoured to be hiding among the crowd, but at the time of the photo shoot his Island debut was still several months down the line.

November 1969 saw the release of another Island sampler, *Nice Enough To Eat*, which included, as well as King Crimson, Mott The Hoople, Jethro Tull, Fairport Convention, Traffic and Free, Nick's 'Time Has Told Me'. It was on this album that the bulk of late-sixties record buyers first chanced upon the music of Nick Drake. With their roster growing, Island were confident enough to make their third sampler a double album: *Bumpers* was released in early 1970, featuring Nick's 'Hazey Jane', and was followed in 1971 by *El Pea*, which included 'One Of These Things First'.

These were the records which made their way into back bedrooms and student digs, to be played and replayed as the all-important decision was made: which full-price album to buy? The problem was that while Nick Drake was alive and well and releasing records, there were a lot of calls on the purse-strings of his potential audience. Aficionados of singer-songwriters had new albums by Leonard Cohen, Al Stewart, James Taylor, Tim Rose, Tim Hardin, Michael Chapman, Ralph McTell and Van Morrison all competing for a place on their turntable. Nick was only one of a number of new acts trying to break through, and if he was to stand any chance at all it was with *Bryter Layter*.

The album is Nick Drake's masterpiece. *Bryter Layter* is a record of timeless tranquillity and unimpeachable atmosphere, which merits comparison with Van Morrison's moody and meandering *Astral Weeks* and Love's unclassifiable and mysterious *Forever Changes*. Robert Kirby acknowledges a debt: 'We were certainly listening to

Astral Weeks heavily at that time . . . the string-bass playing, the violinist. It's funny, that's got a track about walking around Ladbroke Grove, and Nick's got "At The Chime Of A City Clock". There are similarities. And yes, we were listening to it a lot at the time . . .'

Bryter Layter extends beyond rock and folk. In its wistful mystery is a timeless, beatific calm; yet what chance did that have against the blitzkrieg steamrollering of the third album from Led Zeppelin? As an indication of what *Bryter Layter* was up against, among the albums which held sway on the UK charts during 1970 were Simon & Garfunkel's all-conquering *Bridge Over Troubled Water*, *Motown Chartbusters Volume 5*, The Rolling Stones' *Sticky Fingers*, The Moody Blues' *Every Good Boy Deserves Favour*, Rod Stewart's *Every Picture Tells A Story* and John Lennon's *Imagine*. A heady mixture of crowd-pleasing compilations, student favourites, and ex-Beatles.

Aside from the rock-steady rhythm section of Pegg and Mattacks, and the sterling lead guitar of Richard Thompson, one other intriguing name which appeared on the sleeve of *Bryter Layter* was that of ex-Velvet Underground founder John Cale. The Velvets had yet to be deified, but those in the know, knew their importance. Cale went on to a peripatetic solo career, and cropped up – like Woody Allen's Zelig – at all the crucial moments in rock 'n' roll history. The Velvet Underground's white-noise enthusiast, he kicked the door open for David Bowie's later experimentation (Bowie acknowledged the Velvets on the sleeve of his masterly *Hunky Dory*). Cale was also there at the birth of Punk, producing the debut albums of Patti Smith and Jonathan Richman, either of which could lay strong claim to being the first Punk album. Cale was also there for Squeeze and The Happy Mondays; Brian Eno and Nico; Lowell George and The Stooges . . .

Cale already knew Joe Boyd, and came to *Bryter Layter* immediately after producing Nico's *Marble Index* album. In an interview with Mike Barnes for *The Wire*, Cale talked about his work on *Bryter Layter*: 'I was doing a lot with Nico and it was on one of those trips that I met [Drake] . . . I had a 12-string and he'd never seen a D12 before, a Martin. And you know that very complicated picking he had? He just picked up the guitar and it was just like this orchestral sound coming out. He went nuts. He was sitting there stunned by it . . . I hardly ever dealt with him. I think it was Joe . . . One other way of developing what I did with *Marble Index* was to do Nick Drake and The Incredible String Band and whatever came around. Joe seemed to appreciate what I was doing. Everything he showed me was very interesting.'

The lushness of *Bryter Layter* seemed to make a strong impact on Cale: certainly his best solo album, 1973's *Paris 1919*, was the most lavishly orchestrated of his career. Journalist Nick Kent remembers talking to him about his work with Nick Drake: 'Cale said he was a genius musician, but you couldn't talk to him, he was like a zombie, like he just had no personality left.'

Richard Thompson's playing on *Bryter Layter* was singled out for praise, but he was dissatisfied with it. Talking to Connor McKnight in *Zig Zag*, while Nick was still alive, Richard talked about working with Nick: 'He is a very elusive character. It was at Trident, I think, and I asked him what he wanted, but he didn't say much, so I just did it and he seemed fairly happy. People say that I'm quiet, but Nick's ridiculous. I really like his music, he's extremely talented and if he wanted to be, he could be very successful.'

Linda Peters, who would later marry Richard, was at that time going out with Joe Boyd: 'I remember being at the Nick Drake session, and it was difficult, because Nick didn't talk, and Richard didn't talk. I think that Richard felt that his work was very perfunctory on it . . . There was definitely a bit of rivalry there too, because Nick was Joe's darling.'

Anthea Joseph, who knew both Nick and Richard, also observed some tension: 'The rivalry between Richard and Nick . . . it was very difficult because they were all such babies – terribly young. They did get jealous . . . And Joe had made a great deal of Richard, quite rightly so, because he was so good, you could see it – a little jewel. But Nick required serious, hands-on looking after. And he trusted Joe, he trusted him implicitly, and I think that was really the base of their relationship. Joe was an extraordinary man, warts and all, and he took Nick on because he knew he'd got something rare . . .

'Joe lavished himself on these people, and Nick in particular. But it was that sort of late teenage "He's mine", "No he's not, he's mine", you know. Joe never showed any favouritism to anybody – but both the kids did feel – because they were both songwriters, good-looking . . . And they were at that rather tender age.'

Linda Thompson, who went out with Nick for a while, was another who noticed how much he and Richard had in common: 'It was funny, going out with Richard and going out with Nick, there were those similarities. They were both very withdrawn and very remote, and they both had these glamorous older sisters, both very outgoing. When Richard would do a solo on Nick's album, Nick would smile, he would like that.

'There was a point when I thought Richard could go Nick's way . . . Richard used to walk around with uncashed cheques, he never changed his clothes, he didn't speak . . . I think it was very hard for him to pull himself out of that, but he's a survivor, Richard, and he latched on to people who were outgoing, outgoing enough to pull him out of it. I think he made a definite effort to do that, and Nick didn't. Couldn't.

'There are people I know, like Sandy [Denny], who died young, and there are countless stories . . . But it's a bit of a blank page with Nick.'

Dave Pegg remembers Nick as easy to work with: 'The only thing was, you never really knew what he thought about it, whether he was happy or not, because he would never communicate. Probably Joe knew whether he was happy or not . . . It all went down fairly quickly. There were never any occasions where stuff was never going to work, where we had to completely redo the track in a different way, or try for a different feel.

'The people they chose to play on those tracks were all from different backgrounds, that made it really exciting stuff to do . . . It must have been quite strange for Nick, because he'd not have had the experience of working with that many people, all in the same studio, all at the same time. Myself and DM had done lots and lots of sessions . . . *Bryter Layter* was certainly one of my best and most enjoyable experiences at Sound Techniques.

'In a day we'd do three or four tracks, it was all very quick, everything was in those days, there didn't seem to be all the faffing about that you get nowadays. In a three-hour session, you'd be doing two tracks. DM and I would go off and do things with Paul & Barry Ryan . . . I think we used to get £17 for a session, and then you got three quid porterage if you carried your own gear.'

Nick's lack of communication, even about the music, was something that struck Danny Thompson too: 'He was not very communicative about anything musically, which isn't unusual. A lot of people, either because they're in awe of you or something, they stand back in the studio. I reckon I'm a pretty normal geezer, I don't think I'm very difficult to get on with; you just think, well, it's their problem, whatever it is. There's a shyness, and there's something else – a deeper one.'

Bryter Layter is a beguiling record. The three instrumentals may teeter rather too close to Easy Listening, but otherwise the album is an enticing blend of folk stylings, jazz, blue-eyed soul and ballads. There is a fluency to Nick's playing throughout, the Fairport rhythm section is rock-solid, and Robert Kirby's arrangements enhance and enrich the musical textures. It is perhaps more than coincidence that John Cale appears on the album's two best tracks. 'Fly', which is coloured by Cale's viola and harpsichord, also features Nick's most bruised and vulnerable vocal: faltering and stumbling, as if he is making it up as he goes along, the song gains a fragility and uncertainty which repays endless replays. The number begins with a plea, and there is a pleading note in Nick's voice which speaks of vulnerability and the knowledge that commitment can only lead to hurt.

Cale is also to be found swelling out the texture of 'Northern Sky', which lays strong claim to being the finest song to which Nick Drake ever lent his name. Again sounding alone and vulnerable, 'Northern Sky' has Nick pleading for the brightness to come and shatter the darkness of his night-time sky. The atmosphere is dense, suggesting silver moons sailing on a raven-black sea, wind lightly ruffling the hair of the treetops, all stoked by a crazy kind of magic; and the alchemy is fuelled by Cale's hymnal organ and soaring piano figures.

'At The Chime Of A City Clock' is a big-city frieze, a fragmentary London portrait of the Soho streets Nick walked when he hitched down from Marlborough to the Flamingo and the Marquee. There is a sinuous melody, emphasized by Ray Warleigh's fat and sensual alto sax – the sound of a cat stretching itself awake.

A wash of strings, a crash of cymbals, like waves breaking on a distant shore, and Nick's deftly picked descending guitar figures usher in 'Hazey Jane I'. But this is no love song: there is no tortured pleading, nor protestations of unrequited love; it is a baffled attempt to grasp the unattainable. And in the end, as the strings seep away like the setting sun, the bass rises and dies – and all the while, the guitar is plucked like a heart string.

There is a knowing, self-referential humour on 'Poor Boy', as P.P. Arnold and Doris Troy coo on the chorus about the child who is so evidently sorry for himself. Nick knew that by setting the self-pitying lyrics to such a jaunty tune he could dilute the cloying nature of the introspection.

Listening to *Bryter Layter*, you are drawn to its atmospheres and textures. The appeal lies not in the angst, the lyrics or the deftness of Nick's playing, nor even in the subtlety of his melodies. But together, all these factors combine to evoke and sustain a mood, an atmosphere, dense and inimitable. It is like sitting in a deserted attic room, tracing through the detritus of childhood, and as your fingers disturb the dust, the motes rise and float in drowsy shafts of sunlight.

Robert Kirby, who had worked closely on *Bryter Layter*, noticed a buoyancy about Nick just before its release. There was a confidence and optimism which would rarely again be obvious in Nick's life: 'This was going to be the one with a single on it . . . I always rated "Poor Boy", but they could have gone with "Northern Sky", but nothing ever happened . . . I remember being down there to watch Chris McGregor put down his stuff for "Poor Boy", Pat Arnold and Doris Troy wailing away, and Nick sitting there at the back, seeming quite happy.

'Haverstock Hill, recording *Bryter Layter*, altogether quite happy times. Nick was quite high on it. The first one had got his name known. I think he felt this was going to be the one. We were told this was going to be the one.'

Paul Wheeler remembers having a meal with Nick just after *Bryter Layter* came out: 'He said he'd assumed that it would be much more successful than it was. And I do remember being surprised, because I didn't think he was in it for that . . .'

Trevor Dann, who had taken over Nick's room at Fitzwilliam, remembered the first time he heard the second album: '*Bryter Layter* I was horrified by. It was a bit like, oh God, Dylan's gone electric, what the fuck are these brass instruments doing here? It wasn't until I was at Cambridge, and I was in a band, and the bass player was really into *Bryter Layter*, and he hadn't heard *Five Leaves Left*, and one night I was round at his house, and it was foggy, the way that it gets in Cambridge, and it all suddenly became clear: first album, "Man In Shed"; second album, Man in London.

'That's the difference. *Bryter Layter* is the horrible urban environment, and reacting to it. What I wanted was another acoustic album, but I'd got something different, but until then I'd never lived in a town . . . I didn't know what living in a town was like. To me, that's what those two records are about: the first one is very rural. It is about acoustic guitars and trees . . . it just feels pastoral. And *Bryter Layter* is the urban record, it's all about tube trains and city clocks, and the picture on the back, him on the motorway.'

Nick's parents also sensed a new alienation in their son, which they felt dated from his move to Haverstock Hill. Rodney: '*Bryter Layter* he wrote in this room he took out in Hampstead. He shut himself off in this room and it was rather difficult to get at him . . .' Molly: 'We worried so much about him.'

Bryter Layter drew reviews of the praiseworthy sort which generally attached themselves to Boyd-produced, Island Records releases. The reviews were respectful, if a little baffled: nobody seemed quite sure exactly what to make of Nick Drake.

It was little more than a year since Nick had dropped out of Cambridge, and he still kept in touch with university friends like Brian Wells: 'I once asked him if he'd go on *Top Of The Pops*, and he said just: "No way." I asked him a year later, and he said: "Yeah, why not?" I think he saw himself as part of a sort of James Taylor, Van Morrison movement rather than The Stones. People who emanated from Dylan, and folk and blues.'

Apart from the odd one-paragraph album review, music press interest in Nick Drake during his lifetime was focused in a single issue of *Sounds*, dated 13 March 1971. It cost 5p, and boasted 'Music Is The Message'. Neil Young was on the cover, as were the names of Mike Vernon's Blues, Harvey Mandel, Graham Bond, Ian Matthews and Ric Grech. But for Nick's name you had to look inside, where as well as Jerry Gilbert's interview with Nick and his review of *Bryter Layter*, there was an ad for the album.

Gilbert was a leading writer on the folk scene at the time: 'I joined *MM* late '69. I'd bought *Five Leaves Left*, and loved it. When *Bryter Layter* came out, it was a combination of that lush sound, the beautifully cultured songwriting, the open-tuned guitar, and I guess what became the Joe Boyd production sound.' By 1970 he had joined the fifth weekly music paper, *Sounds*, where he achieved the distinction of being the only journalist ever to interview Nick Drake.

The single-column interview, under the headline 'Something Else For Nick?', began: 'Nick Drake is a shy, introverted folk singer who is not usually known to speak unless it is absolutely necessary . . .' The page was swelled by a profile of Gerry Rafferty and a quarter-page ad for '*Suicide*', an explosive new album from Stray'.

Through no fault of the writer, the interview revealed absolutely nothing about the artist; but as this was destined to remain the only interview Nick Drake ever gave, even the vaguest of answers are of interest. Asked why he shied away from live work, Nick replied: 'I think the problem was with the material, which I wrote for records rather than performing. There were only two or three concerts that felt right, and there was something wrong with the others. I did play

Cousins and one or two folk clubs in the North, but the gigs just sort of petered out.'

Of recent appearances at prestigious venues like the Festival Hall, Nick explained: 'I was under some obligation to do them, but it wasn't the end of the world when I stopped. If I was enjoying the gigs it would have made much more sense.' About the recently released *Bryter Layter*, he said: 'I had something in mind when I wrote the songs, knowing that they weren't just for me. The album took a long time to do, in fact, we started doing it almost a year ago. But I'm not altogether clear about this album – I haven't got to terms with the whole presentation.'

The interview winds down with the perennial favourite about future plans: 'I think there'll be another album and I have some material for it, but I'll be looking around now to see if this album leads anywhere naturally. For the next one I had the idea of just doing something with John Wood, the engineer at Sound Techniques.'

And did he plan any gigs to promote the album? 'I don't think that would help – unless they were done in the right way. I'm just not very sure at the moment, it's hard to tell what will turn up. If I could find making music a fairly natural connection with something else, then I might move on to something else.'

Bryter Layter was the thirteenth album reviewed in *Sounds* that week. It was a fairly quiet week for album releases, but there were compilations by The Rolling Stones, The Everly Brothers, Family, Dion, Procol Harum, T. Rex and The Move. Also considered were an Incredible String Band album, Tony Joe White's debut ('swamp rock at its best'), and Barclay James Harvest's second album, *Once Again*.

In his review Jerry Gilbert wrote: 'I get the feeling that only a Joe Boyd–Paul Harris alliance could have produced such a superb album as this. And once again a great slice of the credit must go to Robert Kirby, whose splendid arrangements are as noticeable on this album as they were on Nick Drake's last album. On their own merits, the songs of Nick Drake are not particularly strong, but Nick has always been a consistent if introverted performer, and placed in the cauldron that Joe Boyd has prepared for him, then things start to effervesce. Also joining guitarist Nick Drake on various tracks are Dave Pegg, Richard Thompson, Ray Warleigh, Mike Kowalski, Paul Harris, Ed Carter, Lyn Dobson, John Cale, Chris McGregor, Pat Arnold and Doris Troy; it seems nothing has been spared to make this album a success, and Joe Boyd and Nick Drake have certainly succeeded in their intentions.

'There has been a long gap between Nick's first and second albums, and anyone who has seen Nick performing at Witchseason concerts in the interim will recognise tracks like "Hazey Jane". And this, like all his songs, does take time to work through to the listener, with help from the beautiful backing which every track receives.'

David Sandison was now installed as Island's Head of Press, after a lengthy spell in PR: 'I joined Island in early 1970. We had Traffic, Mott The Hoople, Free, Cat Stevens . . . And because Joe had gone back to the States, we were looking after the Witchseason lot. We had in total – sales, distribution, marketing, A&R and the studios – a staff of something like thirty people, and we had 5 per cent of the UK album market for three years on the trot.

'When *Bryter Layter* came out, the response was good; doing the follow-up: Have you got the album? Yes. Have you heard it? Yes. The general consensus was that it was really nice. But in three years at Island, I only had one phone call for an interview with Nick, and that was Jerry Gilbert. He called and said: "Any chance of meeting him?" So I called Anthea, who said: "I doubt it, darling." So I said: "Can you ask?" and she said: "I don't know where the hell he is." She finally came back and said yes. Jerry had done a very complimentary review, I think, of *Five Leaves Left*. Nick was clearly aware of that, and he'd agreed.

'We sweated through three-quarters of an hour trying to get three words out of him that weren't "yes" and "no" or "um". It didn't strike me as depressive; it was just incredibly vague.'

Gilbert remembers the interview only too clearly: 'It was 1971, it took place in a flat in Swiss Cottage. It was a reluctant interview on all parts: Nick clearly didn't want to do it, but had a new album out . . . You could have cut the atmosphere with a knife . . . Nobody wanted to do it. I was unhappy doing it because I knew Nick would be. I don't think he once looked me in the eye. The questions were stilted, I was desperately trying to draw something from Nick. Nothing he said was in any way positive or upbeat . . . I suppose the interview was exactly as I thought it would be.

'He was stooped, I don't remember what he was wearing, he had long hair, which he played with all the time. His answers were mainly feed answers, monosyllabic. He would never develop a subject. It was almost as if he was denying his very existence. There was a great new album . . . Him and John and Beverley were obviously coming up, working a lot of the same shows together.

'Normally in an interview, there's a bit of chat before and after the tape was rolling, but there was none of that with Nick. As a professional journalist, I hope I had a way of making people feel at home, giving them easy questions to establish a common bond. But with Nick, there was never any kind of meeting of minds, it was just an interview that petered out, because in the end, there were no more questions. He wasn't giving. Probably, it was an interview that should never have taken place.

'I'd love to say that when he walked into the room there was this huge charisma that came with him, but there was absolutely not . . . just a chap with his head down, stooped, very shy, very self-effacing, not wanting to talk much about himself, really uneasy. As you'd expect from a public-school, Cambridge background, he was a very well-spoken guy. He spoke very clearly, albeit into his body, instead of at me.'

Four months after *Bryter Layter* was officially released, Andrew Means reviewed it for *Melody Maker*: 'This is a particularly difficult album to come to any firm conclusion on. For one thing, the reaction it produces depends very much on the mood of the listener. It's late night coffee 'n' chat music. The ten tracks are all very similar – quiet, gentle and relaxing. Nick Drake sends his voice skimming smoothly over the backing. The range of musicians used is apt to catch one unawares. Among the talents employed are Dave Pegg (bass) and Dave Mattacks (drums) both of Fairport Convention, Richard Thompson (ld gtr) ex-Fairport, John Cale (celeste, piano and organ) ex-Velvet Underground, Ray Warleigh (alto sax), Chris McGregor (piano) and Pat Arnold and Doris Troy (backing vocals).' Note the oft-employed 'list all the backing musicians trick', used by hard-pressed hacks when a half-page Groundhogs ad has dropped out and they are given half an hour to review an album by someone they've never heard of.

In the poppier *Record Mirror*, Lon Goddard was more convinced of Nick's abilities on *Bryter Layter*: 'A beautiful guitarist – clean and with perfect timing – accompanied by soft, beautiful arrangements by Robert Kirby. Nick isn't the world's top singer, but he's written fantastic numbers that suit strings marvellously. Definitely one of the prettiest (and that counts!) and most impressive albums I've heard. Remember what Mason Williams did with "Classical Gas"? A similar concept here, but Nick does it better, it's refined. Happy, sad, very moving.'

Another contemporary review (probably from one of the hi-fi magazines) ran: 'Nick Drake was discovered by Fairport Convention some time ago and *Bryter Layter* (Island ILPS 9134, £2.15) is his second album. He sings his own very personal songs in a strange, deep vaseline voice, probably more suited to crooning, accompanied at times by a really funky backing. There's an amazing array of faces featured – Dave Pegg, Richard Thompson, Dave Mattacks, Lyn Dobson playing flute on the title track, Chris McGregor and John Cale on lovely things like viola, harpsichord and celeste. An extraordinarily good hefty folk album. Quality – good. Value for money – good.'

Reading the music press of the time is to glimpse a world far removed from the artistic intensity and isolation of Nick Drake. As Nick persevered with his introspective and finely balanced balladry, the 'serious' music papers – the fledgeling *Sounds*, the *NME* and jazz-heavy *Melody Maker* – were just beginning to sit up and take notice of the impact progressive rock was making, not only on the underground, but more significantly on the marketplace. The other two weeklies, *Disc & Music Echo* and *Record Mirror*, took their cue from the charts, paying only lip-service to the noises emanating from the underground.

Pete Frame remembers that when *Zig Zag* began in April 1969, the only music coverage was in the four weekly music papers: 'The nationals didn't really write about pop. When Frank Zappa came to the Royal Albert Hall in September 1967, the *Guardian* did a review. The other papers weren't interested. There was a guy called Geoffrey Cannon on the *Guardian* who was quite hip – he was writing Velvet Underground articles for *Zig Zag* because no one else would take them.

'*Zig Zag* was intended to put a bit more weight into pop culture, into rock writing. I was a print freak. I'd read *Crawdaddy*. There were papers coming out of every city in America – the *LA Free Press*, the *San Francisco Oracle*, Atlanta's *Great Speckled Bird* . . . People were writing about these records as though they meant something, which of course they did. The music we were interested in was not just entertainment. We wanted it to be part of our lives . . . The pop papers in England did not understand that. They saw it as being entertainment . . . there was no kind of fanaticism or passion, none of that belief in a lifestyle.'

Leafing through *Melody Maker* around the time of the release of *Bryter Layter* makes for salutary reading. These were the days when Elton John was the opening act for Sandy Denny's Fotheringay; when you could see 'Dave' Bowie at Acton's White Hall and Neil Young was being spoken of as 'the American whom many feel will be the superstar of the 70s'. These were the days when The Beatles were 'considering' Lee Jackson (of The Nice) and Klaus Voorman as Paul McCartney's replacement, so that the group could continue; when Loudon Wainwright III was touted as 'the new Dylan?'; John Lennon was in a '4-letter word row'; Ry Cooder was 'the name to watch in 71'; and Lou Reed had quit the Velvet Underground 'following a nervous breakdown'.

The eerie thing about skimming through those old copies of *Melody Maker* is the total and conspicuous lack of Nick Drake, as if someone had gone through the paper and excised his name from the yellowing pages. You would expect – if nothing else – to see details of live dates, announcements of tours, support acts, ticket prices, details of the new album . . . Even on the folk pages, Nick's name is absent – Mr Fox, Stefan Grossman, Ralph McTell, Humblebum Billy Connolly, Pigsty Hill Light Orchestra, Rab Noakes, Bridget St John, Midge & Clutterbuck are all present and correct, but no Nick.

Even at the time, Anthea Joseph was acutely conscious of an almost total lack of media interest in him: 'Nobody was interested in Nick at all; it was just Joe's passion. He felt that the young man really was a bit special, and he was determined to make these records, and he made them. If they'd sold ten I wouldn't have been surprised. They were all beautifully produced, the sleeves were wonderful. And blow me, here we are the best part of thirty years later, and it's a cult.'

The 1970 *Melody Maker* Poll was dominated by familiar names: LP Of The Year was *Led Zeppelin II*, followed by *Let It Be*, *Live At Leeds*, *Abbey Road*, *Ummagumma*, *Live Cream*, *Tommy*, *McCartney*, *Deep Purple In Rock* and *Liege & Lief*. The Brightest Hope category, where the stars of tomorrow were signalled, is where the likes of Nick Drake should have been noted. Once again though, he was conspicuous by his absence. Some of the names were predictable: Mungo Jerry had enjoyed a massive, summer feelgood hit with 'In The Summertime', Emerson Lake & Palmer had been long touted, and Ginger Baker's Airforce had risen from the ashes of the still much-lamented Cream. Both It's A Beautiful Day and Flock had featured on recent CBS samplers and made acclaimed appearances at the massive 1970 Bath Festival. But Wild Man Fischer? Burnin' Red Ivanhoe?

It wasn't for want of trying that Nick's name was missing. Island had as much faith in Nick Drake as anyone, but in those antediluvian times before videos, the only way audiences got to see an act whose record they liked was in performance. Although albums were *the* method of communication back then, time was rarely lavished on their recording. It was usually a simple laying down of the tracks which constituted your stage set, before going back on the road to promote your recently recorded product. And playing live was something which Nick was beginning to have a serious problem with.

For him, the very idea of 'promoting product' was probably anathema; but it was essential for acts to be seen, not just heard. Martin Satterthwaite, whose job was promoting Island acts, feels that Nick's reluctance to play live was the major factor in his lack of success: 'I really don't remember any interest in Nick. The Field Promotion Team created as much interest as possible in artists that were out on the road . . . and of course Nick was one of the artists who was never out on the road, and Island had so many acts who did tour . . .

'Live work, and all the promotional aspects that went with it, were what helped sell records. There was local radio, some local TV, local press. Nationally, there was *The Old Grey Whistle Test*, John Peel, the music press . . . Most of the Island artists would be appearing on the university circuit . . . Someone like Nick, the route would have been working the folk clubs, then getting a tour support. We'd go out armed with posters, point-of-sale boards, which would feature the sleeve of the current album, with "Appearing At" at the bottom, you know – Cambridge Corn Exchange, Leeds University.'

Joe Boyd was also beginning to worry about his protégé's unwillingness to perform live: 'The sales were low, the first two albums didn't do more than 5000 . . . *Five Leaves Left* came out and we were very excited about it, it got very good reviews, John Peel liked it . . . It didn't sell a lot, but for somebody completely unknown who hadn't worked around, it got what I felt was a satisfactory start. To my view, that was a launching pad for him to start working.

'But he felt he couldn't work. He'd been spoiled, his first major appearance was with Fairport at the Festival Hall, where you had a seated audience, very respectful and hushed – it was the first Fairport appearance after the car accident – so that you had a very receptive atmosphere, nobody was going to get impatient. Nobody was going to say: "Tune your fucking guitar, man." It wasn't that kind of an atmosphere. I think John and Beverley [Martyn] went on first, then Nick came on, and it was magical. The audience loved him. He went back on to do an encore, which I remember was "Things Behind The Sun", which was mesmerizing. He didn't say a word, but he absolutely captivated the audience. So I got carried away. I thought, oh great, let's book him around the world.'

9

'It was very much the era of all those desolate souls playing at Cousins,' Jerry Gilbert recalls. 'In that sense, Nick would have fitted in perfectly – the Al Stewarts, Cat Stevens, Paul Simon, John Martyn – all singing into their soundboxes. I would have thought that would have been Nick's natural ambience, his habitat.

'Nick was only wheeled out to play the big shows, he never seemed to play the folk-club circuit at all. I think that is a really important point: he didn't ever seem to gravitate around the folk clubs, which all the other Witchseason acts did, and the Island acts generally – Cat Stevens, John Martyn, Sandy Denny, The Incredible String Band. The whole Witchseason thing was linked to the folk club tradition. But not Nick Drake. He came out and did the concert-hall thing, the opening act, then vanished back into wherever he vanished back into.'

The performing career of Nick Drake was incredibly short. Once signed to Island, he only ever gave a couple of dozen concerts, which were, according to eyewitness accounts, largely desultory and inconclusive affairs. As with so many aspects of Nick's life, specific dates and places are elusive. Nick's friend John Martyn, for example, knew of only two gigs, and in 1986 he spoke in a radio interview about what he obviously believed was the most crucial gig in Nick's career: 'He never felt comfortable in front of an audience. It was embarrassing to go and see him, because he was obviously in such utter discomfort. He just didn't like going on and playing. He primarily played for his own amusement . . . one of the things that contributed to his utter detestation of the whole thing was that he was once booked to play at a Coventry Apprentices Christmas Ball . . . in those days, "Purple Haze" was "in", and there he was singing "Fruit Tree" and all those gentle, breezy little ballads, and I can just imagine them swigging back the Carlsberg Special and giving him an awful time. I know that gig lived in his mind, he'd talk about it quite regularly . . . I'd hate to be affected that badly by one social experience . . . dreadfully sensitive fellow, dreadfully sensitive.'

Nick's long-time friend and arranger Robert Kirby has given a lot of thought to the problems facing Nick as a performer: 'When he was performing, in the studio . . . it was his whole life, but even that was compartmentalized. I don't think he ever had a problem performing well. So it wasn't a question of nerves. And as I said, he practised.

'I have always respected Joe and everything he's done, but I don't think Witchseason ever claimed to have agency networks set up, that kind of management. Fairport were self-promoting. Within their group, there was one of their friends who would get the gig and organize it, get the van. Nick didn't have any of that support. I think Nick did get angry, and resented the fact that he wasn't getting the help he should have. What I felt would have helped is if he had an agent. Marcus Bicknell at Rondo, through his relationship with me, got Nick gigs wherever he could. He was representing bands like The Climax Blues Band, Genesis, so wherever he could, he'd put Nick out.'

Popular myth has long held that Nick was so soured by his experience at the Christmas dance referred to by John Martyn, that it put him off live performance for ever, but Robert Kirby has different recollections: 'It was the Nettlefold Nut & Bolt Apprentices' Annual Dance. He and Marcus . . . knew it was going to be the pits, but it was a gig . . . I can remember they came back to Cranley Gardens after the gig, which was in Sheffield or Derby or somewhere up North . . . This one was a riot anyway, it wasn't Nick particularly they were moaning about. It was just pints of lager thrown everywhere. He came back and was laughing and joking about it – and he'd got paid!

'I don't believe that was the occasion, but I can perfectly well accept that he went somewhere where he was expecting to be listened to, and wasn't listened to, and might have felt that afterwards. I think there was one in London that did sour him. I think they were Hooray Henrys who he would have expected to have listened. And they weren't in the slightest interested – "boo-ha", "get off", that sort of thing.'

The concerts Nick Drake is definitely known to have played number no more than a few dozen. After the Roundhouse gig in February 1968, where Ashley Hutchings discovered him, the most significant date was on 24 September 1969, when Nick supported Fairport Convention at the Royal Festival Hall. Then, on 21 February 1970, he was back on the South Bank supporting John and Beverley Martyn at the smaller Queen Elizabeth Hall, and the same month he opened for Fairport Convention at half a dozen dates. The following month Nick was opening for Sandy Denny's Fotheringay on a five-date UK tour – the other act on the bill was a duo undertaking their final dates together, The Humblebums, featuring Gerry Rafferty and Billy Connolly.

In an interview quoted in the fanzine *Pink Moon*, John Martyn remembers seeing Nick before the Fotheringay show at the Festival Hall: 'It was a good place for him, but he was cripplingly nervous. I mean, he was distraught before the gig. It was rather embarrassing in fact to see him. He was distinctly uncomfortable on-stage. I mean, the music was fine, but he just didn't like being there at all . . . I got the impression it was costing him too much to go on the stage. It was just like no amount of applause or anything else would ever have paid him back the mental effort and energy he had to expend.'

Nick's Royal Festival Hall gig in September 1969 was probably the most prestigious he ever played. This was the much-loved Fairport Convention's first concert since the crash six months earlier, which had taken the lives of the band's drummer, Martin Lamble, and Richard Thompson's girlfriend, Jeannie. It also marked the debut of Fairport's new direction, as instigators of English folk-rock, which would characterize their seminal album *Liege & Lief*, released later that year. It was an important moment for all concerned.

Fairport were too nervous to be nervous about their opening act. Even without the extra anticipation which presaged this particular appearance, the Festival Hall was an intimidating room to play. Advertisements for Fairport's keenly anticipated appearance (Tickets 25/-, 21/-, 17/-, 13/-, 10/- and 8/-) detailed the support acts simply as '& Friends'. There was no mention of Nick Drake.

Witchseason's Anthea Joseph was backstage to witness first-hand Nick's terror of live performance: 'Nick was sick with fright, which I can understand . . . you can't live on glucose and lemon juice for ever. We got him on stage, I think he did four numbers and then fled. That was it – four numbers and off. He was shaking all over. Some people can perform and some people can't, and he was one of those . . . he didn't enjoy the adulation. He couldn't carry it at all.

'The other gig was a club of some sort . . . He just *hated* performing. In a room, if you had him in your own sitting room, he'd sit in the corner and take up the guitar and play you something, and it was lovely, no problem – he did that for me a couple of times. But performing was totally different . . . I remember him sleeping on my floor in Islington, because he didn't want to go home. He crashed there a couple of times, we'd sit up all night, but he still didn't talk, and in those days the meaning of life was all. We'd sit there and I'd be rolling joints, and cups of tea, endless cups of tea . . . Next morning, he'd shamble forth and vanish into the morning.'

Eighteen months after first seeing Nick Drake at the Roundhouse, Fairport's bassist Ashley Hutchings was in a such a state of nerves that he remembers little of that landmark Festival Hall appearance, let alone his 'discovery', the opening act: 'It was our first gig since the crash, the first time we had played the *Liege & Lief* material. It was one of the most anticipated events of my life . . . Nick apparently opened, but it was such a big thing. It wasn't just the resurgence of the band after the crash, it was the beginning, if you like, of folk-rock. So it was such a big event for us that we were all nervously pacing about backstage.'

More municipal than the larger, baroque Royal Albert Hall, the Festival Hall, which was opened in 1951 as part of the Festival of Britain, accommodates an audience of up to 3000, sitting in serried rows, sweeping down to the stage, which is open and exposed. Even from the auditorium, it seems like a mighty long walk from the wings, particularly when you are occupying the platform alone.

Unbeknown to their son, sitting proudly in the audience that September night were Nick's parents. Molly: 'Of course the very first big concert was with the Fairport Convention at the Festival Hall. We didn't dare tell Nick that we were going. We crept along there, quite the eldest by about ninety years. Nick came on first, followed by John and Beverley Martyn, then Fairport Convention were the whole of the second half of the programme.'

Rodney: 'He did very well, all by himself, sitting on a stool. He got a lot of applause, and he just got off his stool, waved his guitar to everybody and wandered off. And they couldn't get him back again.'

Molly: 'He was wearing his same old black trousers that he wore every day.'

Rodney: 'I think he found it pretty difficult appearing in public, and it became more so. Of course Island always wanted him to go round doing these . . . "gigs", is that the word? And he didn't like that. He didn't really enjoy performing . . . He became very withdrawn.'

Although the majority of those who witnessed Nick's performances, or talked with him about them, have a vivid recollection of his extreme unease on stage, there are those who were more favourably struck by his stage presence. Joe Boyd and, particularly, Gabrielle Drake, remember being impressed by Nick's Festival Hall performance.

'Well, I read all these reports, about how Nick shambled on-stage at the Festival Hall,' recalled Gabrielle. 'I was there. I am a performer, I know something about it. It's true he didn't do the pre-chat. He came and sat on a stool and played. And he *electrified* the audience. What he did have was a tremendous presence. Sometimes that presence could be black and very negative when he was deeply depressed, but he was a charismatic figure, there were no two ways about that. There wasn't a smattering of applause from a bewildered audience, this wasn't true. They were enraptured.'

However, Island's new press officer, David Sandison, was less than struck by his new charge in February 1970, when he first saw him performing, supporting John and Beverley Martyn at the Queen Elizabeth Hall: 'The QEH gig, Nick was for everyone who hadn't taken their seat or wanted to go and have a glass of wine to go and do it, because he wasn't doing anything that was remotely grabbing your attention . . . He wasn't projecting, there was nothing coming over the footlights. I know Gabrielle is really pissed off with me for the description which was quoted in the ad for *Pink Moon*, but that was how he was.'

The advertisement Sandison refers to was the official Island ad in the music press, announcing the release of *Pink Moon*. It took the form of a letter from David Sandison describing the impact *Bryter Layter* made on him, and how Nick's third album had come into his possession. He also described seeing Nick perform at the QEH show: 'He came on with his guitar, sat on a stool, looked at the floor and sang a series of muffled songs punctuated by mumbled thanks for the scattering of bewildered applause from the audience who didn't seem to know who the hell he was, nor cared too much. At the end of his last song, his guitar still holding the final notes of the song, he got up and walked off; his shoulders hunched as if to protect him from actually having to meet people.'

Sandison still stands by his description of Nick's performance:

'That is how he was: he looked down all the time. Gabrielle's memory is of a different gig, but that night there was a guy on-stage who . . . he actually looked mortified, frightened, ill at ease. In a room of about fifty or sixty people, it would have worked and it would have been very intimate, but he never came to grips with that aspect of playing to 2000 people, big rooms. He really had no experience of it, he was undoubtedly shy . . . it could have been someone doing a soundcheck, to be honest. He didn't say anything, and at the end of the set he didn't even say "goodnight" – he just walked off. Some people clapped, but not enough, and they didn't clap for very long, the lights went up, and we all went off to the bar.'

The recollections of most of those who saw Nick Drake perform are in agreement: they highlight how ill at ease he appeared on stage and speak of his manifest discomfort when confronted with an audience. Following the publication in early 1997 of a feature I had written on Nick, dozens of readers took the time to write to me with their memories of seeing him in concert. Without exception, they confirmed just how uncomfortable a performer he appeared, alone on the concert platform.

Paul Donnelly saw Nick at the Liverpool Philharmonic Hall in very early 1970, supporting Fairport: 'He came on and said nothing audible to the audience, either before or between songs, and when he'd finished he just got up and walked off. True to all other reports about him. I remember "Cello Song" and "Three Hours", mainly because they were two of my favourites . . .'

'I was a teenager and had just bought *Five Leaves Left* and fallen in love with the songs,' wrote Mick Stannard, who remembered seeing Nick at a folk club – almost certainly Cousins. 'Suddenly, there he was on a stool a couple of yards away. I think he started with "Time Has Told Me". It was great, me being a guitarist, looking at his fingers playing those lovely chords. Later, he was in the middle of "River Man", sitting hunched up, head bowed, not looking up at the audience, when suddenly his capo sprung off the neck of his guitar and fell to the ground. There were a few giggles from some people, but mostly we didn't really know how to react . . . He didn't look up or say a word or . . . make light of it with a laugh, but simply bent down and picked up the capo, reattached it to his guitar and carried on from where he had left off. He was aloof and awkward. After his three songs he scuttled off round a corner and out of sight.'

Like many others, Dave Crewe first became aware of Nick from the *Bumpers* sampler which included 'Hazey Jane'. He saw Nick open for Fotheringay at Leicester's De Montfort Hall in March 1970: 'I do remember the songs "Time Has Told Me" and "Way To Blue". Each song being warmly greeted and with growing appreciation by the audience. About halfway through the set . . . midway through a song, he broke a string on his guitar. Embarrassingly, he carried on until he finished the song and immediately and rather nervously began to replace the string, making a few barely audible quips as he did so. After what seemed ages, but was probably only a couple of minutes, he completed his task and received rapturous applause for his efforts. Unperturbed, he continued and finished the set to a standing ovation with cries for more, but he left the stage and never returned.'

Schoolfriends from Marlborough who recalled the self-assured and talented performer of only a few years before were baffled by accounts of Nick's increasing terror of live performance. Simon Crocker: 'When I read stuff about Nick in performance and mumbling, all I can do is look back and remember that Nick was a natural performer. He was bloody good: he was the band leader, he projected well. He was a confident performer. And I heard about this particular performance at the Queen Elizabeth Hall from people who'd been there who said he mumbled. And I remember saying at the time: "That doesn't sound like Nick at all, he must have been ill." It just didn't connect.'

Perhaps it was after Nick signed to Island, with the realization that he would have to confront audiences by himself, that the chill set in. All alone on-stage, just him and his guitar, with no back line of bass and drums, no horn section, no one else to share the vocals or harmonize with. Certainly at Cambridge, Nick had seemed to enjoy playing for friends and even, on occasion, performing in front of an audience. He was never outgoing on stage, but by all accounts had a certain still, calm confidence, and even enjoyed performing. But something had changed.

By 1970 the fear was there for everyone to see – it was almost tangible. In performance and alone, he seemed so exposed that audiences found it painful to watch. For Nick, it was a waking nightmare.

Nick Drake was never comfortable with the label of folk singer, but the mere fact that he wrote his own songs and accompanied himself on guitar, typecast him as a folkie. For guitar-picking hopefuls like him, the folk clubs which had sprung up in such abundance were the obvious live venues, and following the release of *Five Leaves Left*, it was on to the folk-club circuit that Nick was dispatched.

Folk gave you a freedom, but it also gave you nowhere to hide. Folk clubs were ideologically sterile, with none of the 'showbusiness' trappings. The atmosphere in folk clubs during the 1960s owed more to Bertolt Brecht than *Sunday Night At The London Palladium*. A stage was anathema – why should the performer be elevated? These were fiercely competitive venues at which to cut your teeth as a performer. You had to have stamina for the lengthy journeys from town to town, and you had to have guts to get up before an audience who frequently owned every album from which you had filched your repertoire.

The British folk revival had its own figureheads. Like many fledgeling folkies, Nick was fascinated by the richness of John Renbourn's playing, and his ability to draw on all manner of influences, from courtly madrigals to the blues. An even bigger impact on Nick as a teenager was made by Bert Jansch. On the tape he recorded at home at Tanworth during his first university vacation, Nick included two songs, 'Courting Blues' and 'Strolling Down The Highway', which Jansch had recorded on his 1965 debut album. Jansch's striking gypsy good looks and apparently effortless fluency on the guitar, made a mark on all those who heard his records or saw him play in the folk clubs of the mid-sixties. Neil Young cited Jansch as being as much an influence on his guitar-playing as Jimi Hendrix.

Pete Frame, legendary draughtsman of rock family-trees, jacked in his job as a surveyor with the Prudential Insurance Company to run a folk club in Luton, where Jansch performed. 'Bert Jansch was like the fountainhead of it all, to my mind. Nobody had ever seen anything like it. His songs – the structure of them, the feel of them, the melodies, the words . . . There was no precedent, you couldn't tell what his influences were. Just amazing stuff . . . he played guitar like no one else had ever heard it before.'

In the days before videos, before the national press was interested in pop music, before monthlies like *Q*, *Mojo* and *Record Collector*, the chosen route for young singer-songwriters was to start in the folk clubs, graduate to tour support for a fellow Island act and finally headline in their own right.

Ralph McTell remembers diligently treading this path: 'I just went wherever I was sent . . . I was probably doing 200 dates a year, all over the country, for eight, ten quid a night, driving myself . . . I'd be going up to Sheffield for about a tenner a night . . . I can't speak for Nick, because he didn't do that many gigs, but people like John

Martyn, myself, The Humblebums, were not quite folk and not quite pop. And we worked *all* the time . . . Because it was a youth thing, and the folk clubs were Dylan and all that, it naturally spilled off the universities, which is what really elevated the thing into equal status with what a lot of the pop singers were doing. We could get as big a crowd.'

Nick's wariness of live performance can only have been compounded by the isolation of working the folk circuit. In a band, you had company, but as a solo singer-songwriter you were out there on your own – frequently rolling up at a gig alone, with no minder or record company support. However, there was an unseen record company machine waiting to spring into action, and curiously what triggered it were those tiny, apparently insignificant folk-club gigs. Martin Satterthwaite was on the sharp edge, as a member of one of Island's first Field Promotion Teams: 'It meant visiting the local record stores, making sure they had product, telling them which artists were coming to town. We made sure there were window displays, and visited local radio, which then, of course, was only the BBC.'

In those days touring was what you did to interest people in buying your work – a write-off against record sales. There were no tour publicists, masseuses or manicurists; no limos, tour riders or merchandising. Just look at the back sleeve of Pink Floyd's *Ummagumma*, from 1969: two roadies, surrounded by a phalanx of the Floyd's state-of-the-art live equipment, all capable of being squeezed into the back of a transit van, were pictured to amaze fans with the band's high-tech sophistication.

Martin Satterthwaite: 'We'd have boards at the venues advertising the latest product. This was long before merchandising, of course. The only T-shirts that Island would manufacture then, in the early seventies, were for us to give away to DJs, record dealers – there was nothing for sale to the public. It was long before tour publicists or anything, so if a band was playing, you'd liaise with local media, try and arrange an interview backstage.'

Nick's reluctance to gig is widely believed to have sprung from a single unsettling experience which soured him for future live performances. Robert Kirby's memories of seeing Nick immediately afterwards have cast doubt on the apprentices' Christmas party most often held to blame, but Joe Boyd believes he knows when the watershed came: 'Then, the next thing you know, he's playing a student centre at Warwickshire, and everybody's drinking at the back, people are talking. He was very upset, couldn't handle it. He came limping home, he said I can't go on with the tour. So we cancelled the other dates.'

Nick's reluctance to go out and perform effectively cut off the prime avenue of exposure for any new act, a fact which did not escape his record label. David Sandison explains: 'There was interest from a few people while Nick was alive, but it was limited. It was "Yeah, that's nice, but so what?" . . . And that's understandable. There wasn't any profile. There wasn't anything to grab on to. There wasn't even explaining the songs in interviews. There wasn't any gigging, so that you could make that live connection. And there wasn't radio play. There weren't any slots for the promotional people to get for people like Nick, apart from John Peel, and his time was limited. There weren't local radio stations. There wasn't any commercial radio. There was Radio Luxembourg, but they certainly weren't going to play Nick Drake.'

Even when Nick did get out and gig, it was never a comfortable experience. Ralph McTell remembers Nick opening for him at Ewell Technical College, Surrey, on 25 June 1970: 'That's the only conversation I remember having with him, in the dressing room beforehand. I am a dreadfully nervous performer, still, and I'm always clucking around before a show. But to allay my nerves, I would cluck around other people and say: "Are you all right?" Nick was monosyllabic. At that particular gig, he was very shy. He did the first set, and something awful must have happened. He was doing his song "Fruit Tree", and walked off halfway through it. Just left the stage.'

Bruce Fursman was still at school when his group, Folkomnibus, supported Nick at a gig in Middlesex. The Upper Room Folk Club was held at the Goodwill To All pub, a red-brick thirties roadhouse on the corner of Harrow View and Headstone Lane. This gig, on 4 October 1969, could well have been Nick's first-ever folk-club date, and certainly marked his first listing in *Melody Maker*'s Folk Forum.

An audience of around fifty had paid to sit in the room above the pub. Bruce remembers that he bought matching pink denim shirts in an attempt to make Folkomnibus look 'less like schoolboys and more like professional artists'. These would also have contrasted markedly with Nick's customary dark outfits. Folkomnibus played a set consisting of Simon & Garfunkel, Spinners and Corries covers; some Irish jigs and reels; and their own 'instrumental attempts at being teenage versions of the string-bending John Renbourn or Bert Jansch'.

'Nick took to the floor, or should I say the low chair at the front of the audience,' Bruce recalls. 'He sat, stooped, hunched over his guitar, an almost reverential silence in the place and this low, dark, almost drowsy voice – almost one of the audience, only he was facing the other way. His hair covered his face, and as far as I can remember, there were no in-between song comments – quite spooky in some way. The image of the figure – almost like on the cover of *Bryter Layter* – is very strong: dark, hunched shape, face hidden by hair, voice, audience intently listening.'

Before the gig, Nick was fascinated by Bruce's cheap Italian round-backed mandolin, and picked it up. Bruce remembers him 'holding the delicate, pear-shaped body in his delicate hands, as if it were a new-found antiquity'. When Folkomnibus came offstage, Bruce even remembers Nick laughing good-naturedly and saying: 'You've stolen my set.'

Another handful of confirmed gigs came when Nick opened for Fairport early in 1970, as the band endeavoured to recover from the departure of founder member Ashley Hutchings and cynosure Sandy Denny. Fairport's Dave Pegg remembered those dates: 'He did about six gigs with Fairport. I remember we did the Bristol Colston Hall with Nick. He was very well received, the audience liked him. They loved it, he'd go on and play the songs, he didn't have any spiel. But the songs were strong enough to get people's attention, and in those days people were into listening to music anyway. He didn't have much stage presence . . . he was the opposite of somebody who gets up and tries to gee the audience up, but the fact that he was that way, people had time for him, because the music and his voice were so good, and they'd probably never heard much of it before. It was early days for him.

'He was quite sociable. I remember we went for a curry round the corner from the Colston Hall, and he was very friendly . . . I never saw him lose it, I never saw him become that depressed that he'd walk off the stage.'

Fully qualified survivor Michael Chapman saw Nick perform at a folk club in Hull in 1969. Chapman, who was seven years older than Nick, had given up his job as an art and photography teacher in the mid-sixties, for the life of a travelling folkie. He made his debut with *Rainmaker* in 1968, but it was his 1969 set, *Fully Qualified Survivor*, which marked his card. Recorded for Harvest, EMI's 'progressive' subsidiary, the album is remarkable for Chapman's inimitable, gritty 'Postcards Of Scarborough'.

While ploughing around the British folk circuit in the late sixties, Chapman met Bridget St John, who had just made her debut album for John Peel's Dandelion label. 'I'm pretty certain it was Bridget who turned me on to *Five Leaves Left*, and that was an album I loved,' Chapman told me. 'I saw Nick was on at a folk club in Hull, so my wife and I went down. It must have been sometime in 1969, as I remember the album had just come out. It was at a pub called the Haworth. They were a real silver-tankard and finger-in-the-ear crowd. The folkies did not take to him. Nick came on and played his own songs, but they wanted songs with choruses. They completely missed the point. They just didn't get the gentleness, the subtlety. He played beautifully.

'I don't know what the audience expected. I mean, they must have known that you weren't going to get sea-shanties and singalong songs at a Nick Drake gig! I remember he didn't say a word between the songs. I suppose they were all his own songs, I recognized some from the album. He didn't introduce any of them; he didn't say a word the entire evening. It was actually quite painful to watch. Nick should never have been there. It was obviously not in his nature to perform, especially to a crowd like that. But back then, if you played acoustic guitar on your own and played your own songs, folk clubs were the only places that you could play.'

The folk scene in London was centred on Les Cousins, in the basement of 45 Greek Street. Cousins, as everybody called it, was run by Andy Matthews, a folk enthusiast whose parents ran the Dionysius Restaurant upstairs. The club, which was tiny, had begun life as The Skiffle Cellar during the DIY music boom of the mid-fifties. When Cousins first opened its doors in 1965, it charged '2/6 membership, entrance 5/- and 7/6'. Cousins was *the* folk venue in London during the sixties, the club to which every tyro folkie who could string together more than two Bob Dylan songs gravitated. It was where guitar wizard Davy Graham held court; where Paul Simon visited.

Ralph McTell had made his recording debut a couple of years before Nick and was a regular performer at Cousins at the height of the folk boom: 'Very, very small. You were playing to the wall. There was room for three tiny rows of seats before the back wall. There was a dark corner, a tiny stage not big enough for a stripper. A microphone and a domestic amplifier and speaker . . . A little coffee bar, because it wasn't licensed, although there was occasionally a light ale in there!

'The real strength was the all-nighters, because if you got in on a

Saturday night in Soho, you had shelter, people used to sleep there. Every boy with a guitar came in . . . We were all so driven to play, we were all so young. And, of course, just walking through Soho to go to work. When The Incredible String Band were on, the queues used to go round the block, and the working girls around Greek Street at that time were complaining that they weren't doing the business.'

An advertisement in *Melody Maker*'s Folk Forum of 15 November 1969 has John James at Cousins, supported by 'Nick Drake, a fine songwriter'. Steve Aparicio was a member of Cousins, and remembers Nick's performance that night: 'Nick came on and sat hunched up on a stool on the tiny stage. He played only three or four numbers before leaving the stage in some distress, when he was looked after by John Martyn. John Martyn and Al Stewart both got up and did a few songs each.'

Michael Chapman: 'Me and Al Stewart, Roy Harper, Ralph McTell, we were all out working the circuit. But that gig in Hull was the only time I ever saw Nick. Whenever we went down to London, we'd all drift along to Cousins to check out the opposition – nick a lick, maybe pinch a gag or a bit of patter, but I never saw Nick there. I assumed – or I think I'd heard – that he was still at school or university, because his name was never around.'

Folk singer Steve Tilston released his debut album, *An Acoustic Confusion*, in the summer of 1971, and in a couple of reviews found himself compared to Nick Drake. Steve remembers meeting Nick in Soho: 'It was a Saturday night in 1971, and as I walked down Greek Street, on my way to Les Cousins, I noticed a group of about four people gathered on the street outside the club's entrance. One of these was Andy Matthews, who ran the club, and the only other one I recognized was Nick. He was dressed in a white shirt and black jacket, just like in most of his photographs, and stood out in those "tie-dyed" times. We were introduced and pretty soon we got into a conversation. He was very tall and I have this recollection of him having to stoop a little. He startled me by saying that he liked my album, and I remember saying something along the lines of that being good, given that I was supposed to sound like him.

'My memory is of the conversation being relatively easy – given my own then-mastery of the pregnant pause. One question I remember asking him was concerning a small news snippet I'd seen in *Sounds* . . . I was convinced that I'd read a piece about Nick about to be doing some recording with one of the old black American blues legends – somebody like Mississippi Fred McDowell or Son House, somebody of that stature – and I remember feeling really envious. I mentioned it and recall him laughing at the somewhat bizarre prospect. I remember liking him a lot; my recollection is of us getting along pretty well. I think we all then moved along to the Pillars of Hercules pub, and then the memory fades.'

Only one account survives of Nick Drake actually playing at Cousins. It was written by Brian Cullman, who supported Nick that night in 1970, and appeared in *Musician* magazine in 1979: 'He sat on a small stool, hunched tight over a tiny Guild guitar, beginning songs and halfway through, forgetting where he was, and stumbling back to the start of that song, or beginning an entirely different song which he would then abandon mid-way through if he remembered the remainder of the first. He sang away from the microphone, mumbled, and whispered, all with a sense of precariousness and doom. It was like being at the bedside of a dying man who wants to tell you a secret, but who keeps changing his mind at the last minute.'

An American exchange student, who got involved in the English folk scene when he came to London in 1970, and fell in with John and Beverley Martyn, Brian Cullman has kindly expanded his impression of Nick Drake in performance at Cousins: 'There was a large though not capacity crowd there, and, if memory serves, they were polite, if not overly enthusiastic about my set. If I was amateurish and awkward, Nick was even worse, though in a far more interesting and charismatic way. He made no eye contact with the audience and shrank into himself, looking smaller and more lost and fragile than usual. And he seemed to wander between songs, starting one, then discarding it in favour of another, the way someone might choose between melons at a fruit stand, picking one up after another, trying to figure out which was ripe. He forgot lyrics or, if uncomfortable with what they revealed, he sang away from the mic or simply mumbled. I've never seen a performer as deeply unhappy or uncomfortable on stage (and I've never seen an audience as rapt and spellbound . . . there was a genuine affection and admiration, almost a sense of devotion, and the crowd seemed to be willing him through the songs).

'He played many of the songs from *Five Leaves Left* ("Time Has Told Me", which came across almost as a country song; "Three Hours"; "Cello Song" – I think – "Thoughts Of Mary Jane") as well as some songs that turned up on *Pink Moon* ("Things Behind The Sun", maybe another) though the song that left the deepest impression was nothing more than a fragment. He sang the first few lines of

"Hazey Jane I", over and over again, almost like a mantra, against soft and rolling chords. The effect was chilling, like eavesdropping on someone's prayers.'

A flyer for a Bedford College all-nighter on 8 May 1970 announced Nick Drake at the bottom of a bill which proceeded upwards via John Martyn, Spencer Davis, Jo-Ann Kelly, Group X, Black August, Raw Spirit, East Of Eden and Graham Bond. Five years after he had hitched from Marlborough to watch The Graham Bond Organisation, Nick was sharing a bill with Bond. In another five years, both men would be dead.

Nick appeared at Ewell on 24 January 1970, playing bottom of the bill to Genesis and bill-toppers Atomic Rooster. He shared a booking agency with Genesis, who were just starting on the windy, wuthering route to success. It was to promote their recent album *Trespass*, on the new Charisma label, that the band – then consisting of Peter Gabriel, Anthony Phillips, Mike Rutherford, Tony Banks and drummer John Mayhew – were out working the circuit. Phillips, the original Genesis guitarist, was kind enough to share his memories: 'Maybe it was the same agent, but I seem to remember we shared bills at those big university gigs, where there'd be lots of different acts on different stages. There was no *simpatico* because we were all ex-public schoolboys . . . I remember Nick was *so* shy and retiring . . . It was probably a combination of things, that we were so wrapped up in ourselves, and there wasn't much time at gigs either . . . You used to arrive, get on with things, minimal soundchecks, play, then pack up and set off in the van. We had this ghastly old bread van, with no windows in the back. We never travelled with Nick. My abiding memory is that he was so shy, not the easiest guy to talk to.

'He may have found the fact that he was this one person, and here was this phalanx of group, and roadies, he may have found that difficult. He performed, just him and his guitar. And it was a very crouched, husky performance. In techs, people didn't really listen. You have to stamp on people with volume, unless you're a name. The gigs we did with him – university gigs mainly – even we suffered in our quieter numbers, let alone Nick, doing his one-man thing in his soft, husky voice. It was concert-hall stuff, folk clubs, but not a tech gig, where the lads are there with pints . . . I don't know why he was put on those big, loud tech gigs. It was difficult enough for us.

'When you're playing this quiet acoustic stuff to people who are shouting, it just kills the songs really. We used to start with a quiet acoustic set, and build up to a climax – but we got rid of that quite quickly! . . . We started strong – kick 'em in the teeth, quieten them down, then you can go a little bit quiet. One of our most popular acoustic songs was a very sixties-sounding song called "Let Us Now Make Love" . . . Nick obviously liked that one very much, I remember him coming up to me when he heard that I wrote it and saying . . . "Dangerous!"

'All the gigs I remember with Nick were these big, multi-act tech gigs. He might have got £50 for a gig, maybe a bit more, certainly more than us, because we had to split it. I don't remember Nick surrounded by anybody else. There was contact with Robert Kirby and Marcus [Bicknell], who were at some of the gigs. But I can't remember who got the gigs. I don't remember Nick with an entourage. I just remember this very sweet, but rather shy, tall man, who sang in this engaging husky voice, who you could never really hear properly!'

Bridget St John was playing the same circuit as Nick at roughly the same time, and she remembers Nick performing, and the sort of response he got from critics: 'My memories of him playing are of a tall, lanky, long-legged young man – always seated cross-legged. I loved a lot of his music – especially from the *Bryter Layter* period: it was John and Beverley [Martyn] who introduced me to him. I remember we both opened for Fairport Convention in Croydon, and both of us felt good about our performances. Karl Dallas reviewed it and obviously hated both of us equally: "There's only one question in my mind after having heard the Fairport Convention's superlatively excellent performance at the Fairfield Halls last Friday: why the hell did the organisers make us sit through almost an hour of sheer tedium before the interval instead of letting the Fairports have the whole show to themselves?" '

The *Croydon Advertiser* was rather kinder. Reviewing the 10 October 1969 gig, the local paper's reviewer noted: 'The first half of the evening's programme was devoted to another folk direction – that of the solo composer/guitarist/singer. Unfortunately, Bridget St John and Nick Drake were too similar in outlook, and thus each robbed the other of impact. Both sing sad, personal songs in rather deep, hushed voices, interspersed with the slightly amateur incoherencies one associates with this sort of performance. Both are pleasing enough artists, with above-average skills at the guitar and composition . . . Nick Drake, a Cambridge undergraduate, wore youthful cords, an open neck shirt and jacket, and a rather anxious expression . . .'

Nick is also rumoured to have played a short, unbilled set at an open-air festival in Yorkshire, headlined by Free, who were Island labelmates. It could have happened: solitary guitarists who sung their own songs were cheap, didn't need much in the way of PA, and could be slotted in between showers. There are other rumoured appearances, but even some of the ones advertised in *Melody Maker* may not have materialized. What does emerge from eyewitness accounts is that the weight of opinion about Nick's live performances is at odds with that of his sister. Gabrielle remembers Nick electrifying the audience with his tremendous presence, and recalls that at one point he had wanted to become an actor, but she too recognized her brother's intense vulnerability: 'He did very few performances. What put him off, I think, was that he did a working men's club somewhere, and they talked all through the performance. I always think if you're going to be a performing artist of any sort, you have to have an inside that's like a jelly, and an outside that's as tough as nails. And I think Nick's trouble was that he never had that tough outside. He was born with a skin too few . . .'

The solitary nature of Nick's craft probably added to his feelings of being adrift and isolated. Following his appearance at the Haworth folk club in Hull, Michael Chapman remembers his wife seeing Nick on the pavement outside, alone with his guitar, looking quite forlorn: 'She went up and said how much she'd enjoyed the gig and he said he didn't have anywhere to stay; they hadn't booked him a room or anything, so we asked him back to stay for the night. He was very quiet, well-spoken, but as soon as he came in and saw my guitars lying around, we were off. He was quite easy to be with. Once we were in the house, and he was away from an audience, he was fine.

'He was playing a Martin guitar, and I had a Gibson, which for guitarists are two totally different philosophies. As soon as we sat down we started jamming, improvising scraps of songs. We played all night, from midnight to 5a.m. I have to say that substances did play a part in the proceedings. He played some lovely stuff on the guitar, interesting, Brazilian-type tunings.'

Nick was hauled out regularly and put in front of audiences keen to witness Fairport Convention, Fotheringay, John and Beverley Martyn . . . Support acts are the timid Christians thrown to hungry lions in the auditorium, and even tiny club audiences could be pretty doctrinaire in those days. For anyone without the necessary chutzpah, folk clubs could be fairly unforgiving places.

Jerry Gilbert, a regular observer on the folk circuit, saw Nick play half a dozen times: 'I always remember him seated on a stool. He always seemed to be the token opening act, which was sad, as he was worth more than that. I don't ever remember a showcase for him. He was out there as a stooge to whet the crowd's appetite . . . There was always a huge amount of nervousness . . . let me qualify that: Nick's performances were always very accomplished. I don't recall huge amounts of shaky fingers and bum notes or anything at a Nick performance. I think once he got into the song, he lost himself in his own world – he could have been in Sound Techniques recording, he shut the audience out entirely, created this cocoon around himself . . . then he thought, oh God, there's got to be a link here, a bridge, between here and the next song. The actual performance of the songs I remember as being pretty OK.'

For career purposes, the dozens of gigs, most of them supporting other people were not nearly enough – though for Nick personally they were obviously far too much. But to put it in some sort of perspective, Nick's Island labelmate and contemporary, Cat Stevens, racked up 145,000 miles of travel in one calendar year alone, touring to promote his albums. Venturing out from Little Hadham, Fairport Convention also clocked up the miles, hacking across the country during 1970. With little likelihood of picking up airplay for their albums, they recognized that their heartlands were the university campuses and regional clubs.

Dave Pegg: 'We were in a band, and bands are like a different thing. If you're not in a group, you're always an outsider – you don't spend five hours in the van together. Bands develop their own sense of humour, it's difficult for an outsider to get in on stuff like that. I think Nick used to come in the van with us occasionally, but he did take things very seriously, whereas we were the opposite . . . They were very, very happy days, we just seemed to be working all the time. That year we were at the Angel, we must have done about 300 gigs.'

As a live performer, Nick Drake's career fizzled out barely two years after the release of his debut album. The ability to face an audience across the footlights was slowly and irrevocably lost. From then on, the only place for him to turn was in on himself. Back in Soho, Steve Tilston saw Nick for the last time. The elegant young pretender was gone now: 'There was another brief meeting on the stairs going down to Les Cousins. He looked strange and unkempt, given that before he had appeared quite elegant and it was I who had felt like Wurzel Gummidge; and then, I suppose about a year or so later, the word was that Nick was not well.

'He would still occasionally come down to Soho, but then it was specifically to see Andy Matthews – he and his wife Di were very concerned and protective of Nick. The last time I saw him, I remember going into the Pillars of Hercules and spotting Andy deep in conversation with Nick; all I saw were [Nick's] hunched shoulders. I didn't join them, so my last memory is of Nick Drake's back. I didn't see his face again'.

10

In July 1970 Joe Boyd decided that the songs of his Witchseason acts – Fairport Convention, John Martyn, The Incredible String Band, Nick Drake – needed to be better known. He hired a studio and employed a couple of session singers: his then girlfriend, Linda Peters (later Thompson) and Elton John. Reg Dwight had become Elton John in 1968, and was already carving out quite a living, mostly as singer and pianist for those 14/11d 'Can you tell the difference between these and the original sounds?' compilations.

Looking back, with the all the baggage of hindsight, it is hard to remember Nick Drake as anything but a frail, translucent, tragic presence. But there was a time back then when Nick was just another young singer-songwriter, ambitious as any of his contemporaries, and desperately keen to get his material across to as wide an audience as possible.

'I wanted an album of Warlock Music songs,' explained Joe Boyd, Nick's mentor and producer. 'We did Mike Heron's songs, a couple of Nick's songs, a John Martyn song . . . We pressed up 100 acetates, white labels. I never had any. Always the way!'

So 'Elton Sings Nick' were the first covers of songs by Nick Drake? Joe Boyd considered: 'The only cover I'm aware of during Nick's lifetime was by Millie. I think she heard it through Chris Blackwell. She covered "Mayfair" on an album, the one with her straddling a banana.'

Robert Kirby: 'The Millie record came out in 1970. That was one of the first things I did when I left university, thrown in at the deep end with a proper reggae band. That's the album with "Mayfair" on it. I produced and arranged it, and Nick was very pleased – it was a cover.'

The idea was to have something which could be sent out, for managers to play to music publishers, and on to their clients. It was a Tin Pan Alley tradition, and acetates of freshly written Lennon & McCartney compositions regularly turn up for sale at auction. Even the more established acts (Beatles, Bowie, Dylan) still demoed material, which was then pressed up on to acetates and passed around to interested parties. White-label acetates proved a godsend to bootleggers, and latterly, to the compilers of box sets and CD reissues.

The best-known acetate in rock 'n' roll was Bob Dylan's *The Basement Tapes*. Culled from six months of loose-limbed jamming with The Band in the basement of their house, Big Pink, at Woodstock during Dylan's enforced lay-off during 1967, a twelve-track acetate was circulated to interested parties in the UK during early 1968. That acetate achieved notoriety when – as *The Great White Wonder* – it became rock's first bootleg during 1969.

Was the idea to get the likes of Tom Jones or Engelbert Humperdinck interested in covering one of Boyd's protégés' songs? That sort of crossover was not unfeasible; there had been precedents. The first person to record a Paul Simon composition was Val Doonican; the first commercially available cover of a U2 song was by Barbara Dickson; and the first person to cover a Beatles song had been Kenny Lynch – and John Lennon was only too grateful.

Of the 100 acetates that Boyd had pressed up, six are known definitely still to exist and only two have appeared on the open market, the most recent changing hands for £925. The enduring appeal of the Warlock Demo is not so much due to the handful of Nick Drake cover versions, but rather the identity of the singer who, though relatively unknown at the time of recording during 1970, later became Elton John. Elton's days as a session singer used to barely merit a footnote, but the release in 1994 of *Reg Dwight's Piano Goes Pop* imaginatively collected together the best of Elton's anonymous vocal sessions, revealing the unmistakable sound of the man who would be king flexing his vocal cords.

Hindsight lends a curious perspective to the Warlock session: here is a man whose best-known records would fill the radio waves for the next quarter of a century – and, at one point during the 1970s, accounted for an astonishing 2 per cent of all records sold worldwide

– singing the songs of Nick Drake. Elton was in great demand as a session singer for his interpretative ability, which is what makes his handling of 'When Day Is Done', 'Saturday Sun', 'Way To Blue' and 'Time Has Told Me' so striking.

Elton John was 'unavailable for comment' when I tried to reach him for his memories of the session, but he has been quoted as being impressed by the 'beautiful, haunting quality' of Nick's songs. It is believed that when, in 1993, he sold off his collection of some 25,000 vinyl albums (with all proceeds going to AIDS charities), he kept only two back for himself: one was the *White Album*, which Elton had got signed by all four Beatles, and the other was his own copy of the 1970 Warlock Music sessions.

Following his work on Nick's first two albums, Robert Kirby found himself producing and arranging a number of records during the early 1970s. Grateful for the start given to him by both Joe Boyd and Nick, he did his best to return the favour. Besides managing to place 'Mayfair' on the Millie album which he arranged, Kirby also remembers managing to get Nick some much-needed session work: 'Everybody was a singer-songwriter. I did very well at that time . . . There was a guy called Mick Audsley on Sonet, a bluegrass player. I produced two of his albums, and Nick did session guitar on them. He's not credited, but I got him some sessions playing rhythm guitar on those. The first album was *Deep The Dark And Devilled Waters*. He then brought out a single on Sonet called "The Commissioner He Come", and I know Nick played an extra acoustic guitar on that. The second session for Mick Audsley was 1972, in Sound Techniques. I produced "Sugar Me" for Lynsey De Paul, the only thing I've ever earned a reasonable sum of money on, but Ralph McTell played rhythm guitar on that!

'Arranging in those days was heaven. Everybody wanted strings! "Eleanor Rigby" and "Yesterday" were very English styles of string arrangement . . . I love American stuff, American orchestrations, like "Bridge Over Troubled Water" . . . but this country was different. Very little in America got string quartets, they always got the full Hollywood treatment . . . They always approached it differently . . . lush. The UK has always been more prepared to accept a chamber sound. I put that down to what George Martin did . . .

'The other session I got Nick was for Longman, the educational publishers. I was singing, pretending to be a swagman, Nick played guitar, and a childhood friend called Rocking John played banjo . . . I was going out with a girl who was an editor at Longman, and it was

recorded, I think, at their offices in Harlow. It was done within a year
of us leaving Cambridge, so 1970/71.'

Interplay, The Longman teaching anthology record, is an intriguing and previously unsuspected addition to the known recorded
works of Nick Drake. Nick plays on three songs: 'Full Fathom Five'
and 'I Wish I Was A Single Girl Again', both sung by Vivien Fowler;
and the traditional Australian pioneer song 'With My Swag All On
My Shoulder', sung by Robert Kirby. The accompanying teachers'
notes for 'Full Fathom Five' reads: 'This dirge, which has so many
different musical settings, is here sung in folk style . . . Pupils could
also suggest "modern" settings of traditional songs or tunes: the Top
Twenty usually has at least one example'. Released in 1972, this
Longman double album is probably the rarest of all Nick Drake's
recordings. So rare that even Robert Kirby does not own a copy.

'Another thing I know Nick played on was a musical I wrote,
which was never released . . . A guy had got a lot of money, and had a
friend who wrote lyrics, and they needed twelve songs to go with
them, which I wrote and linked them together. We had this grand
design, it was going to be the new *Hair*. Nick came in and played
acoustic guitar on that. I was trying to turn it into a medieval Mystery
Play – it started with birth and ended with death . . . It never got as
far as having a title.'

As a teenager, Nick grew up listening to the pirate radio stations,
particularly Caroline and London, both of which first went on air in
1964, broadcasting offshore from ships outside territorial waters, to
escape stringent government regulations. As a performer, though,
Nick came too late for pirate radio, which was finally forced off the
air by the Labour government in 1967. That same year saw the launch
of BBC's Radio 1, which was the only national channel playing pop
music. Exposure on Radio 1 was crucial for any act hoping to happen.
If you lived in Kirkcaldy or Bodmin Moor, you might be able to read
all about the latest pop sensations in the music press, but likely as not,
the only way you would ever get to hear them was on Radio 1.

To ensure that only music of the highest quality would be heard
over BBC airwaves, acts had to submit to a trial by jury. The panel of
BBC producers could approve a new act in two ways: either by
assessing a recording by a producer who felt strongly enough about a
new act to book them for an inaugural session; or by listening to a
tape sent in by the artist concerned when they applied for a BBC
session. Nick Drake's BBC audition was his Radio 1 debut, which he

recorded on 5 August 1969. Three of the four songs broadcast were then submitted to the BBC panel on 14 October, and six days later received a unanimous pass.

The panel's report on Nick stated the obvious ('sings his own songs and accompanies himself on guitar'), noted his 'professional behaviour' and 'attractive vocal quality, somewhat reminiscent of Donovan'. Another anonymous producer saw Nick as 'the type of artist who would appear on a John Peel record label', finding the music 'good of its kind, but limited appeal'. The report concludes: 'At last, something that holds one's interest from the start.' Nick fared considerably better than David Bowie, who four years before had been rejected by the BBC panel as 'a singer devoid of personality'.

Radio 1 was essential for disseminating your name if you were just starting out. The newly formed folk supergroup Pentangle, for example, played eight Radio 1 sessions for John Peel in 1968 alone. Not that there were that many opportunities for a left-field, album-orientated act like Nick, for while the name of producer Joe Boyd and the cachet of Island records guaranteed some press interest, that interest just didn't translate into those all-important airplays.

Despite the listening panel's approval, Nick's radio debut remained a one-off, something with which Ralph McTell could sympathize: 'We didn't get any radio play. I got one play on my first album, and that was John Peel. I remember sitting at home and it came on the radio, and I went: "That's me." I was so excited.'

David Sandison shared the artists' sense of frustration: 'Nick wasn't being played on the radio, because he wasn't releasing singles. There may have been the odd John Peel play, but I think Bob Harris is playing Nick Drake more now than Nick Drake was ever played when those albums were out. How were people going to hear about him?'

In the early days of Radio 1, stringent Musicians' Union regulations limited the amount of airplay which could be devoted to playing records, and what little needle-time there was, had to be shared with easy-listening Radio 2. To fill the remaining hours and ensure that the new sounds were heard, live sessions became the lifeblood of the new network. As marked as the split between Radio 1 and Radio 2 was the division on Radio 1 between the daytime Top Forty pop fodder – purveyed by Dave Lee Travis, Tony Blackburn and Noel Edmonds – and the underground sounds, as relayed by John Peel, Pete Drummond and Stuart Henry.

During the afternoon of 5 August 1969 Nick Drake made his way to the BBC's Maida Vale Studios. The studios, where the bulk of Radio 1's sessions were recorded, were only a few hundred yards from EMI's Abbey Road Studios, where, that same day, The Beatles were recording 'You Never Give Me Your Money' and 'Because' for what proved to be their final album together, *Abbey Road*. Nick spent a couple of hours at Maida Vale's Studio 5, recording four songs for broadcast on John Peel's Radio 1 programme. Sitting alone, and accompanied only by his own guitar, he performed 'Time Of No Reply', 'Cello Song', 'River Man' and 'Three Hours' – the last three from his debut album, *Five Leaves Left*. When the session was broadcast the following night, 6 August 1969, it was the last time 'Time Of No Reply' would be officially heard until it became the title track of Nick's posthumous fourth album.

Pete Ritzema was the BBC Radio staff producer who booked Nick for his radio debut: 'I thought the *Five Leaves Left* album was amazing, so I booked him on the strength of that. I remember being slightly disappointed by the session because rather than come in and do free-flowing spontaneous versions of the songs, he just did the arrangements as they were on the record. So he left gaps for the string arrangements, while he'd just strum away. He was very concerned that he didn't have the strings, he wanted to do it like the record, which is understandable, but I thought he would be a folkie, and come in and improvise, but he wasn't up for that.

'It was just him and an acoustic guitar. I was pleased that he did it, because his voice was so fantastic, but funnily enough I did have that feeling of disappointment at the end of it . . . I didn't realize he'd never done another session. I hope I didn't put him off. He was a gloomy fellow, very, very quiet. I don't know of the whereabouts of any tape – I haven't got one.'

Long after Nick's death, rumours persisted that the Radio 1 tape still existed, and was to be made available on record. Certainly the Strange Fruit label were allowed access to the BBC's archives during the 1980s, and began releasing half-remembered and legendary sessions on disc. Cult figures and contemporaries of Nick, such as Syd Barrett and Tim Buckley, had their Radio 1 sessions made available. Not the Nick Drake session, however. Radio 1 archivist Phil Lawton told me: 'The Nick Drake tape doesn't exist. The tapes were junked. Very few artists have a complete archive, not just Nick, but Pink Floyd, David Bowie, Led Zeppelin . . . Corporation policy in those days was to reuse tape – they were very concerned about storage space. You have to remember, in those days, and in their eyes, pop was very disposable. Radio 1 started in 1967, and I think that the BBC mandarins rather hoped that in two years they could go back to the Light Programme.

'Some producers in the sixties and seventies didn't agree with the BBC policy of reusing tape, so rather than junk sessions, they kept them, and they are filtering back to me. There is also the possibility that somebody could have a tape of the Nick Drake session which they taped off the radio at the time.'

Early in 1997 Jason Creed, editor of the fanzine *Pink Moon*, received a letter from Steve Greenhalgh, who claimed to have a recording of Nick's Peel session, recorded on a reel-to-reel tape from a microphone placed in front of the radio speaker. Although half of 'Time Of No Reply' is missing, and the tape apparently ran out during 'Three Hours', Greenhalgh began selling copies of the incomplete tape for £9.50, which prompted a number of letters from subscribers calling it 'a bloody rip-off'.

Witchseason's Anthea Joseph, who was still 'nannying' Nick as and when required, recalls him recording another Radio 1 session, which appears never to have been broadcast: 'Joe said to me: "We've got Nick in the John Peel prog. You've got to take him down there." It was at the Paris Studio, in Regent Street . . . I got Nick there, took him out, gave him dinner, and we went down there and he said: "I don't want to do this." I don't want to do it. I'm not playing. It was just in the studio, there wasn't an audience – but because it was going to be on the radio, in his mind that was like being in the Albert Hall.

'It took *hours* to get this twenty-minute session. Bernie Andrews and John were wonderful . . . endless patience, the kindness – and every now and again Nick would get up and say: "I'm going now", and head for the door, and I was like a whipper-in. I'd crack the whip on the door, going: "Back, back", and he went back. We did actually finish it, but it was absolutely exhausting. I had to take him home too, because I wasn't sure that he'd actually get there if I let him loose.'

For nearly thirty years that August 1969 John Peel session was believed to be Nick Drake's only radio appearance – by the time independent local radio was introduced to the UK in 1973, Nick was in no fit state even to consider any radio work. Then, in 1997, Iain Cameron contacted me with details of a radio session he had undertaken, accompanying his old Cambridge contemporary: 'I started doing sessions for Radio 2. Alec Reid had all these funny folkie types coming in . . . I said to Alec: "There's a guy called Nick

Drake, you should get hold of his record", so that's how Nick got the session, and because I'd made the lead, Alec said do you want to play on it?

'So I went to his flat on Haverstock Hill. I guess it's summer, so it might be a year after the May Ball, May or June 1970 . . . I found him much harder to work with in London. There was a . . . stranger atmosphere around. It's the sort of thing that's hard to put into words, but when you're trying to work like that, you detect quite readily. He wasn't giving anything . . .

'In the studio was a celeste, a little keyboard. Nick saw this, and started fiddling about with it. And he did a version of "Saturday Sun" on this celeste. I didn't know he played the keyboard, so that was quite a surprise. He had the song down as well on piano as he had on guitar . . . We did maybe four to eight songs. My impression is that Alec didn't find him unbearably difficult to work with. He was a bit more communicative in the studio than he was at Haverstock Hill. I sensed that drugs could have been a factor there. That was the climate of the time; it may have been contributory in his decline.'

On 23 March 1970 Iain Cameron and Nick Drake spent most of the day in Studio S2 at Broadcasting House. The session was then cut up and broadcast between midnight and 2a.m. on the night of 13 April 1970. Disc jockey Jon Cruyer hosted that night's edition of *Night Ride*, which was broadcast simultaneously on Radio 1 and Radio 2. As with the Radio 1 session, the tapes have long since been scrapped by the BBC, and producer Alec Reid told me he certainly has no copy of the session himself. BBC mandarins at the time were very strict with producers who wanted to keep sessions, reminding them of the illegality of the act.

Nick's perception of his own failure was a lacerating wound, but with so few people actually getting to hear his music there was little that anyone could do about it. Island themselves, from Chris Black-well down, were always strongly supportive of Nick, but they were also slightly baffled about what to do with the quiet young man who loathed performing. Blackwell told me: 'He was very introverted . . . I liked him very much and also liked his music, although other than John Martyn, Island had never handled his style of music and I told him I was unsure that Island could do a good job for him.'

Tim Clark, Island's production manager at the time of *Bryter Layter*, summed up the label's feel at the time Nick was struggling to gain a foothold: 'Marketing then was servicing stores with cardboard cut-outs of your acts, advertising in *Melody Maker* and so on. We knew the market. We knew who was going to buy the stuff, most of all we knew which shops they were going to buy it in . . . The independent shops were a lot more important then, back before the megastores and chains. There were some extremely good independent shops that stocked this new music; they were very enthusiastic. There were always pockets, London obviously, and university towns played a very important part. The university circuit was very important in those days . . .'

Meanwhile Nick Drake's records sold in tiny, tiny numbers to people probably more attracted by the producer's name than that of the artist. Pete Frame remembers how much cachet attached to the name of Joe Boyd: 'He was the ultimate in taste and cool. Everything he touched, I thought, was fantastic. I loved The Purple Gang. Elektra Records was the best label ever . . . The Incredible String Band's *The 5000 Spirits*, that was another of those instances of "Where have these songs come from?", "How do people write these songs?" They were just so original and unique. Fabulous songs, and so off the wall instrumentally. You thought the guy was a genius, everything he had his name attached to you thought was brilliant.'

11

Respectful reviews, a tiny, loyal audience, but gnawing at Nick Drake following the release of *Bryter Layter* in November 1970 was a tangible sense of failure.

Looking back, it wasn't simply that he had failed – it was as much to do with what he had to compete with. Even as an introspective singer-songwriter, Nick was beaten on his own turf. With Bob Dylan in mysterious, self-imposed exile between 1970 and 1973, and the search on for 'new Dylans', the beginning of the seventies was the very time to be a singer-songwriter.

American James Taylor had broken big in 1970 with *Sweet Baby James*, an album whose sweet melancholy found such a warm reception that it stayed on the US album charts for over two years. Following its release in 1971, Carole King's *Tapestry* went on to shift over ten million copies, making it the most successful rock album by a woman up to that date. After his Warlock Music session of 1970, Elton John had conquered the world with *Tumbleweed Connection* and *Madman Across The Water*. Cat Stevens, having dispatched the chirpy pop image of 'I'm Gonna Get Me A Gun' to the dustbin of pop history, was reborn as the sensitive, bearded soul, staring from the sleeve of *Mona Bone Jakon*. His subsequent *Tea For The Tillerman* and *Teaser & The Firecat* helped Island's profits soar.

Paul Simon had shaken off the cosy, easy-listening image of *Bridge Over Troubled Water* with his eclectic, eponymous 1972 solo debut. Leonard Cohen became enshrined in a generation's hearts as the emotional surgeon, using his songs as sensitively as a scalpel. Phil

Marlborough College, C1 House Relay Team, 1965; Nick Drake is standing third from left.

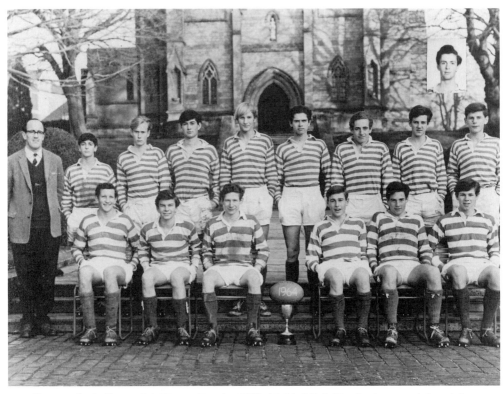

Marlborough College, C1 House Rugby XV, 1964; Nick Drake is seated far right.
Nick's Housemaster Dennis Silk is standing far left.

Nick's parents, Rodney and Molly Drake, at Far Leys.

The Drake family home at Tanworth-in-Arden, photographed from the garden.

Nick's first photo session for Island Records, just prior to the release of *Five Leaves Left* in 1969.

A 1967 lino cut of Nick playing the guitar in Aix-en-Provence.

The boxes of the three original master tapes of Nick's albums for Island Records.

Regent's Park, 1969.

Seated at the photographer Keith Morris's table at the time of *Bryter Layter*.

The final photo session on Hampstead Heath, 1971.

Nick's music room at Far Leys with the original artwork for *Pink Moon* framed on the wall.

An early sketch of Nick in Aix-en-Provence, 1967.

Ochs, Tim Hardin, Van Morrison and Tim Buckley, Neil Young, Joni Mitchell – all were appealing to their own devoted audiences. By 1973 Bruce Springsteen, John Prine, David Blue, Loudon Wainwright III, Jackson Browne, Tom Waits, Kris Kristofferson, John Prine and David Ackles had all released their debut albums.

Undeniably part of the singer-songwriter's appeal was a fascination with the private made public. There was a definite confessional element to the best-selling albums of the period – everyone knew of James Taylor's roller-coaster emotional state and his heroin addiction; but success soon removed the American singer-songwriters from anything approaching reality. Leaving their teenage bedsits far behind, they were installed in luxury hotel rooms, perpetually on the road promoting hit albums.

Nick Drake's British contemporaries like John Martyn, Al Stewart, Richard Thompson, Cat Stevens, Sandy Denny and Ralph McTell were also out gigging to promote their new albums. If ever there was a time for Nick to break through, this was it.

Anthea Joseph: 'I don't think Joe realized how paranoid Nick was about gigging. I don't think any of us did in fact. He knew Nick was difficult . . . Whatever the damage that Nick had done to himself at some point, I don't know, but something happened. By the time we met him . . . it was almost as though he was bricked up. There was a wall round him. I don't know whether Nick had some bad trips that turned him over or not, but it wouldn't surprise me. Certainly his drug habits were considerable. Not just smoking . . . I don't think he was a junkie, but I mean there was an awful lot of Mogadon around and things like that, you know. But he was never straight – you knew – you could always tell when someone was stoned. I don't know, but it may even have been prescribed by that time.

'Nick didn't twitch – he was always very still. And isolated. That's what I mean about being bricked up, he could be in a room, and there'd be Fairport there, String Band, all sorts of people falling in and out of the building, and Nick would be still, completely on his own, surrounded by people . . . shrieking with laughter . . . sitting on the floor and saying: "Here, what do you think of this?", and playing a verse of something. And Nick would be there – but he was always over there – he was not part of it.'

Around the time of *Bryter Layter*, Island Records recognized that Nick Drake was never going to reach the wide audience of Cat Stevens. Tim Clark, production manager at Island, recalls a meeting to discuss the second album's sleeve: 'We met in Joe Boyd's office, in

Charlotte Street, Joe, Anthea, myself, Keith [Morris] and Nick. Nick
sat there looking down, barely looking up. All his answers were
monosyllabic – occasionally not even monosyllabic, sometimes just
grunts. We were all trying to coax replies out of Nick. Ideas came up,
were discussed, and Nick sat there, and we tried hard . . . "What do
you think?" It was difficult to get him to do more than grunt to say yes.

'There was absolutely no heaviness . . . Everybody was very
sensitive to Nick . . . And Joe, who was a fairly quiet man himself
. . . certainly never raised his voice or anything like that. We all
thought Nick had potential . . . and that Nick was a very important
artist. A lot of the time, decisions weren't terribly commercial, and
that's why we staggered from one disaster to another. We did spend
too much on sleeves, we did spend too much on advertising, and we
did spend too much on the artists that we absolutely believed in
ourselves. If we had stood back I suppose we would have recognized
that actually to sell huge amounts of Nick Drake records, Nick *had* to
get out and tour to promote those records.'

Nick's state of mind during 1970 and 1971 could best be described
as delicate, though Gabrielle points out that at one point his problems
seem to have stemmed from a physical source: 'There wasn't a sea
change in Nick. It was a gradual thing . . . I think the crux came
around the time he produced *Bryter Layter*, and he was quite ill, he
had kidney stones, which caused my parents terrific concern. He
would disappear in London, and nobody would know where he was.
That was the first time I came in touch with Island. We were trying to
find out where Nick was.'

In the light of the frequent allegations of record company indifference, it is interesting that Gabrielle feels strongly that Island could
not have been more supportive of her brother: 'Mum and Dad were in
London, very worried, and I rang up Island because we thought that
he was deeply depressed at that time because Island weren't supporting him, that he'd brought out a record, and they'd never give him
dates and things like that . . . They said we'd do anything for Nick,
give him publicity, but he won't do it. Chris Blackwell said if he
doesn't want to do public performances, fine, we'll put him on a
stipend of however much it was a week. And I suddenly realized that
on the contrary, Island were prepared to do anything. And that that
was not where the problem lay.

'I read about Nick railing that he wasn't more famous, but in the
end, you jolly well have to set about becoming famous. As a young
artist of any sort, you have to push. I think he was very lucky – he was

also extraordinarily talented – but he found somewhere like Island who were prepared to support him, to nurture him, and not mind that he didn't do the publicity.'

Although his real success came with the re-release of 'Streets Of London' in 1974, Ralph McTell was fiendishly busy throughout this period. By 1972 he had moved up from the folk-club circuit to the Royal Albert Hall, but he still kept a watchful eye on his contemporary singer-songwriters: 'There was definitely this thread of guys who dressed reasonably smartly and sang in this particular style. And I would say Nick was definitely there. He would have hated Cousins and that folk circuit. It's a strange paradox: you really want to get your ideas across and record them. But playing in public, performing in front of an audience . . . the terror of actually going on.'

Even at Cambridge, friends had sensed that Nick's shy and soulful nature had an element of conscious image-building to it. As someone who had seen him close-up, had Ralph McTell ever felt that? 'I always thought all of it was. I thought we were all affected in some way . . . Bert was the only one who wasn't mannered. He revealed himself in different ways. He was unable to talk in a fluent way, that's why he wrote songs . . . On reflection, perhaps Nick was the same. But I doubt it. Bert was not an articulate man. He's not someone who enjoys conversation. Whereas somebody who's been to Marlborough and then on to Cambridge . . . It's almost like slumming it somehow, they should be doing something else.

'There was that element when people were being deep and dark, you thought at what point are they going to say fuck this, I've got to go and have a drink and have a bit of fun. Some of them just never did – Nick would be one of them. If Nick didn't have a job to do, you wouldn't see him round and about. You'd bump into other people at gigs, but Nick was very outside of that, on the edge.'

Brian Cullman, who had supported Nick at Cousins, was a fixture around the London folk scene at this time, and thanks to his friendship with John and Beverley Martyn he saw a lot of Nick: 'I would often go round to John and Beverley's basement flat in Hampstead in the afternoon and listen to music and drink tea, get stoned and watch the sun set over the heath . . .

'The third or fourth time I stopped by . . . Nick was there, hunched up in the corner of the room, smoking a joint. He had an odd way of sitting that made him seem smaller and frailer than he was (it was always a surprise, when he stood up, that he towered over John and nearly everyone else) . . . Nick asked to try out my guitar, and I passed it over to him, curious to hear what his music sounded like, both because he seemed so self-contained and distant, but also because John treated him with such care and deference, as if, at any moment, he might fade away . . . Nick ambled over, took my guitar, then walked out of the room and closed the door. I could hear the faint sounds of fingerpicking, like the ocean, far away . . . Ten, maybe fifteen minutes later, the sound stopped, and he walked back in, nodding to himself. Nice, he said handing it back. Then he studied the front, as if he'd just noticed the design on the pickguard. "Gibson," he said. And then he left.'

How much of that air of mystery Nick cultivated, and how much of his remoteness sprang from genuine shyness is hard to say. Certainly Cambridge friends and colleagues from Island thought they detected an element of contrived mystery; a sense that he was always conscious of the impression he was making; a feeling that Nick knew, by dressing almost entirely in black, saying little and smiling inscrutably, he was aiding and abetting the myth-making process.

Paul Wheeler: 'This just comes to mind, someone talking about a Rolling Stones concert, you had Mick jumping about all over the stage, and then Keith just moved one step, and the whole place went wild. And I think there was an element of that with Nick. I'm not saying it was conscious, but I think he knew how to play the crowd . . . The one comment that Nick would add to the conversation you would really hear, because he said so little the rest of the time.'

John Martyn was quoted in *Dark Star* as saying of Nick: 'He was quite conscious of the image portrayed in his songs. He was not a manic depressive who picked up a guitar; he was a singer-songwriter in every sense.'

From the moment he first heard the demo tape, Joe Boyd worked as closely with Nick as anyone. Joe was the person who put Nick on the map, the man who encouraged and nurtured his talent, and as such was well placed to observe him at close quarters, but even with Joe, he does not seem to have moved beyond a close working relationship: 'I got along very well with Nick, but a lot of the dialogue was not outside of specific, concrete stuff to do with production. There was a lot of one-way traffic. He struck me as a very shy and – dare one say it – even repressed upper-middle-class English person . . . He didn't stutter, but he had a little hesitation at the beginning of his sentences.

'He certainly liked being around people who were a lot more

relaxed and outgoing than he. In particular, there was a semi-retired, East End minor villain that I had befriended, where we used to go round and play Liar Dice, smoke dope, drink tea, and Nick loved going there. Because this guy geed him up all the time, cuffed him on the shoulder. "C'mon Nick, what's up? Spit it out, boy" . . . He loved playing Liar Dice and the congeniality of that situation, but he remained very quiet. He could be very funny and very witty when he did speak, but I never found him the life and soul of the party; he was a very reserved guy.'

Perhaps at some level Nick felt that if he spent enough time with ebullient, larger-than-life characters, he might acquire some of their vigour and robustness. Danny Thompson was another who Nick seemed keen to get close to. Older by ten years than most of the singer-songwriters he was to work with, Danny had begun playing in the skiffle era after National Service. By the time Pentangle formed in 1967, he was nearly thirty, and had worked with everyone from Cliff Richard to Rod Stewart. While working on *Five Leaves Left*, Danny sensed that Nick was keen to forge a friendship: 'He wanted to get close. I know that. Either he liked the way that I was or for whatever reasons. I don't want to come over as some important bloke in his life, but he really did want to know.

'He said could he come out to the house – I lived out in Suffolk, in a manor house, with loads of acres – so I said yes. I thought it would be a good opportunity for him to come out, go down to my local pub . . . but it wasn't his sort of thing. He didn't open up at all – the whys and wherefores of life, the tragedies of being . . . no, none of that.'

Danny felt that by getting Nick away from London, he might be able to get to know him better and help him come out of himself. But even the Suffolk countryside could not break through the cocoon into which Nick had withdrawn: 'He was very shy, very quiet. I had the feeling his mum and dad wanted him to get a proper job, finish off at university, and had pretty much laid a path for him to follow. I have no proof of this at all, but I just felt he was under pressure. I know he used to smoke a lot, which I wasn't aware of at the time, and that in itself is an indication, trying to get lost in it. Me, I used to like a few pints and know what was going on – each to his own. He could never be a close mate of mine, because I wasn't into dope. I wasn't into being a lost soul. I wasn't into all that deep and meaningful stuff, and I never have been.

'I felt it all a bit tragic really. Because I'd been in the Army and all that . . . and come from a background of real blokes, and I thought all he needs is a bloody good bacon and chip buttie and a good kick up the arse and a couple of good shags and he'll be all right. And I just thought, well, I'll have a go.'

Try as he might, Danny Thompson was frustrated by his inability to get through to Nick, and also by the effect it was having on himself: 'For people who didn't know him, it's very hard to describe how . . . draining it is on you. When you see someone, and you can't really work out what the matter is . . . In the end, you sort of lose patience and say get on with it, because it takes up so much of your own time. You've got your own problems; particularly then: I was about thirty-something.'

Joe Boyd feels that Nick's natural reserve and inability to make connections was heightened by an awareness of the social class into which he was born: 'For Nick, someone lacking in confidence, it is very difficult to be part of that public-school group, people who are bred, trained; people who behave as though they are the most confident people on the face of the planet. So to be the one who was a bit shy, hesitant, in that context, I would imagine could be very difficult . . . All those songs about longing for contact and longing for relationships, and yet at the same time, a very clear awareness of how difficult it is for him.'

One thing Nick never did, even when cultivating the company of minor East End villains, was to deny, or try to shake off, the marks of the social class into which he was born. He seems always to have accepted his background for what it was: an unalterable accident of birth. The other problem with trying to blame Nick's class or upbringing for his increasing sense of unease is explaining why the signs did not show themselves earlier. Certainly there are some people in Nick's life who only really knew him when he was troubled, but equally there are those who knew him when he was apparently happy and well-adjusted. The fact that there are so few who actually witnessed the change has much to do with Nick's talent for com-partmentalizing his life.

Most of the time Linda Thompson knew Nick he was troubled, but even she has fleeting memories of a happy Nick: 'He was a class act, Nick. The lanky aristo . . . I remember at the beginning when I used to see him, when he did smile, or he laughed, you just felt thrilled for weeks. It used to make me so happy when he smiled or laughed. He was an adorable person.'

Linda was well placed to observe Nick in and around London as he started to make his way as an Island artist. A singer herself, Linda was

engaged to Joe Boyd before marrying Richard Thompson in 1972: 'I
can't remember the very first time I met Nick, whether it was with
Joe, or at this drug dealer Bob's house. We'd all go there to play
cards, and people would sing. Nick would sing, Richard would sing,
John Martyn. I really don't know if Nick was getting drugs off Bob –
Richard and I certainly didn't; we must have been awfully stupid,
because we didn't really know he was a drug dealer.'

Later Linda and Nick would embark on a somewhat half-hearted
relationship: 'The fact that he came to my flat once a week, lots of
people, myself included, thought we were boyfriend and girlfriend
. . . We would drink macrobiotic tea, and I'd put on records for him.
And if he didn't like it, he wouldn't say anything, he'd just shake his
head, and I'd have to rush over and take the record off.

'He made monosyllabic seem quite chatty. And he was still fairly
up then, he wasn't too bad at all. We'd sit on the bed . . . we'd have a
bit of a cuddle. But it was always strangely detached . . . He never
said very much. Then I'd see him the next week, same night, and then
it just got a bit too much like hard work . . . Instead of thinking to
myself, God, this isn't right, he's not well.'

Though Nick's sexuality has increasingly become a focus of
attention in the years since his death, there is no real evidence that
he was gay. Friends from Marlborough are agreed that he showed no
homosexual tendencies and they feel sure that in the hothouse public-
school atmosphere, it would have been apparent. David Wright: 'I do
remember that Nick wasn't of the "little boy" persuasion. At
Marlborough in those days, before girls came along, the main topic
of conversation wasn't weather, it was little boys. Though very little,
if anything, actually happened . . . it was a classic girl-substitute
during term time. Certainly I don't recall Nick being interested in
that.'

Contemporaries from Cambridge even recall Nick's enthusiastic
heterosexuality; one even remembers 'getting laid at the same party'.
But just as many are convinced that he was sexually ambivalent,
unable or unwilling to commit himself to the demands of a sustained
relationship, with anyone, of either sex. There is no real evidence of
any sustained relationship in Nick's life. Linda Thompson remembers
that he went out with one of her friends and that he played them off
against each other. Schoolfriends remember a girlfriend in Aix in
1967, and Nick's friend from Marlborough, Jeremy Mason, met a girl
in Beirut, shortly after Nick died, who spoke of being engaged to him.

Twenty years on, attempts to contact her for this book failed, and

Jeremy felt that without her permission it was unfair to reveal her name: 'Nick was meant to have got engaged to her towards the end of his life. She was in Beirut while I was there with an exhibition, and she talked about Nick a lot, because she saw him for the last few months of his life. She was a very sensitive girl . . . I think she met Nick's parents. She knew all about the end. She was very good looking. We got quite close to her in Beirut, over this brief period of time . . . Her eyes used to fill with tears every time she mentioned his name.'

Unfortunately, this account cannot be confirmed, though its timing seems to lend it credence. Molly Drake had noticed that in the last few months of Nick's life, he seemed to have attained a degree of happiness, but until now it has been assumed that the reason for his contentment was his visit to Paris in the months immediately preceding his death. This possible romance would offer another reason for Nick's brief happiness just before the end.

By the beginning of 1971 Joe Boyd was feeling the pressure. Witchseason was struggling, and he was labouring under a heavy burden: Richard Thompson and he had been at loggerheads over Fairport's last album, *Full House*, and when Richard announced he was quitting the group, Boyd's primary interest in Fairport went with him. He was having problems with Sandy Denny and her plans for the future; to his concern, The Incredible String Band were becoming increasingly immersed in Scientology; and Nick had already announced that his third album would be a solo effort, with little need for any of Boyd's production flourishes.

After selling Witchseason to Chris Blackwell at Island Records, Boyd left London to take a job with the music division of Warner Brothers films. By all accounts, one condition of the sale was that Nick Drake's records should never be deleted from the Island catalogue. It was a condition to which Blackwell, a long-time admirer of Nick's work, readily agreed.

Anthea Joseph: 'Joe got this offer to go to the States, and that's when we all broke up – he told me at London Airport . . . We sat down on those awful plastic seats . . . and he said: "I've taken a job in Hollywood." And that was it. And I said: "You've gotta do it – if you get an offer of that kind you've got to do it." He said: "Are you sure?" and I said: "Well, of course, it's an experience you can't turn down – we'll all survive somehow." And that was the end of Witchseason.'

Some who have suggested that Nick – whether wittingly or not –

was homosexual, have seen Nick's evident fondness for Joe Boyd as a manifestation of such feelings. Certainly Nick did admire Boyd, and not just for his proven ability at producing records. But if there was more than simple affection on Nick's part, it seems likely that it was not secret desire, but secret envy. For how could he not envy the consummate ease with which Boyd managed his life? With his high cheek-bones and face framed by long, fair hair, Boyd was strikingly good-looking. His cultivated Boston upbringing lent him self-assurance, and he was capable of communicating swiftly and with a personal commitment which made you feel you were the sole object of his concern. In short, Joe Boyd was everything Nick Drake was not. And when Boyd left London, it removed another strand from Nick's already unravelling life.

Nick's parents were both fond of Boyd and they appreciated how much he had contributed to their son's career, but they were worried by how much Nick missed him when he went back to America. Anthea Joseph also noticed Nick's dependence: 'Nick relied enormously on Joe. He was emotionally tied to Joe, it was a mental thing, a brain thing. I mean, neither of them were homosexuals, by any stretch of the imagination. Joe rang a bell in Nick, I think, and vice versa. Joe really did care about him and tried to look after him as best he could.'

Linda Thompson, who knew both men, told me: 'All those stories that Nick had a crush on Joe. I don't think Nick ever had a crush on anybody . . . Fantastically good-looking man, unbelievably good-looking. Tall and lanky. He was just gorgeous. Long, tapered fingers. A fabulous-looking bloke. But he was totally other-worldly, Nick. He really, really didn't seem like he belonged.' Linda, like so many others who knew him, seems to discount the theory of Nick being gay: 'The time I knew him he was twenty to twenty-five. I think you would have seen him give a loving glance to some bloke, or being somehow involved. Somebody would have come out of the woodwork by now.'

So many people speak of Nick's unwillingness to communicate, that there is frequently a tangible sense of frustration when they remember him. A well-spoken young man, educated at public school and university, who wrote such beautiful songs, should have been able to articulate his feelings.

Brian Cullman remembered seeing Nick in London towards the end of 1970, and how he seemed to phase in and out of groups: 'Over the next few months, I'd run into Nick at John and Beverley's or sometimes see him on the streets of Hampstead. He'd appear and disappear from rooms, from restaurants (I had dinner with a group of musicians at an Indian restaurant once and only realized that Nick was there with us when he got up to go) always by himself, always quiet, deep in his own world.'

Throughout 1971 Nick grew more introspective. His friends and his family discerned the changes, but felt powerless to do anything. Linda Thompson: 'It seemed almost like a kind of autism in a way. It just got progressively worse and worse . . . One didn't see the signs in those days, we just thought he was really cool . . . People would say, oh, you've got a relationship with Nick, that's unbelievable. He put his arm round you? That's practically frenzied lovemaking for Nick. At the time I was playing the field a lot, and I'm ashamed to say I don't much remember what went on. But I remember I used to get quite cross with him, because he didn't talk enough . . .

'He did the odd gig . . . But it really wasn't very good. It was like watching somebody who was very ill in public . . . It wasn't enough. He didn't talk. It was OK on record, but for live gigs, you can't really cut off your audience that much. I was around Sound Techniques a lot and he was fairly, well, not animated, but he had fairly strong feelings in the studio. He knew what he wanted.'

His family recalled with fondness a streak of determination which would reveal itself in certain circumstances, and which he had shown occasionally since childhood, but except in the recording studio, that too seemed to be fading away. Far away from it all in Tanworth, Rodney and Molly Drake were increasingly concerned at their son's withdrawal. 'Then, of course, came *Pink Moon*,' recalled Rodney. 'Where and how and when he wrote that is difficult to say. He was beginning to get very withdrawn and depressed then. He was very down when he wrote *Pink Moon*. But some people say it was his best thing . . .'

12

'*Pink Moon* does remind me of Robert Johnson,' says Peter Buck, 'and the fact that they recorded him in a hotel room, facing the wall, too shy to look at the people recording him; and I understand that's pretty much how they recorded Nick for *Pink Moon*. There is that loneliness. Close up, intimate. Scary.'

Buck, REM's guitarist and the band's musical archivist, is only one of a new generation of musicians who are coming to appreciate Nick Drake. He also made that fascinating connection between Nick and the late Robert Johnson. Although he only ever recorded twenty-nine songs, at five sessions between November 1936 and June 1937, such was the passion and intensity of that music that Johnson's position as the King of the Blues remains unassailable.

King Of The Delta Blues Singers, a sixteen-track album released in 1961, was the record which marked out the parameters of the British blues boom which followed: Eric Clapton, The Rolling Stones and Led Zeppelin were just some of the white boys who hailed Robert Johnson's influence as seminal.

To the sheer quality of Johnson's music, you must add a palpable sense of mystery, for his short life and hard times were shrouded in an impenetrable mist of myth. Columbia Records' A&R chief, John Hammond, was intrigued by the blues he heard on Johnson's recordings and went looking for the man in 1938 so that he could highlight him at his Carnegie Hall 'Spirituals & Swing' concert showcase. But by the time Hammond's interest had been piqued, Johnson was already dead.

Johnson only ever made it to twenty-six, the same age as Nick
Drake. But otherwise, their lives could hardly have been more
different: Johnson was born in poverty, black and illegitimate –
some say it's a miracle he lasted as long as he did in the lynch-happy,
Jim Crow American South of the thirties. As Peter Buck pointed out:
'Blues is the music of the outsider, and you can't get to be much more
of an outsider in our country than a poor, black guy in rural America
in the 1930s, which is where Robert Johnson came from.'

In view of the enigma that was his life, it is little surprise that the
circumstances of Johnson's death were also mysterious; though it
now seems certain that he was murdered by the jealous lover of a
woman who was showing too much interest in the bluesman. Before
his death in August 1938, Johnson transferred some of the visions
which haunted him in life on to shellac. Vocalion's Don Law was the
man who tracked down the bluesman and lured him into a makeshift
recording studio.

Johnson's first recording session took place at the Gunter Hotel in
San Antonio, Texas, in November 1936. Johnson was young and
nervous, and he mistrusted the motives of any white man who seemed
interested in him. Law eventually persuaded him to record, but the
singer was so nervous that he asked if the recording engineers could
be located in the room next door. Finally, Johnson was coerced into
singing, but not before he had turned his back to the engineers. He
recorded facing the wall, lost in a world of his own, unobserved,
wrapped in the isolation shared only with his music.

Although Johnson's music was available in the Deep South during
his lifetime, it was only posthumously that it became widely available
and appreciated. Aficionados appreciated the high, lonesome quality
of his keening singing and the strength of his guitar-playing, which
came in part from his astonishingly long fingers. Throughout his life,
and in the sixty years since his death, mystery has attached itself to
Robert Johnson like wool to Velcro. The most enduring question is
how he learned to play the guitar in that eerie, other-worldly way of
his. They say that when he came out of Hazlehurst, Mississippi, he
couldn't play guitar worth a whit. Then the boy vanished. The next
time Johnson appeared, folks said he must have sold his soul to the
Devil to play guitar like that.

Like many poor boys, he believed that having his photo taken
imperilled his immortal soul, and it was only in 1986 that a picture
emerged which could be authenticated as that of Robert Johnson.
After all those years, if this wasn't an image of Johnson, then it

should have been. Staring at you from a photo from over half a century ago, the eyes are rigid and inflexible, but what compels you to keep staring is not his eyes; rather it is the fingers of his left hand, which grasp the neck of his guitar like the throat of an enemy.

Nick Drake, like so many young white boys growing up in the 1960s, is known to have loved the plaintive blues which came up off the Mississippi Delta, and he was particularly fond of Johnson's *King Of The Delta Blues Singers*. Friends speak of Nick's penchant for the blues during his lifetime, and it is more than coincidence that 'Black Eyed Dog' was one of the last songs Nick ever recorded, and one of his best. It was a song which drew heavily on the blues tradition, and particularly that of the late, great Robert Johnson.

Johnson's blues are desolate and windswept, none more so than the chilling 'Hellhound On My Trail'. Like the music of Nick Drake, you sift through the work of Robert Johnson looking for omens. In his case you don't have to look far. From his youthful pact with the Devil, chronicled in 'Crossroads Blues', to the end-of-life fatalism of 'Hellhound On My Trail', life and death are marked out clearly on the sparse recorded legacy of the man.

A friend who encountered him during the dark days, remembers Nick comparing himself to the doomed Johnson, and claiming that he too had a 'hellhound on my trail'. 'A little shiver ran down my back,' Ben Lacock told Mick Brown. Those echoes eventually become too loud to ignore: a sound of aching loneliness and solitary desolation. Sung by one man and his guitar to an empty wall.

Nick Drake's third and final album, *Pink Moon*, was recorded over two nights at Sound Techniques studios. With only a smattering of piano on the title track, *Pink Moon* too is the sound of one man and his guitar, pouring out his despair into a studio microphone.

Though unable to articulate his despair in any other way, Nick was clearly aware that there was something gnawing away at him. Unable to cope any longer on Haverstock Hill, unwilling to answer the door, reluctant to communicate on any level – with his parents, his record company or his dwindling audience – Nick finally left London and returned to his family home in Tanworth.

Anthea Joseph: 'When Joe left there was no one really looking after Nick, but he had a family, you see. I mean, it wasn't as though he was an orphan of the storm really - he may have felt like one, I don't know. I mean, it wouldn't surprise me if he did. He wasn't mentally stable. You can't take - nobody can take – responsibility for that, apart from immediate family, and he did have a family who loved him dearly.'

In the period between the release of *Bryter Layter* in November 1970, and *Pink Moon* in February 1972, the depression continued to corrode. Despite his distaste for the mechanics of promoting his records, Nick was upset at the poor response which had greeted the release of both *Five Leaves Left* and *Bryter Layter*, and the transparent lack of success ate away at him. He saw poor record sales as a personal failure, and could not accept that for any singer-songwriter at the beginning of their career, it all took time. You could not expect to make it overnight: building a career involved doing just that, from the foundations up. Before the video age, touring was what gradually brought your name to a wider audience, and with Nick's reluctance to perform, that most obvious avenue was cut off from him.

The reluctance to face the hard facts of commercial consideration became internalized, and where others might have taken advice or bided their time, he saw no future, only failure. 'I've failed at everything I've tried to do,' he told his mother. A terrible admission from a young man barely into his twenties. Concerned at their son's unwillingness or inability to communicate, his parents consulted their local GP, who felt that Nick might benefit from seeking psychiatric help. During 1971 Rodney and Molly Drake took Nick to see a psychiatrist at St Thomas's Hospital in London. His mother later admitted that 'it never really worked . . . what do psychiatrists really know? They are fumbling in darkness too.'

What did come out of those first sessions was a prescription for anti-depressant drugs. Nick was prescribed three types of drug, which he reluctantly began to take daily. Friends recall his embarrassment at taking the pills in their presence. It was a very English, a very middle-class response to a depressive illness: to be seen to be taking anti-depressants was an admission that there was something wrong; an admission of weakness.

Friend and musical colleague Robert Kirby, who had worked closely with Nick and Joe Boyd on the first two albums, felt that Boyd's decision to go to Los Angeles to work for Warner Brothers left a significant gap in Nick's life: 'That is one important thing: the length of time that Boyd was in America. I think that Nick felt sadly out of touch . . . He also admired Joe very greatly, and I think when Joe was in America, it did leave a big hole.'

When Nick did not respond well to the anti-depressants, his father consulted Boyd, who agreed to try to help: 'I spoke to Nick a few times from LA. He was obviously having difficulties. His parents got on the phone to me once and said they really wanted him to seek help, and that he was afraid that everyone would look down on him if he went to a psychiatrist. He was reluctant, and they would appreciate it if I would speak to him because they said he respected me so much. So I spoke to him and said: "I don't want to tell you what's right or wrong, but you should never feel people are judging you. You have to deal with things from your own point of view, and if you need help you should get help." The guy he went to, I think, was the guy who gave him the anti-depressants, and I think we know a lot more about anti-depressants now. Then, they were doling them out like candy, not aware of how dangerous they are.'

As someone who remained a close friend until the end of Nick's life, and has also trained as a psychiatrist, Brian Wells has memories of Nick at the time that are perhaps doubly revealing: 'My view is I don't think Nick Drake had what I as a psychiatrist would view as a biological depressive illness. I think he became more and more uncomfortable around people, and withdrew because he felt safety in his own company. A bit isolated, not for any particular reason . . . I think he got himself in a rut. If you are presented with that as a psychiatrist, there's nothing else you can call it, other than depression. But I don't think he had a biological depressive illness of the type we would normally prescribe anti-depressant drugs for. I'm not criticizing his doctor, because I think when his parents brought him to this psychiatrist up in Warwickshire, they were worried [because] he was at home. He'd had all this lively sort of stuff, he'd been at Marlborough, he'd been at Cambridge, you know. What had happened to this guy?

'Psychiatrists are trained to think in terms of diagnosis. What would explain this behaviour? Well, he's either got schizophrenic illness, which he didn't have: he wasn't listening to voices. The most obvious diagnosis to make with Nick was one of depression. I don't think it was. I mean, it was a depression, but it was more a sort of existential state that he'd got himself into, rather than it being the kind of depressive illness that medical students learn about when they're training to be psychiatrists. I would not have given him Tryptizol, which was an anti-depressant of that time . . . You hear stories that "it seemed to be making a difference". But I don't think that was the kind of depression he had. I think he was a sensitive, rather precious guy who became increasingly withdrawn. And I think that was diagnosed as depression.'

For a time, though, it did seem to those around Nick that his mind was made marginally clearer by the anti-depressants, and Nick himself began to feel that a change of scene might help. Following Boyd's sale of his Witchseason roster before returning to America, Island Records boss Chris Blackwell had maintained a fondness for Nick and his music, ensuring that he continued to receive a weekly stipend. Now, concerned by Nick's visible deterioration, Blackwell allowed him the use of his villa, in Algeciras, near Gibraltar. Barely seven years before, Nick and David Wright, his friend from Marlborough, had planned to use the area as a springboard for their round-the-world trip.

On his return from Blackwell's villa, his mood perhaps slightly brightened by the Spanish sun, Nick began to think about recording again. In the absence of Joe Boyd, who was now installed in LA, he decided to make contact with one of his few remaining conduits to the music industry, John Wood. The mythic version is that Nick turned up out of the blue to record the third album in 1971, insisting that it be sparse and straightforward. 'No frills' is Nick's most frequently quoted comment on *Pink Moon*. In fact, it seems that as early as 1970 Nick had determined that the new album would be much simpler. Back then, though, he was not to know just what torments lay ahead.

Even at the time of its release, Nick had felt that his second album erred towards the more lavish production favoured by Joe Boyd, rather than the simplicity he himself favoured. In an interview with *Musin' Music*, Boyd remembered: 'Nick came to see me before we'd even released *Bryter Layter*, as soon as we'd finished the record, before the cover was done or anything, he said to me "The next record is just going to be me and guitar . . ." I think he may have found *Bryter Layter* a little full, or elaborate . . . I know he liked it, but he did feel, "OK, we've done this, now we're going to do something completely different . . ." Nick wasn't somebody you really argued with, but again he could do that with John Wood, he didn't need me to do a record with just him and guitar.'

Robert Kirby did not learn until later that there would be no place for his sumptuous arrangements on the new album: 'I remember after *Bryter Layter* hoping there would be things for me to do, and I remember him saying: "No, it's only going to be myself and guitar." I don't think this was immediately after *Bryter Layter*; it was more shortly before *Pink Moon*.'

As far back as Cambridge in 1968, Kirby remembers Nick

performing guitar pieces and fragments, which he recognized four years later on the final album. One he particularly recalled was the guitar phrase which appeared as 'Things Behind The Sun'.

'I think at the time *Bryter Layter* was out, most people said it wasn't up to *Five Leaves Left* . . . I think the decline began with the response to *Bryter Layter*. The decline had set in prior to *Pink Moon*. Nick . . . took less care of himself. In the early days he always looked immaculate. Towards the end, he looked ill. He looked haggard, unkempt . . . I don't think he was eating, which didn't help.

'Between *Bryter Layter* and *Pink Moon*, he would come round, stay for a week, and not say anything. Nothing. I knew him. My friends knew him . . . He might get the guitar out and play. If we were in the front room, enjoying listening to sounds, he'd come and sit down and enjoy listening. If we went to the pub or restaurant, he might come with us. But he would quite often not say anything.'

The period bordered by *Bryter Layter* and *Pink Moon* marked the almost imperceptible decline of Nick Drake. The outside world showed no real interest in that decline – merely curiosity. But those who knew him well, especially his family, found the change hard to bear. Gabrielle Drake: 'The public image of Nick really stems from the years of his depressive illness because a lot of that coincided with his record-making. And of course one's later memories are clouded by this - he was very depressed. But that wasn't the essence of Nick as I knew him as a child . . .'

Formerly dapper and strapping and perhaps just a tad too aware of his own image, Nick now had so many real problems that simply making it from day to day was difficult. There was no longer space for worrying about a public image. Each and every day was a struggle, a period to be endured, to get through with gritted teeth. Nowhere was the grinding determination more evident than in the enormous personal struggle it took to record the songs which became *Pink Moon*.

Remembering Nick in happier times, John Martyn told Andy Robson: 'He was extraordinarily lovable. And the most lovable thing about him was that he was so shy.' But the sweet shyness had long gone, and now Nick seemed to have gone too. He was so totally withdrawn that he seemed to be teetering on the edge of something horrible, which he could barely discern and was fearful of truly comprehending. But some impulse - to work, to communicate, or to save himself - drove him to record. And determination, though never a part of the romantic myth, was always very much part of Nick

the human being. Tremors of uncertainty, jarring discord, nagging
awareness, fretful concerns, must have filled Nick's head, for together
they create the mood which saturates *Pink Moon*.

If *Five Leaves Left* - released a scant three years before Nick made
this final album - is melancholy, but with the comforting glow of a
November bonfire for comfort, *Pink Moon* is Manderley without
lights, burned and razed, a hollow shell where once had dwelt
happiness. Talking to Connor McKnight for his *Zig Zag* appreciation, John Wood recalled the sparse sessions which led to *Pink Moon*:
'He arrived at midnight and we started. It was done very quickly.
After we had finished, I asked him what I should keep, and he said all
of it, which was a complete contrast to his former stance. He came in
for another evening and that was it. It took hardly any time to mix it,
since it was only his voice and guitar, with one overdub only. Nick
was adamant about what he wanted. He wanted it to be spare and
stark, and he wanted it to be spontaneously recorded.'

Singer-songwriter Clive Gregson first worked with John Wood a
decade after *Pink Moon* was released: 'I knew his name from Richard
and Linda records, John Martyn, Fairport, Nick. We'd got a deal,
and the record label wheeled in producers and said who do you like?
They'd brought John in because he'd done the Squeeze stuff, which
had just done so well – "Cool For Cats", "Up The Junction", great,
great pop records. As soon as they mentioned his name, I just
thought, yeah, great. I realized I probably had more records with
his name on than anyone else.

'He did the first and last Any Trouble records, then left the record
business. He came out of retirement briefly in 1995 to do Boo
Hewerdine's record. I think he got to a point in the mid to late
eighties, when records were so dismal . . . The kind of records John
liked doing were: you get a band who could sing and play, who had
good songs, and you mic it up right; they perform, and you get it on
tape. But by then, you could take any old bollocks and make it sound
glossy.

'Talking to John about Nick, it was always how the records were
made, and I think that he felt very proud of those records. I always
got the impression with John that he felt Nick was probably one of
the most talented people he'd ever worked with - and that's very high
praise when you look at the people he did work with. I got the
impression that he admired the way Nick could translate the ideas
and arrangements that were in his head.

'Around the time of *Pink Moon* I think Nick's health was

obviously failing. John told me he thought Nick was having problems writing songs. I mean, *Pink Moon* is an incredibly short record. He just said: "That's it. That's what I've got. That's how I want it to be. No overdubs. No nothing. Voice and guitar." John always said that Nick had a very clear idea of what he wanted to do.'

As the last album Nick ever recorded, *Pink Moon*'s status is ensured. But like the house on the cover of Led Zeppelin's *Physical Graffiti*, it is ever-changing, never static. Nothing is certain, there are few glimpses into the lives behind the blinds. The names on the doorbells bear little relation to the current occupants of the rooms.

Nick's final album issued forth from a well of despair, a cell of isolation. Its songs were fashioned in an anonymous north-west London bedsit warren. The shifting, transitional nature of the location left its mark on Nick and the songs he was writing. There is no permanence on *Pink Moon*. It is too uneasy and restless.

Nick's voice never sounded more consoling than here. But, knowing what was behind him and fearful of what lay ahead, it is in the fragmentary instrumental 'Horn' that he encapsulates *Pink Moon*'s terrible, desolate beauty. You can picture him bent over his guitar in a recording studio late at night - long, sinewy fingers moving slowly and deliberately across the neck of his guitar, evoking his own desolation in a way words never could.

Knowing this to be the final album, you search for those omens and portents which seem to so dog Nick Drake's career. Here is a bleakness and unspoken tragedy to match any found in the blues. Here is raw grief and unassuaged anger. 'Horn' is music communicating the incommunicable, inarticulacy articulated. Here is Drake groping for a thread to guide him out of the maze of despair. Maybe the music could do it. Or maybe it would desert him, and leave him as alone and isolated as before.

For all its bleakness, and the outright despair of the voice begging, pleading for comprehension and understanding, *Pink Moon* concludes on a note of optimism. The final track, 'From The Morning', speaks of a beautiful new day dawning. Is it simply hindsight which finds us snatching at straws of hope? Or is there a real sense that, bad as things get, low as you can go, there is always a way up, always the brightness of a new day to follow even the bleakest night?

Is it significant that the song is placed last? Is Nick trying to tell us something? Or is that just the listener hoping that out of all the darkness which engulfed him during the final three years of his life, somewhere, however far in the distance, Nick Drake saw a beacon burning?

Hearing *Pink Moon* play, late at night, with the headphones wrapped tight around your head, so that you are isolated and alone, is chilling – and eerily intimate. It is a testament to John Wood's skill that you feel as though you are part of the mood, and there is nothing between you and those songs, or the man performing those songs.

Pink Moon has all the hallmarks of a finely crafted beauty, a sombre resonance which finds echo all these years on. The songs are pale and wistful, like the late light of a Warwickshire afternoon. It is like watching smoke coil up from a hand-rolled cigarette, as the chill fog of a late-autumn evening sneaks up and wraps itself around you, like an old friend keen to betray you. Hearing Nick Drake's voice here conjures up again the lost boy, creating a mood as irredeemable as childhood, as plaintive as unrequited love, as tragic as lost promise.

The starkness of *Pink Moon* sets it apart. Along with John Lennon's *Plastic Ono Band*, Bob Dylan's *Blood On The Tracks* and Syd Barrett's *The Madcap Laughs*, it stands as an iconoclastic record. A record made to shatter the myth of the invincibility of the artist. All are albums made at times of great personal stress in the songwriters' lives. But whether they were cathartic, or simply compounded the turmoil, only John, Bob, Syd and Nick could say.

Pink Moon is a *cri de coeur*. There was, transparently, no commercial consideration in its creation. This was not the record of an artist intent on alerting the world to a change in his personal life or private philosophy. This was a record which Nick Drake seemed to have no choice but to make. He had once told his father that there was music running through his head all the time.

Because of its harrowing nature, and the bleakness of the circumstances surrounding the record, it is no surprise to learn that Nick's final album was his parents' least-favourite. Writing to Scott Appel in 1986, Rodney Drake noted that: 'The material on *Pink Moon* has always bewildered us a little (except "From The Morning", which we love)'. Two lines from that song form the epitaph on Nick's headstone in Tanworth churchyard.

In a Dutch radio broadcast of 1979, presumably aired to commemorate the release of the *Fruit Tree* box set, John Wood expounded further on his memories of those sessions: 'The most startling conversation I ever had with him was when we were making *Pink Moon*. And as you've probably read, we made the record in, I think, two evenings. Nick was determined to make a record that was very stark, that would have all the texture and cotton wool and sort of tinsel that had been on the other two pulled away. So it was only just him. And he would sit in the control room and sort of blankly look on the wall and say: "Well, I really don't want to hear anything else. I really think people should only just be aware of me and how I am. And the record shouldn't have any sort of . . . tinsel." That wasn't the word he used, I can't remember exactly how he described it. He was very determined to make this very stark, bare record and he definitely wanted it to be him more than anything. And I think, in some ways, *Pink Moon* is probably more like Nick than the other two records.'

Even the circumstances in which Island Records acquired *Pink Moon* have become the stuff of legend. The tale runs that Nick delivered the master tapes to Island, but left without talking to anyone, and it wasn't until days later that the receptionist realized that the package she was holding was the new album from one of the label's acts. It is suggested that Island was indifferent to Nick Drake, failing to nurture him while he was still alive.

Nick's press officer at Island, David Sandison, remembers the event differently: 'I saw him in reception after I came back from lunch . . . I saw a figure in the corner on the bench, and I suddenly realized it was Nick. He had this big master tape box under his arm, and I said: "Have you had a cup of tea . . . Do you want to come upstairs?" So we went upstairs to my office . . . and he just sat in my office area for about half an hour, then said: "I'd better be going . . ." He went down the stairs with the tapes under his arm, and about an hour later the girl who worked behind the front desk called up and said: "Nick's left the tapes behind", so I went down and it was the big sixteen-track master tape box, and it said: "Nick Drake: Pink Moon." So they called John Wood and said: "What's this?" and he said it was the new album. So we ran off a safety copy and said let's hear it.'

In the dangerously deep waters of analysing what Nick Drake's records 'mean', there is much to be gleaned from *Pink Moon*. The title track, particularly, lends itself to ominous symbolism: the 'Pink Moon' which is going to get the singer is widely taken to be the harbinger of Nick's own death. *The Dictionary Of Folklore, Mythology & Legend* notes that during eclipses of the moon, 'the earth's shadow casts a dark reddish colour on the moon, dimming its light or blacking it out altogether. These "bloody" moons, or other aspects of the moon when the atmosphere makes the moon's face seem red with blood, are evil omens, portending catastrophes. The Chinese, for example, see in an abnormally red (or an abnormally pale) moon, a warning of evil.'

Pink Moon, released on 25 February 1972 as ILPS 9184, appeared in a busy month for Island re-releases. The label was more concerned with re-promoting Emerson, Lake & Palmer's *Tarkus*, Jethro Tull's *Aqualung*, King Crimson's *Islands*, Sandy Denny's *The North Star Grassman And The Ravens*, Mott The Hoople's *Brain Capers*, Mountain's *Flowers Of Evil* and Fairport Convention's *Babbacombe Lee* than the new album by Nick Drake.

In an extraordinary move', *Pink Moon*'s official full-page advertisement, which appeared in the music press in the month of the album's release, took the form of an open letter from David Sandison under the heading 'PINK MOON – NICK DRAKE'S LATEST ALBUM: THE FIRST WE HEARD OF IT WAS WHEN IT WAS FINISHED'. The letter included a warts-and-all account of Nick's Queen Elizabeth Hall gig, before telling the tale of the new album: 'The last time I saw Nick was a week or so ago. He came in, smiling that weird smile of his and handed over his new album. He'd just gone into the studios and recorded it without telling a soul except the engineer. And we haven't seen him since.

'The point of this story is this: why (when there are people prepared to do almost anything for a recording contract or a Queen Elizabeth Hall date) are we releasing this new Nick Drake Album, and (if he wants to make one) – the next?

'Because, quite simply, we believe that Nick Drake is a great talent. His first two albums haven't sold a shit. But, if we carry on releasing them, then maybe one day someone authoritative will stop, listen properly and agree with us. Then maybe a lot more people will get to hear Nick Drake's incredible songs and guitar playing. And maybe they'll buy a lot of his albums, and fulfil our faith in Nick's promise.

'Then. Then we'll have done our job.'

Dave Sandison – December 1971

Island's Press Officer.

It was as if the sheer naked honesty of Nick's record had simply made hyperbole impossible. But perhaps even more strange is that a record company would simply accept the tape, press it up and release it immediately, exactly as it was, without any attempts at interference. In that context, the ad begins to seem quite ordinary, though Sandison does admit now that it was a bit of an admission of failure: 'I don't know what else I could have done. It was a statement of faith as much as anything: we'll stay here as long as he wants to make records. Whether long-term and realistically, it would have been like that, I don't know. Probably not.'

Gabrielle Drake was touched by the concern Island Records displayed over Nick during this dark period; Chris Blackwell particularly wanted to ensure that Nick was looked after. But as David Betteridge pointed out, the label did have other priorities at that time: 'So many things were happening at Island. Nineteen seventy-two was an extremely busy year for Island. We had Sparks, Roxy Music, Cat Stevens . . . I mean, Cat Stevens amounted to something like 20 per cent of our sales that year. Worldwide, he was huge.'

No one at Island was really clear just what was wrong with Nick. Many of the people I spoke to who saw him around this time assumed it was a drug-related problem. His increasing isolation meant that even keeping the lines of communication open was a nightmare, as Sandison pointed out: 'He was very difficult to contact. He was living in one of those places, four floors of flats, a couple of flats on each floor, and people only stayed for three weeks. It wasn't a squat, but it wasn't far off . . . so when you called, nobody was really sure whether Nick was there. Somebody would tramp off, and come back about ten minutes later and say: "Well, I've knocked on the door and there was no reply." But that didn't mean anything. You didn't know if he was there or not.

'But then he would just pop up. He would arrive at Witchseason, out of the blue . . . or he would swan off to Paris. He was together enough to organize that sort of thing. Whether after having become a "recording artist", he just didn't want to do it. And because he was so incredibly lucky to fall into Witchseason's hands, and then Island, where this sort of thing was indulged. I mean, any other record company that might have signed him at the time wouldn't have pursued him past the first album, given the fact that he wasn't going to do any gigs or interviews.'

With the benefit of hindsight, you can see why *Pink Moon* and Nick Drake were so marginalized. The same issue of *Melody Maker* which carried Sandison's letter down a whole page featured advertisements or reviews of other albums released that week – Paul Simon's solo debut, Jethro Tull's *Thick As A Brick*, Neil Young's *Harvest*, Ry Cooder's *Into The Purple Valley*, Carly Simon's *Anticipation*, Al Stewart's *Orange*, as well as debut albums from singer-songwriters John Prine, Steve Goodman, David Blue and Judee Sill.

The number-one album that week was from Nick's labelmate, Cat Stevens: his breakthrough *Teaser & The Firecat*.

The music industry was biding its time, treading water, following the break-up of The Beatles and Simon & Garfunkel, Bob Dylan in hiding and The Stones in tax exile. No one was sure if Glam was a flash in the pan, or how much longevity you could expect from Savoy Brown or Jonathan Kelly. Wherever the bright lights were shining, though, Nick Drake was well out of sight, edging into the shadows.

In his *Time Out* review of *Pink Moon*, Al Clark was clearly aware of the problems surrounding Nick: 'Sadly, and despite Island's efforts to rectify the situation, Nick Drake is likely to remain in the shadows, the private troubador of those who have been fortunate enough to catch an earful of his exquisite 3a.m. introversions.'

Even Nick's most loyal supporters in the press were hard pushed to be unequivocally enthusiastic about *Pink Moon*. In his review of the album for *Sounds*, Jerry Gilbert wrote: 'Island appear to have forgotten about Nick Drake until he ambled into the offices one day and presented them with this album. No-one knew he'd recorded it except the engineer and it's a long way removed from the mighty sessions that Joe Boyd used to arrange for him. Nick Drake remains the great silent enigma of our time – the press handout says that no-one at Island even knows where he's living, and certainly he appears to have little interest in working in public again.

'The album consists entirely of Nick's guitar, voice and piano and features all the usual characteristics without ever matching up to *Bryter Layter*. One has to accept that Nick's songs necessarily require further augmentation, for whilst his own accompaniments are good the songs are not sufficiently strong to stand up without any embroidery at all. "Things Behind The Sun" makes it, so does "Parasite" – but maybe it's time Mr Drake stopped acting so mysteriously and started getting something properly organised for himself.'

Within a couple of months of the release of *Pink Moon*, Nick had suffered a breakdown, and was hospitalized in the Warwickshire countryside. Like an ocean liner, slowly and inexorably, he was slipping the ropes which connected him to the shore. David Sandison's poignant press statement had only confirmed the rumours which were already percolating around the music industry. With so much else happening – the first post-Beatles hysteria accompanying Bowie and Bolan; the increasing interest in the progressive movement epitomized by ELP and Yes – the absence of the already shadowy Nick Drake wasn't exactly headline news.

In *Melody Maker*, Mark Plummer's review of Nick's last album was strikingly foreboding, given that Nick was still alive and only believed to be temporarily absent: 'John Martyn told me about Nick Drake in ecstatic terms and so it seemed the natural thing to do, bag the album when it came in for review that is. It is hard to say whether John was right or not. His music is so personal and shyly presented both lyrically and in his confined guitar and piano playing that it neither does or doesn't come over. Drake is a fairly mysterious person, no-one appears to know where he lives, what he does – apart from writing songs – and there is not even a chance to see him on stage to get closer to his insides. The more you listen to Drake though, the more compelling his music becomes – but all the time it hides from you . . . It could be that Nick Drake does not exist at all.'

13

'He was the most withdrawn person I've ever met,' John Martyn said of Nick. To Andy Robson he said: 'We were never that close. Except, I was as close as anybody could be. He was an impossible man to get close to . . . In another age he would have been a hermit.' Martyn and his then wife Beverley, near neighbours to Nick in Hampstead, were among the very few who were ever really close to him. Martyn, three months younger than Nick, was always one step ahead of him during his early career, and was the first folk-related signing to Chris Blackwell's Island label.

His early albums – *London Conversation*, *The Tumbler* – were cut from the folkie cloth, but soon Martyn got the hump, and working with bassist Danny Thompson, switched direction: 'I was actually very shy and retiring,' he told *Q*, 'and ever so sweet and gentle until I was 20 then I just got the heave with Donovan and Cat Stevens and all that terribly nice rolling up joints, sitting on toadstools, watching the sunlight dapple through the dingly dell of life's rich pattern stuff . . . I'm not really that nice, and I very consciously turned away from all that.'

That change was marked by 1973's *Solid Air*, which Colin Escott in his booklet to accompany 1994's double compilation *Sweet Little Mysteries* described as 'John's masterpiece'. Escott went on to explain that 'The texture of the title song was dictated by Danny Thompson's bass, mixed way up. Inasmuch as the lyrics offered themselves up for interpretation, they were for, or about, John's Island labelmate, Nick Drake. Nick lived near John for a while, and died mysteriously, if not altogether unexpectedly, the following year.'

Martyn's song was a cautionary note to Nick. Knowing him now to be unreachable, perhaps he hoped Nick would respond to a message written in a form he understood. Talking to *Zig Zag*, while Nick was still alive, Martyn said: 'Solid Air was done for a friend of mine and it was done right with very clear motives and I'm very pleased with it, for varying reasons.'

In 1986 Martyn told biographer Brendan Quayle: 'Nick was a beautiful man, but walking on solid air, helpless in this dirty business, an innocent abroad. He was killed, like [Paul] Kossoff, by the indecent, parasitic opportunism that pervades the music business.'

When I approached Martyn about being interviewed for this book, he rang to say that he felt he had said enough about Nick Drake over the years and was reluctant to run the risk of turning his memories into anecdotes.

Chas Keep, who is currently working with Martyn on his authorized biography, wrote to me in June 1997 with a memory of Martyn's response to Chas's profile of Nick in *Record Collector* : 'I think the thing that sticks in my mind the most is the image of John reading my article on the day it was published in 1992. Driving back to his house, he sat in the passenger seat reading, with tears in his eyes, the silence only broken by his occasional muttered "Poor Nicky, poor Nicky . . ." Poor John, he does so blame himself for being unable to prevent Nick from withdrawing from the world.'

Following their move from Hampstead, John and Beverley Martyn relocated to the sleepy South Coast town of Hastings, where Nick became an irregular visitor. Fond as the Martyns were of Nick, it seems that by the time he visited them during 1972, he was in a place that they could never hope to reach.

David Sandison: 'John Martyn told me a story about when Nick was staying with them, and they were all sitting round watching telly . . . and Nick got up and left the room, and he thought he'd gone to have a pee, or make a cup of tea, but then he suddenly realized that an hour had passed, and Nick hadn't come back. He was slightly concerned – he didn't suspect he was going to kill himself or anything – but just wondered where the hell he was. And Nick was sitting in a foetal crouch outside the door, and it kind of freaked John, because he said that it was almost like he was listening to see if we were talking about him. There was a hint of paranoia. There was also that kind of . . . vague insult that we were his friends, but he didn't want to be with us.'

Rodney Drake wrote that Nick was 'very close' to John and Beverley Martyn during 1971–72, and that he was living near them in Hampstead around the time he was recording *Bryter Layter*. He had fond memories of Martyn, and recalled him visiting the Drake family home in Tanworth when Nick was at his most withdrawn: 'They knew each other very well, and when Nick was up here, and was pretty bad, we got John Martyn to come up. We'd never met him, and he came up here, and he was a very charming person.'

Molly Drake recalled: 'Nick, having said he could come, then went into the most awful torment of worry, because . . . Nick always went on about his two worlds, and he thought John Martyn's one world, and you're another world, and it simply won't work. But in actual fact, it worked like anything, we absolutely loved John Martyn, we got on dreadfully well . . .'

Rodney: 'He kept us both entertained, and Nick was very amused, and the next morning, Nick wanted him to go . . .'

Molly: 'Nick was very bad, and John Martyn is a tremendously vivacious, ebullient character, and at that stage, it was more than Nick could take. It was all right for one evening, and the next morning he couldn't take any more of it.'

Interviewed on Radio 1 in 1985, Martyn remembered Nick: 'He came and lived with me in various locations, and was just distinctly unhappy in all of them. I think he distrusted the world. He thought it had not quite lived up to his expectations.'

Joe Boyd had settled in Los Angeles, and after years of scraping by with his Witchseason acts was finally on a regular salary from Warner Brothers. But in London, in the early 1970s, with Boyd gone, Nick felt even more isolated. Nick's decision to record *Pink Moon* without the lavish Boyd production which had been such a feature of *Bryter Layter* meant that Boyd could leave for America with a clear conscience, though in later years he admits to wondering if Nick did in fact feel abandoned: '*Bryter Layter* took a very long time. It was very off and on, doing little bits here and there, over the course of a year. And so by the time it was released, I was on my way to Los Angeles, so when it actually came out and didn't sell, I wasn't around as a manager . . . I guess I feel badly that I couldn't totally follow through on it.

'I think he did feel abandoned. You can look back and see how . . . I didn't think of myself as being that important to the people you were dealing with. You were young, you think things go on and you do this and you do that. I was a little frustrated, because a lot of the groups, and Nick, wanted to do things that I didn't feel necessarily involved me that much. Nick had already announced that he wanted to do his next record stark, so I said, well, you can do that with John, you don't need me for that.

'Nick loved *Five Leaves Left*. I don't know what he thought of *Bryter Layter*. Whether he thought that his music was being a bit overwhelmed, by the arrangements, by the visiting artists, by John Cale, by Pat Arnold and Doris Troy . . . I just don't know. But definitely by the end, when we finished *Bryter Layter*, he said: "The next record's going to be different. It's going to be very simple." This was before i left, before *Bryter Layter* came out and didn't sell, before any of that. And that was one of the things which added to my feeling of well, why not take this job with Warner Brothers.'

Simon Crocker had lost touch with Nick since the release of *Five Leaves Left*, but assumed that, signed to the prestigious Island Records, with his third album just out, things couldn't be better for his old schoolfriend: 'Then I met Robert Kirby . . . and we had a long chat about Nick and he told me everything, and I was absolutely flabbergasted. One of the things was, Joe Boyd going to America really caught Nick on the hop. Basically he depended very heavily on Joe . . . and he was kind of lost after he went. I don't think you can point the finger at Joe: he did what was right for him at the time . . . I don't think there's any blame to be placed. He can't be responsible, but in a way the impression I got was that Nick didn't really grasp what was happening until it was too late. He didn't realize the gap that was going to be there.

'What amazed me looking back was that Nick never had a manager. Nick needed people to get his act together. Nick was just not someone who was going to do that by himself . . . Anyone who knew him would realize that he needed someone to really help him, to structure his life . . . I'm sure if he had had the right manager with a bit of money, and he could have had other musicians playing with him, he could have performed very, very well indeed. Is it because Nick said: "No, I don't want it?" I don't know that.'

Another friend from Marlborough and Aix was Jeremy Mason. He was equally shocked when he saw Nick for the first time in two years: 'He had changed completely. This would be early 1971. We couldn't get anything out of him at all. He didn't like the pub. He said it was a class of people he was not interested in any more – it was a pub for the Chelsea set, what you'd call yuppies today.

'We did go back to his flat. He actually only loosened up when we got back to the flat. Whether he had just moved in, or whether this was it, but it had nothing in it except the boxes in which his stereo had come. You sat on the bed, and had coffee off the boxes.

'I remember introducing him as my great buddy from school; and realizing that I had nothing further in common with him came as a bit of a shock . . . He had certainly gone a very different path by then . . . He had turned, from the time I knew him, from a relatively laid-back chap, with whom I had no trouble communicating . . .

'I must emphasize that when we were at school and went to see Graham Bond, and we went to the Flamingo, and we came down to France, played the guitar . . . he was pretty normal. It was Aix that started it. He became more and more . . . "obsessed" is the wrong word. More and more interested in the music. It went from a schoolboy thing, to something he did more and more.'

Brian Wells had been close to Nick at Cambridge, and kept in touch when they both moved down to London. Knowing how abrasive the music industry could be, Wells knew how it could impact on such a sensitive individual as Nick, but he also remembered him as withdrawn and reclusive, even during their university days together: 'It's difficult for somebody to say he wasn't depressed – any psychiatrist quite reasonably would have said this is a depression. But I think it was more to do with . . . you know how Howard Hughes just withdrew? I think it was more like that.

'I think he was always slightly sensitive, not aloof, but distant from it. I've been in pubs with Nick, and he would laugh and joke and things, but he would then go after a while . . . Whereas most people would hang on for another hour, he would get up and go. From the minute I met him, he would get up and go, because you got the impression that he thought it was uncool to stay there getting pissed, or whatever. It had to do with cool, and image, a lot of it.

'It's interesting, isn't it: Why wasn't he a well-integrated, well brought-up English public-schoolboy who went off to do the same as everybody else? But, you see, he was. He was, and it seemed to change once he got into the music business. And I think the music business is a great place if you've got some rough edges. I think the music business is a much easier place for working-class lads to be . . . I think you've got to be quite tough and almost ruthless to be successful in the music business.

'I think he got into this arena with a fine, chiselled talent. I mean his music is not . . . he was not getting up on-stage and playing loud

chords and boogying around or being sexy. He wasn't into rock 'n'
roll. He was sitting there, a kind of . . . timid figure, dressed in black,
playing beautiful weird-tuning-type acoustic guitar stuff . . . He was
never a rock 'n' roller.'

For those who only knew Nick after he arrived in London to make
a career as a musician, the decline was less striking, but nonetheless
still shocking. Because of his chosen career, many assumed that
Nick's problems could be put down to drugs. Only a 10/- cab ride
away from Nick in London at this time, Linda Thompson remains
convinced that his problems were not drug-related: 'I never saw him
do drugs. I saw him smoke dope, but I never saw him do anything
else. I suppose he did. But then you know, looking back on him now,
right from the start, there was something wrong

'If he did take a lot of drugs, he wasn't an overt drug user. Then as
time wore on, he was taking drugs for his depression. It was hard to tell.
Then he had his Howard Hughes phase, which was really scary, with the
long fingernails and the dirty clothes and stuff. At the time I certainly
felt, oh, that's disgusting – those long fingernails and the dirty clothes –
instead of thinking it might be nice to try and help this person.'

'I've known a lot of drug addicts . . . and I think he was ill. Clinical
depression. If he'd been in a rehab, if he'd had lithium or something,
maybe counselling, maybe something would have helped. But in those
days, vegetarian food and shrinks were still very much fringe things.
He must have found that hard, because he had to try and keep himself
together on his own.'

At Cambridge, a mere three years before, Nick was fastidious
about his nails because of his guitar-playing – Paul Wheeler laughed
when he remembered that Nick would never do the washing-up
because it might damage his nails. In London, by early 1972, Linda
Thompson noticed that Nick's nails had grown so long that it was
hard to imagine he would ever play the guitar again.

It was Nick's parents more than anyone who bore the brunt of
their son's depression. When he was back at home in Tanworth,
Rodney and Molly Drake were the only people he saw regularly, and
it was they who watched his tragic decline in his last three years.
Rodney: 'God knows where the depression came from . . . The
experts didn't seem to know much about it, because he did agree
to go and see some very eminent people . . . and they didn't seem to
know what was wrong with him. They gave him pills to take, one of
which, of course, was the cause of his death, and they did seem to help
him, these pills.'

Molly: 'Hampstead was the beginning . . . He took this room, all alone, and he decided to cut off from all his friends, and that he was just going to concentrate on music. He had a tremendous number of friends and at one stage he was very gregarious almost, and then he suddenly said this is no good, and he went off to Hampstead, which was where he started to get so depressed, and that was when we really started to get so terribly worried about him.'

Rodney: 'He was depressed about the world . . . I think he thought deeply about things, but he couldn't talk to us about it . . . He did feel that everything was going in the wrong direction . . . He always thought 1980 was going to be the time . . .'

His parents were sad, but not surprised that they could not communicate with their son. But even his contemporaries were unable to get through to him. Iain Dunn had lost touch with Nick after he left Cambridge early to record his debut album, but kept buying the records of the boy he remembered playing his songs in college rooms: 'You could tell in the music as well, as soon as *Pink Moon* came out, you thought, this is . . . desperate. Most of the intelligence I got back was from Paul [Wheeler], who was still seeing him quite a lot, and was desperately, desperately worried.

'I think an awful lot of people got their brains severely fried at that time, because most people didn't really know what they were taking. All they really knew was that it felt good. I remember after leaving college and getting my first flat, sharing with some guys who worked on the *NME* . . . I mean I was the only person there who knew what time of day it was . . . People matured a lot later in those days, even by the time you went up to university, you didn't really know what was going on in life. So you were coming to terms with all that; huge changes going on in society; this vast ingestion of all kinds of illegal substances . . . I don't think Nick was alone in having his brains done in by this . . . cocktail. I think there were a lot of people who were just as badly affected; unfortunately for him it was far more severe in terms of where it went.'

On 3 September 1971 John Lennon and Yoko Ono left Britain for New York. Lennon was never to return. For the last two years, the couple's home had been at Tittenhurst Park, a Georgian house on a sprawling seventy-two-acre estate near Ascot. Lennon's personal assistants there were Nick's friend from Cambridge, Paul Wheeler, and his then wife, Diana.

Tittenhurst Park played a substantial role in Lennon's last years in the UK. It was in the grounds there, on 22 August 1969, that the four Beatles gathered for what proved to be their final photo session. During early 1971 the Lennons had much of the ground floor gutted, and it was there, during the course of one week in July, in one enormous white room, that Lennon recorded his best-loved solo album, *Imagine*.

After the Lennons moved out, Ringo bought the house, and when he in turn moved out in the late eighties, Tittenhurst became a recording studio. Set amid landscaped gardens, the house was everything you would expect of the sixties rock-star aristocracy. From the master bedroom, you looked out over lawns which descended like an enormous green staircase to the sweep of cedars for which the property was famous before the Lennons' occupancy. Next to the window were a pair of switches for turning on the garden lights; rather touchingly, one was labelled 'John', the other 'Yoko'.

The Lennons' departure was connected with the long-running custody battle for Yoko's daughter Kyoko, and there was every reason to believe that they would return to live in verdant Royal Berkshire. While Paul and Diana Wheeler were in residence, Tittenhurst – like Charles Foster Kane's Xanadu – was kept in a state of permanent readiness in case the whim of the master and mistress dictated a swift return. It was during this time of limbo that Nick visited Paul Wheeler there.

Another Cambridge visitor to Tittenhurst was Brian Wells, who was still studying to be a doctor: 'We used to eat cannabis, I was getting this cannabis extract . . . and we'd put it into cookies and eat this stuff, and wander round the arboretum. There was all this Beatles memorabilia – the statues from the cover of *Sgt Pepper*, the Pepper uniforms and in John and Yoko's bedroom there was a wall of Rickenbacker guitars. I said: "Oh, there's John Lennon's Rickenbacker", and some guy said come and see this – and there's a whole *wall* of them!'

Paul Wheeler remembers Nick being impressed by Lennon's work even before he visited the house: 'I remember when he wrote "Cold Turkey" late in '69, Nick heard it and said what an amazing thing to do, to write about that . . . it's a really tough song. And I was quite surprised to hear Nick saying it was a really interesting thing to do, because I didn't associate Nick with that kind of pain.'

There is a striking incongruity in the image of Nick Drake stalking the corridors of Tittenhurst during 1971. From an early age Nick had been no stranger to home comforts, but surely even he would have

been impressed by the opulence on display. The long corridors
gleamed with gold records. The interior was so white that a casual
visitor might have imagined he had strayed into an asylum – even the
grand piano was white. No noise intruded. Here was the tranquillity
of Tanworth and the beguiling other-worldliness of Cambridge, but
on a scale which mere mortals could barely comprehend.

With record sales that scarcely registered, a career that hardly
merited the name, and a darkness which seemed set to fill his
horizons, Nick Drake wandered around the empty mansion of a
millionaire rock icon who would never return.

'John and Yoko had gone,' Paul Wheeler recalls, 'and Nick seemed
to fit in with the "ghost house" image of Tittenhurst, the empty
palace. It always stuck in my mind as an allegory of the times, this
abandoned estate . . . They hadn't definitely gone for ever, which is
why we were still there, they could have come back any day. When he
came to see us in Ascot, there were people he met there who were
fascinated by him, by his presence. "Who is this guy?" He had very,
very strong presence. There is this idea that he was just this
shimmering, ghost . . . No, no.'

Fashionable as it has become to seek out conspiracy theories to
explain Nick Drake's lack of success during his lifetime, at a distance
of twenty-five years you gain a perspective lacking at the time. By
1972, Island Records were enjoying their most successful year ever.
Island had been very much an album-based label in the late sixties,
but they had made the transition and were now making substantial
inroads into the pop charts, selling singles to teenagers.

Some may feel uncomfortable remembering just how popular Cat
Stevens was at his peak. Now, as Yusuf Islam, he is best known for
condoning the fatwa passed on British author Salman Rushdie in
1989; but during the early 1970s he released a series of compelling and
enormously popular albums which came to epitomize the sweeping
appeal of the introspective singer-songwriter.

David Betteridge remembers Island being bullish about their
chances in the American market at the beginning of the 1970s: 'In
the States, Traffic went out on United Artists; Free and Cat Stevens
went out on A&M, we were placing act by act, which is why Nick
finished up on Warners.'

Asylum Records founder David Geffen was known to be a fan of
Nick's work, and was keen to ensure Nick's product was available for
the American market. Geffen knew a thing or two about promising

singer-songwriters, having graduated from the post room of the William Morris Agency to manage Laura Nyro, Joni Mitchell, Jackson Browne and Crosby, Stills, Nash & Young. With Asylum, Geffen had championed Tom Waits, David Blue and Judee Sill. He thought Nick's records were 'fabulous . . . I thought Nick Drake should have been a star, and that I could help him.'

Only a compilation of the first two albums – imaginatively titled *Nick Drake* – was released in America during Nick's lifetime. The cover was the 'running man' shot from the back sleeve of *Five Leaves Left* and the album garnered a glowing review from Stephen Holden in *Rolling Stone* of 27 April 1972: 'British singer-songwriter Nick Drake's American debut album is a beautiful and decadent record. A triumph of eclecticism, it successfully brings together varied elements of the evolution of urban folk rock music during the past five years. An incredibly slick sound that is highly dependent on production values (credit Joe Boyd) to achieve its effects, its dreamlike quality calls up the very best of early Sixties' jazz-pop ballad. It combines this with the contemporary introspection of British folk rock to evoke a hypnotic spell of opiated languor . . .'

Holden went on to draw the inevitable Cat Stevens and *Astral Weeks* comparisons, picked out Nick's 'softly seductive' singing and his 'densely textured guitar' and suggested a 'head cocktail . . . in a pool of sweet liqueur after a couple of downs and a few tokes'. Asking if this could be 'the Muzak of 1984', Holden goes on to find similarities with the work of Donovan and Astrud Gilberto, before concluding: 'Drake's greatest weakness – one he shares with all too many of today's male lyric troubadors, especially those from England – is the lack of verbal force in his song lyrics, which by and large could be characterized as art nouveau. In the case of Drake, this is less serious a liability than it is for the artists who are more up front vocally. The beauty of Drake's voice is its own justification. May it become familiar to us all.'

Unfortunately, Nick's resistance to gigging even wrecked his chances of making it across the Atlantic, for as David Betteridge pointed out: 'Generally speaking, you've got to break it in your own territory before you can break an act overseas . . . and touring was the way to do that.'

So if Nick hadn't been so shy and hadn't so obviously hated live performance, the plan would have been to release his records in America, tied in with a prestige showcase gig around the time of release, at the Troubador in LA, or New York's Bottom Line, and then to land him some prestige support slot with, say, Carole King or James Taylor, where he could reach an audience sympathetic to his sort of music? 'Yes, precisely. That's exactly the way it worked. But not with Nick.'

Peter Buck thought back to being a teenager growing up in Athens, Georgia, and remembered just how little Nick was appreciated in America then: 'I don't think Nick's albums came out here in the States while he was alive, and if they did nobody reviewed them, but then journalists, particularly music journalists, are great ones for rewriting history. Everyone says: "Oh yeah, *Exile On Main Street* is THE Stones album", but you go back to the original reviews of 1972, and they're all "Well, Side Two doesn't rock", "It's kind of a muddy sound" . . . Go look for a review of the first Velvet Underground album, everyone thought they were these circus freaks from New York. At best they were irrelevant, at worst, a total con job, junkies, Andy Warhol's puppets. If today's journalists went back to 1968 and said: "We're from the future, we're going to tell you the names of the important artists – James Brown and The Velvet Underground" – they would all drop fucking dead.'

In his essay which accompanied the posthumous *Fruit Tree* box set, Arthur Lubow wrote of Nick Drake's American launch: 'When a compilation album was released in the US . . . the reception at the Troubador featured a cardboard cut out of Nick on stage as the record played. If he wouldn't tour, perhaps his reclusiveness could be commercial.'

The fifteen months which separated the release of Nick's second and third albums was the period of the most marked decline in his health and state of mind. Still living alone in Haverstock Hill, Nick was drawing further inward, curling up foetus-like in his own world, a world bordered by the four walls of his room.

Brian Wells: 'He never said: "I'm utterly pissed off and I wish I'd sold more records", you know – that wasn't cool. I think he was very aware of what was cool, and I think he found safety in actually appearing to be withdrawn. And I think he was quite uncomfortable around people. In Cambridge he wasn't one for sitting round and just shooting the shit. It would run out of steam, and then he would look nervous, and then say, right, I've got to go. And you knew that he wasn't going *to* anything. He just wanted to withdraw from the situation. That went on in Cambridge, and I think became more and more the norm for him. I think he would withdraw from situations, but still feel awkward having done so. And he'd go back to his room on Haverstock Hill and stare at the wall for ages . . . A guy called Rick Charkin went to Morocco with Nick before Cambridge, and he once said to me that he went round to see Nick in Haverstock Hill, rang the bell and no one answered, so he went round the back and there was Nick in his room staring at the wall, just not answering the front door . . .'

A record as bleak and initially intimidating as *Pink Moon* was never going to get radio play, aside from the odd spin on John Peel's late-night Radio 1 show; and with Nick refusing to perform live, the chances of anyone even being aware of the existence of the third album grew more and more remote.

Linda Thompson: 'I saw him around the time of *Pink Moon*, we were doing *Bright Lights* around that time. We were both in the same studio. Nick did those sessions very late at night, so he'd be going into the studio as we were coming out . . . I would grab him and tickle him, but he was . . . incommunicado.

'Sound Techniques itself was fairly big . . . You walked in, and you went up a very windy staircase, and then there was a big studio, a big ground-floor studio, the control room was set up, so that you could look down into the studio. Then you went up some more windy steps to the kitchen. It was a lovely studio, in two parts, a front part and a back part; mostly they used to do vocals in the back part. Nick liked that studio. He was always very close to John Wood. John had a sixth sense about what you wanted for the record.'

Trevor Dann was still at Cambridge when Nick's final album was released, and remembers how uneasily its sombre mood sat with the times: '*Pink Moon* I didn't care much for when it came out. I'd gone all Mahavishnu Orchestra, if I wanted to be cerebral, and Roxy Music if I wanted to dance, and *Pink Moon* was just so bleak. The other bloke of my acquaintance who was completely besotted by Nick Drake was another guy from my school, Dick Taylor, who was also at Cambridge, and we used to spend nights arguing which was his best record. Dick would always plump for *Pink Moon*, 'cos it was the darkest, the most in touch with the psyche. Dick was a fairly boisterous, rather upper-class bloke, the same age as me, and when he was thirty-eight he shot himself. I hadn't seen him for ten or fifteen years, I had no idea what had been going on, but almost my first thought about it was – Nick Drake! That Dick had been so obsessed by that really dark stuff.'

To their credit, Island had not given up all hope. Garrell Redfearn was a young assistant to Muff Winwood in radio promotion, who remembers being dispatched to Hampstead to try to interest their most retiring act into doing something, anything, to help awaken interest in his new album. The idea was to get Nick along to the BBC's Maida Vale studios – where he had gone in such high spirits barely two and a half years before – to record a session plugging *Pink Moon* on one of the nightly *Sounds Of The Seventies* programmes. One day during the early part of 1972 Garrell went along to Haverstock Hill. He was one of the last people from Island ever to see Nick Drake: 'By broadcasting a session, you could get more than one track played from an album, maybe three or four in one broadcast. As he was known to be very difficult about performing at that stage, and I can't quite remember why, maybe because we were about the same age . . . I was asked to see if I could chat to him and persuade him to do a session. I think it was a request from one of the producers to try and get him on.

'I went along to the big, old run-down house on Haverstock Hill, the bottom end, near to Chalk Farm Tube . . . I don't think he said an absolute no, but we never did get him into the studio again. I remember the flat being extremely grotty: tatty, filthy bits of fabric covering the windows as curtains, keeping the light out. All dark inside . . . There was a big, heavy, old Victorian sideboard. It was on the ground floor, as far as I remember. It wasn't a bedsit, because he'd got up and out of bed to let me in, and the bed wasn't in the room that we sat in.

'He sat in a chair with very long hair, head down, hair falling over his face so I couldn't even really see his face. A few mumbled responses. He wasn't being difficult or unpleasant, he really just had difficulty talking to anyone, just making that contact. I just explained the situation, how it would really help if we could get him to do a session because it would mean a lot more exposure for the album . . . He said something like "I don't think so at the moment, maybe in the future" type of thing.

'It was almost down to nods and shakes of the head, grunts. I remember saying to him: "Do you *want* the album to sell?" . . . It seemed illogical to me that you take all this trouble to record your music and you don't make any effort to try and help it get exposure, for people to hear it. But I think he may have got to a stage where . . . if it was important, it wasn't important enough for him to overcome whatever the inhibitions were that stopped him performing and promoting it.'

Alone and isolated, Nick rarely left his hideaway. He would

venture out occasionally, but otherwise he waited, and let the world come to him. And waited. And waited. With no involvement on Nick's third album, and his own career as an arranger burgeoning, Robert Kirby had seen less of his friend since the release of *Bryter Layter*. But he was quite used to Nick just turning up, a silent visitor: 'I think Nick regarded groups of people and places as bolt-holes. After I left Cambridge, I lived for a long time in Cranley Gardens in Muswell Hill. Nick lived on Haverstock Hill, and then towards the end – his very last place in London – was a very grim bedsit on Muswell Hill Road. It was only about 100 yards from where I lived. That was very grim . . .

'He would arrive at all hours, quite unannounced, totally unexpected. He'd stay for one day. One week . . . And then he'd be gone. Then you'd find out he had gone to John Wood's house, out in Mildenhall in Suffolk. He'd stay there. Then you'd find he'd gone home. Then you'd find he was staying somewhere near Brian [Wells] . . . and I'm sure there were other totally independent groups of friends that we didn't know anything about at all. I think he did compartmentalize them a bit. Maybe by the time he got bored with one group he'd move on.'

Molly Drake attributed Nick's decline to the solitary years spent living in and around Hampstead: 'He once said to me that everything started to go wrong from the Hampstead time on.'

'His parents were wholly supportive the whole of the time,' Robert Kirby recalled. 'I was never privy to the family at home, but the phone calls that I had from the dad were . . . "Have you seen Nick? Don't get him. Don't tell him I called, but is he all right?"

'I think underneath it all, Nick did have a hankering that maybe he should have got a proper job . . . He did try to please his father. But I didn't believe that his father pressured him. I remember when his father got him this job working in computers in London, and Nick disappeared, his father phoned quite distraught. "Have you seen him? Ask him to get in touch. Can you try and help?"

'I feel elements of guilt about not doing more . . . I was always very overawed by Nick. I always admired him, looked up to him, and so if he wasn't saying anything, I said to myself: "This is what a genius does." The first thought wasn't, oh, he's ill . . .'

A particularly painful glimpse of Nick Drake's decline was provided by Nick Kent. Probably best known as the chronicler of excess during those sybaritic seventies, Kent never met Nick, never saw him perform, but was captivated by the three albums. 'Requiem

For A Solitary Man', his *NME* piece about Nick, appeared in 1975 and some years later he got John Martyn to talk about their friendship: 'I met Martyn, and he was very emotional about the whole thing – you know he wrote that song "Solid Air" – and I tried to get him to sit down and talk on the tape about it, but he was very close to tears whenever the subject was brought up. It was an incredibly emotional thing for him, and so what he did was he said: "I'm going to take you to some friends of Nick's. I'm going to take you to a place in London. I'm going to introduce you to some friends of Nick Drake's who knew him up to the end, and you can make up your own mind there."

'He took me to this place in Ladbroke Grove, which was kind of a squat. It was not a particularly pleasant place to be in. And these people were mostly . . . they were all drug addicts . . . they weren't heroin addicts, but they had barbiturate problems. They were good people who'd had a bad time with drugs. They basically just told me this story: Nick would come round to their place a lot, and he would just sit there. He wasn't a drug addict. He wasn't a big druggie himself. But my understanding was that he had been involved to some degree with obviously smoking dope, and taking acid, not a lot . . . and these things had turned him. The whole thing had turned him.

'And what I remember is that there was a woman there who seemed to know him very well, and she spoke very, very affectionately about him . . . It's awfully, awfully sad. The thing that she said to me . . . I just started crying when she said it, because she said he came round to this flat three days before he died, and he said to these people: "You remember me. You remember me how I was. Tell me how I was. I used to have a brain. I used to be somebody. What happened to me? What happened to me?" '

14

Muddled and muffled by the anti-depressants as he now was, his career non-existent, and with little hope left for the future, it is hard to imagine what it must have taken to make Nick Drake return to the recording studio. At a time when it seemed to everyone who saw him that he was quite, quite lost, from somewhere deep within himself he found the impulse to write and record again.

In 1994 Joe Boyd cast his mind back twenty years and told me about his memories of Nick's final recording session: 'He came to see me when I was in London and he was in a terrible state. That's when he blurted out a kind of . . . a direct version of the lyrics of "Hanging On A Star", which were basically his bitterness and his anger about not having enough money and not having sold enough records, and everybody says he's so great, but if he's so great, why is he broke and unrecognized? He couldn't understand it, he felt very aggrieved about it. I was astonished, because he'd never expressed any anger to me about anything . . .

'I always had this objective overview of "Well, of course Nick doesn't sell records because he doesn't tour, because *Pink Moon* was so introspective." It's very easy for me to have that objectivity, because I'm working with a lot of different artists. But for Nick it was devastating. It was his whole life. I guess I wasn't quick enough to see that as a problem to be dealt with, until he brought it up.

'Then a few months later I spoke to John Wood, who said Nick had been in touch with him about recording some new songs, so I spoke to Nick and asked him if he wanted me to come along. John and I were

there for that last session, and Nick came in. It was chilling. It was really
scary. He was so . . . He was in such bad shape he couldn't sing and play
the guitar at the same time. We put down the guitar parts and
overdubbed the voice. It was all one day: we started in the afternoon
and finished about midnight – just for those four tracks.'

When these four final tracks appeared on *Time Of No Reply*, the
session date was given as February 1974. However, contemporary
evidence suggests that July is more probable, and this seems to fit in
with the chronology of Nick's last year. One factor which may have
encouraged him to pursue his thoughts of recording again was
Connor McKnight's *Zig Zag* feature of June 1974. One of the few
pieces on Nick to appear in his lifetime, it was a rare indication that
anyone outside his immediate family even knew who he was, and as
such it must have an impression on him.

Of the four songs Nick recorded in 1974, 'Rider On The Wheel' is
one of the most beguiling of his short career. Ironically, he sounds
relaxed and in control, as a rolling folk melody is delicately picked on
guitar. The slowly spinning essence of a dance is suggested by the
lyrics, as round and round it goes. 'Hanging On A Star' does indeed
express the anger and frustration Boyd remembers Nick expressing:
all the bitterness at the lack of recognition and poor record sales, the
abject sense of failure that he felt so keenly in his final years. All this a
bare five years after he had first begun recording. You can imagine a
drum pattern underpinning 'Voice From A Mountain', the final track
of the four; Nick's singing voice sounds strained, whereas before on
record he had always seemed in control. After this, there would to be
no more.

In 'Black Eyed Dog' there is the real sense of the hellhound close at
hand. The dog which was always one step behind Robert Johnson,
Nick too had heard howling. Dangerous and other-worldly, the song
is as chill and sparse as a midnight crossroads. He keens for home, but
seems to know he is beyond the point of rescue. Behind him snaps the
hellhound; ahead, the fearful unknown.

In ancient times a black dog was frequently a symbol of the Devil,
and by the early eighteenth century the term was being used to
describe depression. The image of death personified by a stalking
hound has been popular in rock 'n' roll since Robert Johnson
recorded the chilling 'Hellhound On My Trail', while 'Black Dog
Blues' was a familiar ragtime guitar tune from the early thirties. The
term was also, most famously, Winston Churchill's euphemism for
the depression which plagued him throughout his life.

Incongruous as it may seem, Churchill, hailed as one of the greatest Englishmen of the century – Nobel laureate, Prime Minister and Peer of the Realm – was prone to acute bouts of black depression, into which he plunged arbitrarily and from which he could find no escape. This darkness was such a familiar caller that Churchill named his bouts of depression 'black dog'. According to biographer William Manchester, Churchill could not bring himself to stand on the platform's edge as a train hurtled by, or to glance downwards from a ship at sea, because 'a second's action would end everything'.

I had always assumed that Nick's depression hadn't really taken hold until around the time of his bleak final album, *Pink Moon*. But talking to those who knew Nick during his early years in London, I found that the depression seems to have begun to afflict him quite early in his creative life. I was struck by how unhappy Nick had seemed, even around the time of *Bryter Layter*, widely perceived as his most 'up' record.

The corrosive depression was apparently something which ate away at him during most of his adult life. But that is not to say that Nick was never happy. To the frustration of those who have constructed an elaborate cathedral of misery around him, he was plainly happy during his four years at Marlborough. Cambridge and France were also places that seemed to bring him pleasure. Even the early days in London, buoyed by the prospect of a career making music, while barely out of his teens . . . All were places and times which brought Nick contentment and happiness. There were friendships and fun and a family apparently devoted to his well-being. There were occasions aplenty which brought a smile to the face of the young Nick Drake.

From this distance, Nick does appear, in his sister Gabrielle's words, to have been born with 'a skin too few', too sensitive for his own good, too acutely aware of his failings, too willing to find fault with himself. But these things alone are not enough to explain away the illness which drove him, literally, to despair.

'It was a very sad world . . .' Rodney Drake said. 'I think really he became – I don't know whether a "depressive" is the right word to use . . . He was certainly extremely depressed, in a way that the word "depressed" isn't sufficient to describe it really.'

Following his breakdown early in 1972, family and friends speak frequently of Nick's withdrawal during his final two years, of him being in a place where they could no longer reach him, of his isolation and inability to communicate. Their accounts of him simply sitting for hours at a stretch, silent and staring, have all the hallmarks of clinical depression.

Visible scars and physical suffering are not necessarily easier to handle than mental anguish, but they are easier to grasp. Terence Rattigan wrote: 'Do you know what "le vice anglais" – the English vice – really is? Not flagellation, not pederasty – whatever the French believe it to be. It's our refusal to admit our emotions. We think they demean us, I suppose.' Yet, strangely, Nick's parents do not seem to have been embarrassed by their son's illness. It would not have been surprising for people of their age and upbringing, in those days before mental imbalance was much discussed, to be lacking in understanding. But by all accounts, Molly and Rodney did their utmost to understand, sympathize and help with Nick's pain and suffering. His mother, particularly, agonized every step of the way with Nick during his last tragic years.

Depression is an illness to which adolescents are particularly prone. It strikes at the root of an existence which is already tremulous, a time when life is divided sharply into black and white; when shades of grey equate to old and lacking principle. It all goes back to Hamlet, the eternal adolescent, and the crucial question of that stage of life: whether to 'be' or not. Such stark choices appeal to the adolescent in us all. Suicide is rather flippantly described as a permanent solution to a temporary problem, but at an age when emotions are at their most exposed, temporary isn't a state you recognize. Pragmatism comes only with experience: 'this too will pass' is a discovery of middle age.

Today at least the symptoms are better recognized, the treatments more sensitive, less draconian. But when Nick Drake began suffering from the depression which would eventually kill him, there were few places where sensitive, introspective youngsters could gain help and sympathy. The majority of GPs were of an age to be unfamiliar, and in some cases, unsympathetic, to any problem which was not manifestly physical.

Tim Lott, who documented his obsession with suicide in *The Scent Of Dried Roses*, explained in an interview: 'The only way to preserve the person I was, was to die. Suicide is a way of avoiding change and Auden says we would rather be ruined than change. The act of will it required would be proof that I was still real; it would be an act of heroism, like going over the top at the Somme.' Lott's image drew me back to Nick. The Somme, where so many of his predecessors at Marlborough had perished; where the flower of a generation had withered on the barbed wire; where there was no elegant, eloquent choice, but rather courage to be found in the inflexible face of duty.

Back to duty. Back to letting nothing show. Back to class.

The only available recording of Nick Drake speaking comes on the various bootlegs which came out of the Tanworth bedroom recordings during 1967–68. The first surprise is that after years with only the records and a few photographs to beguile us, Nick Drake suddenly is given voice. The voice is as you would expect, but perhaps rather more so: polite, hesitant, clear-cut, well-enunciated, unassuming, upper-middle-class. Like many of his class and background and time, Nick has a tendency to sound like a not very confident member of the Royal Family ('one has one's reservations when one has quite enjoyed oneself . . .').

As he speaks into the tape recorder in his bedroom at Far Leys, after returning from a neighbour's party, Nick is clearly drunk. The surprise is, again, that there are no surprises, no insights. For all the world, Nick Drake sounds like any one of a thousand well-educated, softly spoken public-schoolboys. Coming home pissed, he imparts sozzled wisdom into the microphone. Whizzing around in the background is an intrusive pop record which sounds like it is spilling over from Radio 2 (the effect is rather like hearing *King Lear* cutting into the fade of 'I Am The Walrus').

The subject of his discourse is driving, late at night: 'I must have drunk rather a lot, or although it seemed so, at the time I felt myself quite sober, but when I leapt into the car to drive home, after my merry abandon, I found the task extremely difficult. And it was extremely fortunate that, um, there was nothing else on the road because looking back at it, I seem to remember I had a mental brainstorm, and I didn't realize at the time, and I think I drove the whole way home on the right-hand side of the road, which is something, of course, which comes from driving in France too much, which is what I've been doing recently, as you probably know, driving in France, you know. And in moments of stress, such as this journey home, one forgets so easily, the lies, the truth and the pain, and so I'm wavering from the point.'

The lies, the truth and the pain – profound philosophizing, signs, intimations of mortality? Sometimes a cigar is just a cigar. And this is just the sound of a squiffy teenager, playing around, waiting for his life to begin.

Talking to Len Brown in the *NME* about Nick's final four songs,

Joe Boyd pointed out: 'He's someone whose story really is in the songs. He could talk through his songs but he had a very great difficulty in talking to people. The songs in a way became less about other people and more about himself as time went on.'

His songs were the only way Nick knew to tell his story, and the final four are the most eloquent of all.

From then on, the tale would be told in other people's voices.

Robert Kirby was shocked at the swift decline: 'I remember him saying after *Pink Moon* that he'd got material for a new album. So maybe he was planning on something else . . . But I've always thought that things accelerated from that point. Up until then, there had always been something there that drove him on, and then it disappeared, and you can actually attribute the decline to the treatment. I do think he was writing. He might have been digging himself deeper into a hole with "Black Eyed Dog" and not coming out with other types of stuff.

'He upped sticks, and moved back to Tanworth. I only ever visited him there around the time of *Bryter Layter*. I did rather sadly lose touch at the end. I still saw him, probably each time he was in London, but not for any length of time. He wasn't talking. Sometimes he would actually stand in the corner, facing out on the room, but looking down. With hindsight, you think if only I'd said: "Come on, lad. Pull yourself together, let's go down the pub." At the time though, I thought, he's writing his next album, he's writing a brilliant song. It sounds so naive now . . .'

Like a thief in the night, Nick Drake just quietly disappeared. Anthea Joseph remembered her last meeting with the 'very beautiful young man' she had first encountered in the Witchseason offices in 1968: 'The last time I saw him was at Island, must have been '72 . . . It was a very hot August day . . . I got inside and there was this body sitting in a chair with a newspaper virtually glued to his face. And I thought, I know that mackintosh. Went up to him and slowly, he heard my voice, and he lowered the newspaper. "Hello Anth." I said: "Hello Nick, are you waiting?" He went: "Mm", and the newspaper went straight back up again and I thought, what's he doing here? Brenda Ralfini told me he just comes in, and he used to do that at Witchseason as well: for no particular reason, he would just come in and sit.

'And that was the last time I saw him. You couldn't even give him a hug, you know. He was totally non-tactile. Now most people don't have any trouble really saying: "It's lovely to see you." But with Nick you couldn't – again, the brick wall. And thinking about it, he probably did feel bereft when Joe went to America because Joe was an anchor – an anchor of sort of sanity, a man of infinite patience.

'You could see the difference. I mean . . . the difference between when he first came into Witchseason . . . and the young man I saw at Island. The deterioration was quite something. But he was still beautiful, he was incredibly thin, the skin was translucent.'

Simon Crocker, who had been in a number of Marlborough bands with Nick, was stunned when Nick turned up at his London home one day in 1974: 'In either April or May I got this phone call out of the blue. And it was Nick. He sounded very incoherent. But he said: "I'd like to meet." So I said: "Great! Fantastic!" But he sounded a bit shaky. Anyway he came round to meet me in Chelsea . . . I'm amazed he even found his way there. He turned up, and he was completely incoherent. It was the most awful thing, because I wanted to take him and look after him. He sat there, completely shaking . . . He couldn't put a sentence together.

'I really tried to say, Nick, is there anything I can do? It was just awful, awful, lonely . . . The last memory I had of him was of a completely different person. I didn't realize till later how bad things were. I said, look, if there's anything I can do. I'm involved in the music business, maybe we can do something together. And he said: "Oh yeah, that'd be great." And he went. And I never saw him again.'

BOOK III:
AFTER

15

The withdrawal of Nick Drake did not lead to the frenzied speculation in the rock press which attended Bob Dylan's absence during 1967, or John Lennon's house-husbandry between 1975 and 1980. Nick did not vanish so much as fade away. For the last years of his life he took refuge in the family home in the quiet Warwickshire village where he had lived as a toddler.

From the time he left London in early 1972 until his death in late 1974, Nick's most prolonged absence from Far Leys was during the breakdown he suffered shortly after returning home, when he spent five weeks in a nearby psychiatric hospital. Brian Wells visited him there and recalls: 'I know that he had at least one admission, I think it was just the one. I visited him in the hospital, and gave him this book about Bob Dylan by Anthony Scaduto . . . It was in Warwickshire, near his parents, because I went to his parents' place first, and they hadn't wanted to tell me he was in hospital, because Nick had asked them not to tell anyone. I rang Nick, and he said: "I'm not in a nut house, this isn't a nut house." I said: "No, OK. Can I come and see you?" He said: "Well, all right." I said: "I want to give you something, I've got this book I want to give you." When I got there, it was a regular psychiatric ward, and a regular Victorian loony bin, and he was fine. He'd been unforthcoming for some time before, and when I got there, it was more of the same really. I didn't talk to any of the staff or anything like that. I was just there as a supportive friend. I went back and talked to Molly and Rodney, I think I stayed the night with them, and then came back to London.'

After Nick returned to Far Leys from the hospital, his parents remained terribly worried by his visible decline, although they dared hope that the prescribed anti-depressants would keep him on a more even keel. To an extent, the Tryptizol did appear to put some balance back into Nick's life, but the side-effects produced a torpor and absent-mindedness which must have been hard to bear.

Molly Drake remembered one evening when Nick, having ex-pressed an interest in learning to play the violin, asked to borrow her car so that he could drive down to London and buy an instrument. The following morning Molly asked if he was still going to London to buy a violin, only to be met with a blank, uncomprehending stare. Nick had no recollection of the conversation. On another occasion Gabrielle was contacted by the police: Nick was marooned at a zebra crossing, unable, uncertain, and unwilling to cross the road. He had been standing there for an hour. In fact, she had already seen her brother in a similar state of detachment. She had not been frightened, and had spoken with some pride to Mick Brown about the time that Nick came to see her at the BBC canteen while she was rehearsing: 'He was this stony presence, not saying a word, and very quickly everybody else just left the table. It was a positive negative presence. It was almost impressive in a peculiar way.'

The final eighteen months of Nick Drake's life are characterized by slow and steady decline. His inability to communicate, and his tendency to withdraw completely in on himself, were a daily drain on his parents. Rodney and Molly felt themselves trapped in a waking nightmare, forced to witness the deterioration of their only son. Molly: 'I remember him striding up and down one morning saying: "I've failed in every single thing I've ever tried to do." It was the most terrible heart-rending cry, and I said: "Oh Nick, you haven't, you know you haven't." But it wasn't any good, and he had that feeling that he was a failure, and that he hadn't managed to achieve what he'd set out to do. And how much that was a contributory factor in his final depression and death I don't know. I really don't know. There are always so many questions unanswered, and of course it was a terrible time, because whatever you did, you always felt you were doing the wrong thing. You always had this awful feeling that you were somehow letting him down.'

Rodney: 'He used to go for a long time without talking to anybody, when he was very bad. He used to play a lot of music. He used to sit there, leaning back against that piano, with those two speakers on, and the record player on . . . Times when he was prepared to talk at all were few and far between, and when they happened, you had to be ready to try and help him as best you could.'

Molly: 'He was very, very bad when he wanted to talk, you knew he was. Sometimes he'd say: "Are you busy?" And, of course, whatever I was doing, I wasn't busy, and just let him talk, because you so longed to be able to do something to try and help him.'

It had all happened so swiftly. Less than three years after quitting Cambridge delighted with his new recording contract and full of optimism about his new career, Nick was back home, sleeping in his boyhood bedroom. A gaunt and silent figure who haunted Far Leys and then disappeared unexpectedly, driving long into the night. Even that solitary pleasure was reliant on his parents' good graces. Nick would frequently break down, or simply run out of petrol, and then he would phone home, waking his father, and ask to be collected.

Time and again Nick would take off in the family car, or later his own, and as the flat blackness wrapped around him, he would drive, and drive and drive. Yet there was rarely any purpose to the journeys. He was quite likely to simply turn around and make his way home again. If he did arrive anywhere, and stayed, it would usually be a wordless visit, the silence which shrouded him unsettling his friends. Then, after an hour, or a week, he would return to the car, again without speaking, and head off into the night.

Nick's fondness for driving is mentioned repeatedly by those who knew him. Did he perhaps find peace in the mechanics of driving, or was it simply a means of escape? Apart from music – and his schoolboy athletics – driving was pretty much the only hobby or passion anyone seems to have noticed in Nick, and it remained a love all his life. From teenage odysseys through France to solitary late-night venturings trying to escape the darkness, Nick welcomed the freedom which driving brought. Perhaps it was the solitude he liked, or the speed, which effectively blocked out reality; or simply being in control of something in his life.

'He was a very good driver, quite nippy,' Paul Wheeler recalls. 'It was like sprinting in the car. He wasn't reckless . . . He had a little white car I remember, I can't remember the model, but it wasn't at all flashy. He did like driving, and was not at all hesitant. He would say: "Let's go somewhere", like when we went out to the coast . . . When we were in Ascot, he wouldn't think twice about driving down from

Tanworth, and that must have been quite a long drive. I don't recall that he ever asked for more than the address, never asked how to get there, which is quite interesting. It goes against this "lost boy" image. He could find his way very well!'

Following James Dean's death in a car crash, *The Times* wrote of 'a lonely young man, haunted by insecurity, longing for affection, yet thrusting it away from him, gifted yet suspecting his gifts, ambitious yet preferring to live like a tramp, in love, like T.E. Lawrence, with speed, and hugging a surly manner around him like a protecting cloak'. There are echoes of Nick Drake in that appraisal, as there are in the life of T.E. Lawrence. During his life as a gentleman ranker in the aftermath of his desert triumphs in the First World War, Lawrence of Arabia loved what he called the 'voluntary danger' of driving fast along country roads. For Lawrence, there was a certainty in speed, a pleasure in the isolation of hurtling along, in control of his vehicle and lost in the momentum. In 1935 Lawrence was killed by that momentum, when his motorbike swerved to avoid two young cyclists, and he was hurled over the handlebars to his death.

Paul Wheeler: 'That sense of just going off. Of feeling abandoned. He certainly did that more and more towards the end of his life. I know that his parents talked about him setting off from home, going somewhere, and ringing up and saying bring me back.'

Brian Wells was married and living in Eastbourne at the time, and became used to his old friend ringing and announcing he would be driving down from Tanworth: 'Nick would come quite late at night, and he'd run out of petrol two miles up the road. He resented going to garages and putting petrol in the car . . . so I went off and helped him fill up the car with petrol. And we all went to bed, and by the time we got up in the morning, he'd gone. That sort of stuff happened a lot.'

Nick's ambivalent attitude to his friends extended also to the form of transport he relied on so much. Brian Wells explained that when he wasn't using his parents' car: 'Nick drove clapped-out cars. The last one he had was quite pokey but he blew it up, he just ran out of oil. I'm sure he did it deliberately . . . Impulsive: "Fuck it, I'm just going to keep driving it. I'm not going to put any oil in it" – almost out of frustration, bloody-mindedness. And from time to time this would appear, this kind of frustratedness. It was almost an arrogance, because he would wait for twenty-four hours, sleep on somebody's floor, then ring up Rodney, and Rodney would bail him out. To some extent it was taking advantage of his parents.

'It was slightly irritating . . . because we were all driving clapped-out Mini vans and things, and there was Nick . . . just not taking any responsibility, knowing he was quite capable of doing so, and then when asked: "Why didn't you put any oil in?", "Oh, I just couldn't get it together." It was almost as though it was kind of rather cool: "Oh, I'm just so untogether, man, I just couldn't get it together to put any oil in." That it was far too mundane a thing.'

Rodney: 'He had his own car, and he'd then make a decision to go away somewhere, and he'd get into his car and drive off, sometimes he'd get about two or three miles, and come back. Sometimes you didn't know where he'd gone. He used to travel tremendous distances. It used to be a sort of therapy to him to be able to drive. He used to set off with the idea of going up to London to see some friends, sometimes he'd get to London. Sometimes, we heard subsequently, there was a girl he knew very well, and he'd just walk into her flat and sit there, and she knew and was accustomed to him. And he'd get up and walk out without saying anything and drive home again. Other times he'd drive out, and run out of petrol, and couldn't bring himself to go and get some more. And then he'd ring us up, and we'd set off, all over the country . . .'

Out of the blue, Nick would turn up on the doorsteps of friends. John and Beverley Martyn were used to seeing him in Hastings. He was a familiar visitor at the Suffolk home of John Wood, Sound Techniques' owner, and his wife Sheila, who had a special bond with Nick ('she was his confidante' Robert Kirby told me). Talking to Patrick Kampert for the *Chicago Tribune*, Wood remembered: 'He would suddenly turn up for a few days. Sometimes he wouldn't say anything. He was very self-contained. He could sit and say nothing for hours. It was unnerving.'

Friends like Brian Wells and his wife were never surprised when Nick just appeared, but it could be a terrible shock for those who were unaware of his harrowing decline. Richard Charkin, who had spent an incident-packed month in Morocco with Nick in early 1967, and remembered him fondly from his time at Cambridge, told me: 'After Cambridge, I'd moved down to London, and we'd lost touch, but one day I bumped into him in the street in South Kensington. He was looking pretty bad, and it was the week before he died. I felt terribly guilty because I said I'd get in touch . . . But when he came to London he was less . . . friendly. In Cambridge, he used to come round and see me as often as I would go round and see him . . . in London that was not the case.'

*

It was not all darkness, even during those last months. Brian Wells recalls, during a day spent with Nick in his bedroom at Far Leys, picking up a guitar and starting to play. Recognizing the riff, Nick took up his saxophone, and for a while the two jammed away on Henry Mancini's familiar, throbbing 'Peter Gunn' theme.

'I think he was a sensitive guy,' Brian says. 'After he'd been in the psychiatric hospital . . . I was talking about *Bryter Layter*, and getting him to play it, and talking about tracks on it, because he would show me tunings. This is when he had gone back to Tanworth . . . and I would go up there just to hang out and have a laugh. And then we'd play tracks off *Pink Moon*, and I remember saying, God, if I'd made that record and it hadn't sold, I'd have been very pissed off. And he said: "Well, now you know what's going on with me." He actually said that. Which was rare for him, because normally he was very unforthcoming.'

For Nick's mother, the only hope came when he felt able to communicate, and tried to share his feelings. Towards the end of 1974 Molly took it as a hopeful sign when Nick asked to borrow her Linguaphone records, to brush up his conversational French. She was even more delighted when Nick felt confident enough to plan a visit to Paris.

For years rumours have persisted that the one relationship Nick had enjoyed during his life was with the *chanteuse* Françoise Hardy. Speaking about Nick for the first time, Françoise denied the stories: 'I was more attracted by Nick as an artist than as a man; even though he was that explosive mixture, which usually seduces me totally, of purity, innocence, beauty – as much exterior as interior – and of a fascination for death. Maybe my subconscious self understood that Nick's instinct for death was too strong, both for himself, and in regard to me and what I could have done to combat it.'

Like most British teenagers, Nick would have become aware of Françoise Hardy when her song, 'All Over The World' became a British hit in March 1965. The twenty-one-year-old Hardy personi-fied all that was alluring and enticing and Gallic. Wistful and with her long, willow hair framing her face, Françoise captivated Beatles, Stones and Bob Dylan (who name-checked her on the sleeve of his fourth album) with her undeniably French appeal.

Robert Kirby: 'He was exactly the same age as me, and I was madly in love with Françoise Hardy . . . She was beautiful, and I'm sure that's where it started. Nick hadn't got a voice, but he used his voice perfectly on his own stuff. Françoise Hardy also hadn't got a voice.

The French also come from a culture where they declaim the words, rather than have to have much of a melody. It's the lyrics that carry the song. French *chanson* culture has always been totally different to German, English, American, Italian in that it's the words that matter. They don't write strong melodies.

'It is the concept, the atmosphere of the whole. It is not based on a catchy tune. The French would latch on to "La Vie En Rose", it doesn't really matter what the tune is . . . you use music to deliver a lyric. I think that attracted Nick as well, because in fact his vocal melodies aren't that strong: if somebody asked you to sing a Nick Drake song, it's very hard to do. I think that made him think perhaps Françoise Hardy could do his stuff well: to deliver, to declaim atmospherically, a lyric.'

Françoise Hardy's first hit, 'Tous Les Garçons Et Les Filles', came in 1962, when she was only eighteen. By 1968 she was moving away from the image of the bruised and vulnerable *chanteuse*, recording songs by Serge Gainsbourg and Leonard Cohen. Joe Boyd: 'I went with Nick to visit Françoise Hardy, who was interested in recording some of his songs. We went and had tea with Françoise. That began because there was a guy called Tony Cox, who was a producer who worked at Sound Techniques, and he played Nick's songs to her, because the album was her attempt to break the English market. She loved them, thought they were wonderful. He put me in touch with her, and I arranged to go visit her with Nick, and we went to Paris together. It was while we were making *Bryter Layter*, I think, May or June of 1970. We climbed to her beautiful flat, at the top of one of those old buildings on the Ile St Louis. We had tea. Nick said not a word the entire time. There was an agreement he would send her more songs; we might have sent her a tape of the rough mixes of *Bryter Layter*, so there was a follow-up, but nothing ever happened.'

Françoise Hardy: 'I no longer remember how I discovered Nick Drake's songs. Maybe I bought his first record at the sight of the sleeve. Whatever it was, I loved it straight away . . . For me, he didn't belong to a particularly British tradition: his style was quite different from that of The Beatles, The Stones and other groups that I was listening to a lot around this time. It is the soul which emerges from his songs, and that touched me deeply. The soul of romantic melodies, poetic but at the same time refined . . . as well as the very individual timbre of his voice, which adds to the melancholy feel of the whole thing.

'I loved all the songs – the early ones as much as the later – but it never occurred to me to record any of them because my vocal and rhythmic limits, as well as my whole personality, make me prefer to sing more simple songs, a bit more "subtle" than Nick's. I don't remember the dates of our meetings, I remember more the circumstances. Every time I get enthusiastic about singers who are, as yet, little known, I talk about them to everyone, including the journalists who interview me. So Nick knew from the press that I appreciated his work. So he came to see me at the studio where I was recording in London. He also came to Paris and I remember we went out to dinner with my best friend at the time, a Brazilian woman called Lena, to the Eiffel Tower restaurant. We were going there to watch a singer – I don't remember which one any more – and as Nick arrived unannounced, we took him with us.'

On his way to stay at Chris Blackwell's villa in Algeciras in 1972, Nick stopped off in his favourite city, planning to visit Françoise. Joe Boyd: 'There was a legend, which I never heard from Nick, that he went to Paris subsequently, in '72 or '73, when he was on his way to Chris Blackwell's house in Spain, and he rang her doorbell, and a secretary or maid came to the door, and he stammered and didn't say anything, left a message, but never came back.'

Françoise Hardy recalled: 'Nick seemed, and no doubt was, so shy, so wrapped up in himself, that in retrospect I'm astonished that he managed to come and see me two or three times, even knowing that I appreciated his enormous talent . . . When he arrived at the studio he would hide in the corner and not say a word. As I am also quite shy, particularly with artists I admire, and because I speak English badly, communication between us was never great. But I had the impression that to know he was appreciated, loved, gave him confidence; and that to feel that his silent presence was accepted, was enough for him.'

In the autumn of 1974 Nick Drake again found a degree of contentment in Paris. His life over the preceding two years had taken on the aspect of a dark, spreading stain. But back on the boulevards he had first visited as a teenager a decade before, Nick was by all accounts relaxed and convivial. The shadows which had engulfed him, seemed to be clearing; and strolling by the banks of the Seine in the mellow early autumn sunshine, he seemed to be revitalized.

True to the bohemian aura of Paris and the romantic image he once had of himself, Nick stayed with some English friends who owned a barge on the Seine near Notre Dame. Leaves lined the streets, thin October sunshine lightened the skies, and in the evenings a slight chill in the air made the sanctuary of the pavement cafés even more enticing. It is a brief period of Nick's life of which nothing more is known, though much has been speculated. It would be nice to believe that during that short stay, he found a degree of happiness, or at least a lightening of his heavy burden.

Françoise Hardy has a vague memory of a dinner with Nick on that visit. Her recollection is darker: she remembers a dinner when Nick sat opposite her in total silence. She did not recall him uttering a single word throughout the entire meal. Despite his grasp of conversational French, during his last visit to Paris Nick had little to say for himself.

Any sunshine he found during that final stay in Paris was all too fleeting. On his return to England, Nick went home to Tanworth, where he would live out the few remaining weeks of his life.

16

Far Leys was a large house but Nick's bedroom was tiny, a simple room, with a small, circular window in one corner. He slept in a single bed, next to which stood a plain wooden chair with a cane seat. Near to the bed, just the other side of the window, was an old, wooden desk over which hung a still life of flowers in a vase.

To the right of the door was an alcove with a built-in bookcase; among its contents were volumes of verse by Browning and Blake, commentaries on the work of Chaucer, Buddhist scriptures, novels by D.H. Lawrence, a copy of that key existential text, *Hamlet*, and the Scaduto biography of Dylan which Brian Wells had given him.

In 1974 Dylan was briefly signed to Island, so for a short while during the last year of his life, Nick was a labelmate of the man who had so inspired him. Dylan was well represented in Nick's record collection, with the sepia-covered *Blonde On Blonde* evident, as well as Tim Hardin's *Bird On A Wire*, Leonard Cohen's first album, Joni Mitchell's *Blue*, Mike Oldfield's *Tubular Bells*, Judy Collins's *In My Life*, Randy Newman's much-loved eponymous debut, Ralph McTell's *You Well-Meaning Brought Me Here* and Island's compilation album *Bumpers*, featuring Nick's own 'Hazey Jane I'.

An album of Bach's Brandenburg Concertos, bought in Aix seven years earlier, was lying on Nick's turntable when he died – presumably the last record he ever listened to. Next to his bed Molly found a copy, in the original French, of Albert Camus' *Le Mythe de Sisyphe*. Camus was fascinated by the myth of Sisyphus, the father of Ulysses, whose punishment in the afterlife of Hades, was to roll a huge stone up to the top of a hill; but as the stone always started to roll down again just as it reached the summit, his task was never completed. Molly kept the book she had found by her son's bed, and in the wake of his death struggled to read it in the hope that Nick: 'might have been trying to tell me something'.

Nick went to bed early on the night of 24 November 1974, and never came back.

The world he left behind knew little of him any more. His name was never seen in the music press now. It had been two years since his last album, *Pink Moon*, and there were other names to be covered. New acts, who went out and gigged, who were seen by their fans and didn't sit at their parents' home staring out of the window.

The twenty-fourth was a Sunday, the day of rest. It seemed for ever autumn, for around Tanworth the lightly rising Warwickshire hills kept the worst of the wind at bay. Over to the east, the countryside around Cambridge was flat and exposed; the wind whipping off the North Sea came all the way from Russia, the Fenland residents boasted. Tanworth was spared the worst excesses of the English winter, but with less than a month to go until the shortest day, the days were already dark. That November Sunday the sun rose at 7.46 in the morning and had set by 4.04 in the glowering afternoon. It didn't leave much opportunity for daylight to shine through. The *Birmingham Post*'s weather forecast for that day was: 'cloudy with rain. Some bright intervals'. In meteorological terms, brighter later . . .

Sunday in England was always a dull day. A vague feeling of tasks left undone or a reluctant return to work the next day, the paucity of diversion, everything closed: a typical English Sunday in the late November of 1974. Radio 1 had been up and running for seven years, but was still forced to split its programming with Radio 2. That day on 'the nation's favourite pop station' Between 5 and 6p.m., it was *My Top 12* with Uri Geller. Manfred Mann's Earth Band were in concert in *Sounds On Sunday*, then between 7.30 and 10 it was 'as Radio 2', before Radio 1 returned to close with two hours of jazz.

The Drakes' local commercial channel, ATV, broadcasting from Birmingham, began its mid-evening programming with the lachrymose *Stars On Sunday* at 7p.m. (Joseph Cotten and Moira Anderson were the special guests). There was a film, *The Professionals*, at 8.20, and at 10.45 jazzman turned critic Benny Green hosted *Cinema*, reviewing the week's big film, an all-star version of Agatha Christie's

Murder On The Orient Express. A rerun of *Marcus Welby MD* ended ATV's evening schedule.

BBC1 was dominated by nearly three hours of *The Royal Variety Show*, boasting the timeless talents of Perry Como, Roy Castle and Paper Lace. There was an *Omnibus* profile of the author Jean Rhys at 10.10p.m., followed by Christopher Chataway talking to the head of British Steel. Closedown came at 11.35. BBC2 began its evening with the natural history series *The World About Us*, followed by a screening of the film *The Asphalt Jungle*. Broadcasting ended at 12.15, with a reading of Dylan Thomas's poem 'Fern Hill': 'Oh as I was young and easy in the mercy of his means, Time held me green and dying, Though I sang in my chains like the sea' . . .

'He went up to bed rather early,' Molly Drake remembered in a 1979 interview for Dutch radio. 'I remember him standing at that door, and I said to him: "Are you off to bed, Nick?" I can just see him now, because that's the last time I ever saw him alive.'

No one will ever know what thoughts went through Nick Drake's mind in the long and solitary, dark hours before dawn. Both Rodney and Molly said that they would not have been surprised had Nick committed suicide some months before, but in recent weeks he had seemed happier. More than anyone else, his parents observed the ebbs and flows of his life.

The world spun on. National and local news continued to be dominated by the killing of seventeen people by IRA bombs which had destroyed two pubs in the centre of Birmingham the previous Sunday. The Prime Minister of the recently elected Labour government was Harold Wilson. The police were 'anxious to interview' Lord Lucan about the murder of his nanny. Helen Morgan, who was briefly 1974's Miss World, was forced to stand down when it was discovered that she was an unmarried mother.

Conservative middle England opened their copies of the *Daily Telegraph* at breakfast on 25 November 1974 and noted that there was 'Support for Mrs Thatcher as leader'; MP John Stonehouse was still missing; following the Birmingham bombings, Home Secretary Roy Jenkins had banned the IRA; Cornelius Ryan, author of *The Longest Day*, had died; and in Cambridge students had thwarted 'left-wing manipulators', with student leaders calling it 'a vote of confidence for moderation'.

'He didn't often get up early – he sometimes had very bad nights,' Molly Drake remembered, 'and I never used to disturb him at all. But it was about 12 o'clock, and I went in, because really it seemed it was time he got up, and he was lying across the bed. The first thing I saw was his long, long legs . . .'

Nick was prone to sleepless nights, frequently prowling the house in the small hours. His mother, alert to his movements, would often get up and sit with him in the kitchen until he returned to bed. But that night, when Nick woke and went down to the kitchen, Molly slept on. He had a bowl of cornflakes, then returned to his room. Sometime before dawn on the morning of Monday 25 November 1974 – probably around 6a.m. – the extra Tryptizol he had taken that night caused Nick Drake's heart to stop beating.

An announcement in the *Birmingham Post* on 28 November read: 'DRAKE – On November 25 Nicholas Rodney (Nick) aged 26 years, beloved son of Rodney & Molly, dearest brother of Gabrielle. Funeral service Tanworth-in-Arden Church on Monday December 2 at 12.15 p.m. No flowers please.'

The funeral took place at the church Nick had known all his life. Canon E. Willmott, who himself lies buried in St Mary Magdalene's graveyard, conducted the service, and afterwards the body was taken seven miles to Solihull Crematorium, where the mortal remains of Nicholas Rodney Drake were consumed by fire.

Rodney: 'Of course we thought the fact that he couldn't communicate with us was possibly something to do with the generation gap and all that . . . his world and our world, which he used to talk about occasionally. But when the sad day of his funeral came, a lot of his young friends came up here, we'd never met many of them. They were wonderful people, and they all said to a man really, in effect, that it really wasn't anything to do with you – we were just the same, we could never get through to him either.'

Molly: 'They said he just went away into a world where none of us could reach him.'

Rodney: 'There was a very close friend called Brian Wells . . .'

Molly: 'I think he was closer to Nick than almost anybody, but he couldn't really get through to Nick'.

Brian Wells: 'I missed the actual funeral. We got to Tanworth just as everyone was coming out of the church. There was Gabrielle in the doorway of the church as everyone was leaving. So we followed everyone else to the crematorium . . . and then went back to Far Leys afterwards, where there were all these different people, from Marlborough or wherever. The only one I knew was Robert Kirby . . . Rodney gave me Nick's guitar at that post-funeral thing. There were about fifty people there, none of whom seemed to know each other.'

Nick's funeral was the first, and final, occasion when all the diverse strands of his life were drawn together. Gathered at Tanworth that December day were friends from school, university and the music industry, all gathered to remember the boy who had barely had time to become a man.

Anthea Joseph stayed away: 'I didn't go to the funeral, but Joe went. I'd had enough of funerals by that point. I just felt that Nick had had enough of this life, which was not getting any better. Again, maybe if, if, if . . . some shrink had got hold of him, sorted him out, but it was physical as well as mental. You know, he was let free.'

17

Rodney Drake had been sufficiently worried about Nick to write to his friend and erstwhile family doctor before Nick's death, asking for advice. On the first day of the new year, barely five weeks after his son had died, Rodney Drake wrote another letter to my uncle, James Lusk, thanking him for his opinion and breaking the sad news of Nick's death.

Written in fountain pen on Far Leys headed paper, Rodney's letter is dated 1 January 1974, although he wrote it on New Year's Day 1975 a common enough mistake to make with your first letter of the year. The first part of the letter reads:

My dear Lusko,
Thank you so very much for your most interesting letter and for the time and trouble you took to give us such a helpful opinion about Nick.

I am very sorry to say that we have lost poor Nick. On the morning of November 25th Molly went in to his room to wake him as it was nearly midday and found him collapsed across his bed and the doctor when he came said he must have been dead for six hours or more.

The cause of death was given as an over dose of tryptizol which was one of the three things he was taking on prescription the other two being stelazine and disipal. You can imagine what a stark and numbing tragedy this has been for us both and of course a dreadful shock for Molly finding him. What made it even worse was that he had seemed so much better during the previous two months; he had been staying with some very kind and understanding friends in Paris where he had seemed to be happy for the first time in three years and after he came back he had been talking about getting back to his music. He had seemed quite all right the night before when he went to bed fairly early but the next morning there were signs that he had had a bad night (as he sometimes did) because he had obviously been down to the kitchen some time and had some cornflakes. More often than not when this sort of thing happened Molly used to wake up and go down to talk to him but alas on this occasion neither of us woke. However we didn't think anything of it at first and left him to sleep late. It must have been done on impulse in the early hours of the morning and, as I said, he was lying right across the bed on top of the bedclothes.

There had been a time a year ago or more when we had feared that something of this sort might happen (when he was really badly depressed) and anyway we always kept sleeping pills and aspirins locked up. I'm afraid we had not realised that tryptizol was dangerous and we're not sure that Nick did either but he certainly did take a heavy dose according to the pathologist.

So now we're trying to come to terms with what's happened and of course it is some comfort to know that all the suffering we've watched Nick go through over the past three years is now over for him and perhaps it is really the best thing for *him*.

We have had some remarkable tributes about his music from various quarters. There was a very long article in a magazine about three months ago and his name was mentioned in an article in a recent issue of the *Listener* and this three years after he has produced anything. He told me once that music was running through his head all the time and I think that recently the fact that he could no longer produce it was one of the main causes of his unhappiness.

I'm afraid I have written rather a lot to you on this sad subject but I was encouraged to do so by your very sympathetic response to my last letter and it is nice to unburden oneself to an old friend particularly when he happens to have been one's family doctor as well!

The letter continues for several pages, with news of Gabrielle and other family members as well as 'the ex Burma brigade', and poignant details of Rodney and Molly's saddest Christmas, spent with friends 'the first Christmas we have been away for many years'. Finally, after offering warm congratulations on the birth of a third Lusk grandson, it concludes:

'Molly and I send our love to you both and thanks again so much for all you wrote about Nick.

'Ever, Rodney'.

An inquest into Nick's death was held on 18 December 1974, after which H. Stephen Tibbits, Coroner for the Southern District of Warwickshire, recorded a verdict of suicide, with the cause of death given as 'acute Amitriptyline poisoning self administered when suffering from a depressive illness'. Unable to obtain a certificate of his son's death until after the Coroner's inquest, it fell to Rodney to officially register, on Christmas Eve 1974, the death of 'Nicholas Rodney Drake, Musician'.

The verdict of suicide was challenged by Nick Kent in his piece for the *NME* which appeared in February 1975; and has subsequently been vehemently disputed by many people. Gabrielle Drake, however, is less certain; talking to Kris Kirk in *Melody Maker* in 1987, she explained: 'I personally prefer to think Nick committed suicide, in the sense that I'd rather he died because he wanted to end it than it to be the result of a tragic mistake. That would seem to me to be terrible: for it to be a plea for help that nobody hears.'

No one will ever know what sad, solitary thoughts preoccupied Nick during his final hours on earth, or what misery and corrosive unhappiness he took with him to the grave. Even the facts of the matter remain stubbornly elusive; the number of Tryptizol he took that night has been variously estimated as anything from three to thirty tablets, neither figure apparently based on any hard evidence – though the tone of Rodney's letter would suggest that a fairly large dose was taken. Curiously, Coroners' reports are not a matter of public record, and the relevant document may not even have been kept this long.

It is easy to get caught up in attempting to understand what went through Nick's mind that night, trying to guess whether it was a bleary, befuddled accident; a rash impulse with little thought for the consequences or the future; or a deliberate, calculated decision to gain control over something which he perceived as spinning, slowly and pointlessly, out of control. The absence of a suicide note only poses more questions. But Nick's Cambridge contemporary Brian Wells, now a consultant psychiatrist specializing in substance misuse and addictive illnesses, makes a very powerful case for focusing purely on the intent, when trying to decide whether the overdose was deliberately suicidal: 'Personally, I don't think he had the kind of depressive illness that should have been treated with anti-depressants; and secondly, I don't think Nick would have . . . you don't commit suicide . . . I think this was an impulsive episode, one night, frustrated, probably didn't sleep very well, took a few, took a few more, thought, fuck it, took a few more.

'Tryptizol is an anti-depressant, but it's a sedative as well, and I think he was taking it to help him sleep . . . If he wanted to kill himself . . . I don't think he would have done it at home. I think he would have buggered off somewhere. I think if he had wanted to kill himself, he would have driven somewhere and put a hose into his car. Or he would have rung me up and said: "What could I take?" He wouldn't have taken an overdose of Tryptizol, which he had no way of knowing was potentially fatal, at home, one night. This wasn't a premeditated suicide, this was an impulsive guy, can't get to sleep . . .

'I can see it: "Oh, who gives a bugger if I don't wake up?" kind of thing. You're a bit stoned, a bit what the hell. That's not somebody with suicidal intent. And a coroner should only diagnose suicide in somebody who's had suicidal *intent* . . . I intend to kill myself: that's suicide. Somebody who accidentally takes an overdose of pills, that's not suicide. You diagnose murder and suicide by the degree of intent, and I really dispute that there was intent there.'

I spoke to journalist Nick Kent, who was one of the first to dispute the suicide verdict but was also intrigued by the drug connection in Nick Drake's life. In the seventies Kent was as much of a star as the people he was writing about. No stranger to the dual addictions of rock 'n' roll and drugs, to get close to the fire Kent zonked out with Keith Richards and Jimmy Page. He danced with the Devil, with a short spoon. For all his dark stuff, Kent had a conduit to the lost and the wasted, the withdrawn and the mislaid. Like Syd Barrett and Brian Wilson. And Nick Drake. 'I've taken Tryptizol,' he said. 'I've taken them once, and they are horrible, horrible drugs, almost overdosed on them, a doctor gave them to me when I was trying to get off heroin once, and I took two and they almost turned me into a zombie for about seventy-two hours, just two of these things. They were supposed to calm you out . . . but they turned you into a brain-dead zombie. Just taking one or two could do that to you . . .'

That Nick Drake died so young is a terrible tragedy; not just because of who he was, but because of what he might have become. The potential of all those years left unlived. But what made the waste even more unbearable for those left behind was the shaft of hope which came immediately before his death, a brief, shining moment of buoyancy which had hinted at a return of the old Nick. In the end, of course, only Nick really knew what happened that night, and that knowledge died with him.

The death of Nick Drake made little impact on the world outside Tanworth-in-Arden. Friends from Marlborough and Cambridge had scattered, and many were not aware for months that he had died. But few were truly surprised when they heard; most had chill memories of the last time they had seen him, transformed from the shy, smiling friend to a hunched, withdrawn spectre with whom they could no longer communicate.

Nick's old colleague from Marlborough's C1 House, Arthur Packard, told me: 'My memories of Nick were very happy, but when I learned his life ended in tragedy I won't say I fell off my chair in surprise. Nick was always . . . you felt there was a very reflective, pensive mode to his psyche. While he joined in the fun and the laughter, he was always a little apart from the crowd.'

Paul Wheeler: 'I don't remember the last time I saw Nick, because you don't think, this is the last time I'm going to see Nick . . . But 1974, when Nick died, was, I thought, a crashing point for loads of people. That was like the end of the dream. I have a personal thing, that my son was born on the day that Nick died. He was called Benjamin Nicholas Wheeler, after Nick . . .'

Iain Cameron, who, like Paul Wheeler, had known Nick at Cambridge, also recalled the anticlimactic air of the 1970s: 'I get *Pink Moon*, and he dies, and I try to make sense of that to myself. And what I see at that time is . . . like everyone's having trouble, a lot of people who were at Cambridge at the time . . . It was more like a cultural trajectory, so you have the optimism, the floweriness of the late sixties, and then people are trying to make it work, and can't really get it to hang together. It all got very grimy in the mid-seventies. We were a gilded, protected generation. Just look at Cambridge: you've got this wonderful built environment, loads of intelligent and articulate people all wafting around. No wonder people managed to write quite well in that environment.'

David Wright, who had taught Nick his first chords on the guitar at Marlborough, and with whom Nick had planned to journey round the world, recalled the last time he had seen Nick: 'That time at the Roundhouse, he was stoned, he wasn't quite with us. I remember thinking at the time, the image which has never actually left me . . . I remember not being terribly surprised when my father told me that he had died. I remember thinking, oh Christ, the music business has got him . . .'

Linda Thompson was another who was not surprised when the news of Nick's death was broken to her: 'The last time I saw him he was looking really awful. Those incredibly long fingernails. He couldn't possibly play the guitar, which was maybe why he did it. He couldn't have played at all. He was filthy, like a hobo really. I wasn't surprised when Nick died . . . He looked at death's door for a long, long time. I don't know how you can live through life not speaking to anybody. It was really a downward spiral . . . It was very sad, there was obviously this extraordinary talent, but also this inability to deal with life.'

The industry which had offered Nick Drake something resembling a career was even less surprised. High-profile rock 'n' roll casualties were no longer unexpected; by 1974, Brian Jones, Jimi Hendrix, Janis Joplin, Jim Morrison, Duane Allman, Gene Vincent and Gram Parsons had already gone.

Ralph McTell: 'I wasn't at all surprised when I heard he died. Not at all. The illness, the going deeper and deeper into himself, only having his back photographed for his albums. I had a family by then, two kids, and when I heard I just thought, you poor sod. I hadn't seen him, but I knew he'd got more and more dependent on mind-controlling stuff . . . and more or less vanished.'

Zig Zag's Pete Frame remembers: 'At that time you kind of got used to rock stars dying, in a sense it was part of the trip. It used to happen with alarming regularity.' In January 1975 *Zig Zag* carried a heartfelt piece by David Sandison, Nick's press officer at Island, entitled 'Nick Drake: The Final Retreat', which began: 'The amount of coverage Nick Drake's death had in the weekly musical comics just about sums it all up really. Jerry Gilbert did a beautiful piece for *Sounds* and they cut it down to half a dozen paragraphs. No-one else mentioned his departure with much more than a cursory nod of acknowledgement.

'OK, so the guy did no more than a dozen gigs before more than 150 people, and they'd raised no ripple you'd notice. He released three albums in four years, and together they probably didn't sell enough to cover the cost of one. What the hell do you want? front page in *The Times*? . . .

'But. The biggest three-letter word in the dictionary, that. But Nick Drake was a lovely cat. But he wrote songs that'd tear your soul out if you relaxed for a second. But in a world full of bullshit, hype, glittery horrors with the talents of dead oxen and the integrity of starving rats, Nick Drake was a man of sincerity, an artist of tremendous calibre and one of the few entitled to be called unique. But what the hell do they care?'

The *Sounds* piece to which Sandison refers, a quarter page by Jerry Gilbert headlined 'Nick Drake: death of a "genius"', was the only contemporary obituary; it began: 'Nick Drake died in his sleep two Sundays ago, leaving a legacy of three superb, stylised albums on the Island label. He had been ill – perhaps weary is a better expression – for some time, but at the time of his death his enthusiasm had never been as high, for he was totally immersed in the prospect of completing his fourth album.' It ended by quoting Robert Kirby: 'He was ready for death all right, I just think he'd had enough, there was no fight left in him. Yet I get the feeling that if he was going to commit suicide he would have done so a long time ago.'

Talking to me more than twenty years after Nick's death, Kirby was not alone among Nick's friends in wishing he had done more to try to help, and regretting that he hadn't fully recognized the depths to which Nick had sunk: 'My memories looking back on Nick are predominantly happy, but stained with guilt and remorse that I didn't do anything. But in 1974 I was twenty-six, and what can a twenty-six-year-old do to help someone like that?

'There is a great element of guilt. I wish that between 1972 and 1974 I'd rung him up and said: "Are you working on anything?" And if he'd said: "Well yes, I'm working on this on my own", I'd have said: "Well, can't we try a few ideas and see if it works?" He would almost certainly have said yes, but I don't think people ever pushed him because they always thought it was going to come from him, because they admired him so much.'

The issue of *Sounds*, dated 14 December 1974, which carried Gilbert's obituary, indicated just how far rock 'n' roll had travelled since Nick first set foot on the highway, and just how far removed he had become by the time of his death. It was now the era of *Topographic Oceans*, the progressive bombast of Yes, Genesis and ELP; the guitar flamboyance of Carlos Santana and Jan Akkerman; the still accessible David Bowie and the silky style of Roxy Music. It was not, and never had been, the time of Nick Drake.

Rodney and Molly Drake continued living at Far Leys after Nick died, though after Rodney's death in March 1988, Molly spent her last years at Orchard House, a smaller home, nearer the centre of the village. Canon Martin Tunnicliffe, who came to St Mary Magdalene in 1979, grew used to fans from around the world coming to the church and vicarage. Patiently, he would point out the grave, and encourage comments in the visitors' book. On Sunday 20 November 1994 a memorial service was held at the church to mark the twentieth anniversary of Nick's death. Molly had died in June the previous year, but the service was attended by Gabrielle, and a tape of some of Nick's songs was played.

As an artist, Nick Drake was thwarted during his lifetime; his glory came posthumously. The tapes of his parents speaking reveal undeniable pride in their voices as they talk of the young pilgrims who make their way to Tanworth, as well as their realization that Nick's single-minded determination in pursuing his chosen career was justified. The tragedy is that it all came too late.

Pete Frame: 'I think he was the archetypal figure who was ignored in his lifetime, and his worth was only seen later. You have to remember that Them could have broken up, and Van Morrison could have gone back to Belfast to be a gas fitter or whatever he was. They had two albums out and split up, and nobody knew the name of Van Morrison. There wasn't that kind of interest in rock history. That's why *Zig Zag* was so unique, because we cared about the footnotes of rock history, which is what Nick Drake was. Because he wasn't generating millions of dollars, people wouldn't care so much.'

How Nick's life would have developed had he lived, is of course the question which continues to fascinate those who have grown to love his music. If he had conquered his depression, would he have wanted to write and record again? Would he ever have felt capable of returning to his former life? Indeed is it possible to imagine a life for Nick which didn't involve music?

When I asked Robert Kirby, long one of Nick's closest friends, what he thought Nick might have done had he given up music, he told me: 'He talked about literature when he wasn't talking about music. In another life, I could have seen him running a very good publishing company . . . I think he would have been able to select potentially good writers.' Kirby also confirmed that one of the strangest tales associated with Nick's last years, a story I had always assumed to be apocryphal, had actually happened: 'He told me he did go into an Army Recruitment Office. That's absolutely true, he was quite seriously considering it. Funnily enough, if he'd decided to do that, he could have cut the mustard. If he had made that decision, he could have been officer material.'

However disenchanted he was with the music business, however angry about his own lack of success, it is surely significant that just months before he died Nick Drake went into the recording studio again. Only four tracks were laid down in that session, but at the time they constituted the start of a new album. Nick may not have been pursuing his career with anything like the hope and enthusiasm which had marked his early years at Island, but he did still consider himself a musician. The prospect of negotiating a contract, a record deal, of being pushed out on tour to promote his records, all filled him with dread; but for all that, music was what he did.

Molly remembered the trepidation which surrounded Nick's last recordings: 'Those four songs were supposed to be the beginning of another album . . . I remember finding a letter after he died from Joe Boyd saying that this was wonderful and that they'd got to have a proper contract, and it was all rather businesslike, and I think it scared Nick to death.

'I think he felt, I can't really cope with this. Joe was obviously very anxious that he should make another record, but I think things had just become too much for him altogether. The idea of having to do all the business of another record, and all the contracts, I think it just was more at that stage than he could cope with.'

David Sandison believes that sometime after *Pink Moon*, Nick's deal with Island had lapsed and with it the weekly retainer. Whether this may in part have influenced his decision to return home is impossible to know. Certainly Island were still interested and Boyd was trying to interest Nick in renegotiating.

Had Nick Drake survived, it is inconceivable to imagine him battling it out as support act to the new wave of British rock 'n' roll attractions. When Nick's old Marlborough rival Chris De Burgh found himself in the unenviable position of opening solo for Supertramp soon after Nick's death, he had to face the slings and arrows of outraged punters.

It is possible to imagine Nick staying offstage, but continuing to function as a songwriter, supplying material to sympathetic acts, but even those who admire Nick's work seem wary of covering his songs, perhaps because they are so very personal and so indelibly associated with their creator. There are precedents for an in-house lyricist (Keith Reid for Procol Harum, Pete Sinfield for King Crimson) and the role of 'visiting genius' was precisely what Pink Floyd initially envisaged for Syd Barrett, and the Beach Boys for Brian Wilson, though neither example was a spectacular success.

As well as being impressed by Randy Newman's debut album, Paul Wheeler remembers Nick's admiration for Newman's refusal to gig, and his awareness of Brian Wilson's role in the Beach Boys: 'That was definitely out of step with the John Martyn, Richard Thompson, up and down the M1 stuff. That concept of a private world, which had nothing to do with the stage, or the road, maybe that was more what Nick was relating to . . . But I could also understand why the road musicians would resent his lack of "paying his dues". But Nick's reluctance to gig could be seen as being ahead of its time, maybe it was the very mystique that attracted . . . Which is why we're speaking now!'

18

The fact that there is no film footage of Nick Drake performing undoubtedly feeds the myth. The photos – and there are few enough even of those – freeze-frame the image of Nick, shy and hesitant before the camera, capturing him for ever in the aspic of immortality: half-smiling at half-remembered memories.

A rumour broke out in late 1997 that there *was* film of Nick Drake in existence. Not performing, but watching. In October 1970 James Taylor – then at his commercial zenith – was filmed in concert by BBC television; and there, so the rumour goes, in the audience, is Nick Drake. The timing fits, and, yes, that shadowy audience member could be Nick, but then, in London in 1970, there were an awful lot of young men who looked like Nick Drake.

In the early seventies television outlets for performers like Nick were strictly limited: he was too arcane for *Top Of The Pops*, too obscure even for *The Old Grey Whistle Test*. But as we approach the millennium, we look to the moving image to provide veracity. Perhaps if we could see Nick move, he would seem more real, less iconic. Certainly the shock of hearing his drunken teenage voice causes pause; reality threatens to intrude.

The idea that some fragment of Nick was caught inadvertently piques the imagination. Like the few precious seconds of moving film which captured the glee of a Dutch schoolgirl, caught by chance observing a wartime wedding in Amsterdam. There is nothing remarkable in the footage. She did not know she was being filmed: the amateur cameraman simply happened to sweep skywards, and in so doing captured on film the only moving images of a teenager whom the whole world would one day know by name – Anne Frank.

Megastores in every mall on every high street are full of the work of brooding, introspective singer-songwriters – though rather disconcertingly, the music which was once regarded as being on the cutting edge is now, often as not, filed away under 'Easy Listening'. So why Nick Drake and not one of the many others? Just three albums released in his lifetime, a grand total of thirty-one tracks; even posthumously only nine new tracks have officially surfaced, and the widely available bootleg of home demos is largely cover versions. These are frail foundations upon which to build a myth. But built it is.

Is it the pin-up appeal? But then pictures of good-looking boys are everywhere, from pre-teen magazines to coffee-table tomes. Is it the premature end which still entices? Sadly, rock 'n' roll is not short of victims: everyone from the late, great Johnny Ace to Kurt Cobain has been called and gone before. Whatever the explanation, it is the development from quiet interest (who, please, is the Olah Tunji of whom Bob Dylan sang?) through curiosity (did The Stones really cover Dobie Gray's 'Drift Away'?) to out-and-out obsession ('Dear Apple, Please release *everything* The Beatles ever recorded . . .') which is disturbing.

With Nick Drake, the obsession can be so strong that it becomes increasingly difficult to separate the life from the myth. He had strikingly good looks, and in photos his innate shyness and reluctance to commit himself to the camera only add lustre. There is something not quite there about Nick in photographs, a suggestion that he is slipping quietly away from the lens, and that when you look again he may have gone. Like trying to photograph a ghost or catch a wisp of smoke.

When you look at the photos, and listen to the records, it is almost as though he was never there. There is an elusive, illusory quality to Nick. The recording of him speaking reveals a voice that is well-modulated, precise, but waif-like and hard to hear – almost as if he is trying to talk himself out of his life. And in photographs, and from the reports of those who saw him on-stage, it seems as though it were the same: as if he was trying to edge himself out of existence.

David Sandison: 'It wasn't a down, it was just a kind of . . . distance. A disconnection if you like. He was going on his way, and if it meant he had to bump into people and communicate with them from time to time, then OK. But he'd rather not. I think that's even true of people who were close to him.'

Meeting contemporaries of Nick while writing this book was like beating a path to an unmarked door, over terrain which bore no previous footprints, and for which there were no maps. As we sat and spoke of Nick, particularly his days at Marlborough, it struck me that these were Nick's exact contemporaries: in the same year at school, born within months of him. And as we sat and talked, it occurred to me that this is what Nick too would have been like had he lived: approaching fifty, established in life, possibly married with children, and probably – like his father – balding. But we will never know, because Nick traded all this for enduring beauty, a striking image of perfect and timeless youth. And, with the surviving pictures, we are left with the first bloom not yet faded; and on record, with the breathless voice of young promise.

Perhaps this begins to explain, at least in part, the degree of obsession. Nick Drake becomes a blank canvas on which admirers can paint their own pictures, project their own lives and troubles; a mirror in which people see their own pain and lost promise. The danger is that in the process, Nick's own life is lost for a second time.

Those who shared their memories of Nick with me have come face to face with their own destiny: surviving and ageing and all these bring; but Nick never lived to make those discoveries. As Laurence Binyon wrote in his poem 'For The Fallen', which commemorated those who would never return from Flanders' fields:

> They shall not grow old, as we that are left grow old:
> Age shall not weary them, nor the years condemn.
> At the going down of the sun and in the morning
> We will remember them.

Once upon a time there was a photograph of Paris, said to be one of the earliest ever taken, sometime during the 1840s. The camera was placed high on a building and took in all the boulevards, sweeping to the horizon as far as the lens could see. It showed trees lining the city streets, and a man caught in the act of tying his shoe. He was only there at all because in bending to tie his laces, he had stayed in one place long enough for his image to register on the lengthy exposure. His name will never be known, and he probably remained unaware of his date with posterity, but in the way of these things, that Parisian with the loose shoelace of 150 years ago is with us for ever.

Before compact discs diminished the imagery of rock 'n' roll, album sleeves were truly wonderful things. The sleeves of favourite records were as much part of their appeal as the music they protected. You were drawn to them, to the minutiae, and the strange, hypnotic power the pictures exerted. The images are so enduring, because when they were released, there was nothing else to look at. There were no long discourses on how the albums were made, or lavish coffee-table books celebrating the rock photographer's craft. There was a record inside, and as it played you studied the sleeve. The covers of favourite albums became so familiar that it is dislocating to find an out-take from the session detailed on the sleeve – like coming home and finding the furniture rearranged.

The iconography of a sleeve became integral to the music's appeal, and rarely was that iconography more powerful than on the record sleeves of the late Nick Drake. On *Five Leaves Left*, a black-and-white picture, perfectly clear and focused, had Nick nonchalantly leaning against a brick wall, quizzical and faintly baffled, while to his right a man dashes past, blurred by his hurry to be somewhere else.

Keith Morris is the man who did more than anyone to preserve the image of Nick Drake and present it to the world. Still snapping after all these years, Keith doesn't do much music stuff now. After his work with Nick, he went on to shoot some classic images: John Cale's *Fear*, Elvis Costello's *My Aim Is True* . . . , but left rock 'n' roll imagery behind him in the mid-eighties. Keith still gets calls from fans all around the world, at all hours of the day and night. They all want to know about Nick Drake. He smiles at the incongruity of it all: two or three photo sessions, barely totalling a day's work, nearly thirty years before, loom large over anything he has undertaken since.

We spoke in Keith's flat in Little Venice, passing contact sheets across the battered wooden table – 'That's where Nick used to sit, if he dropped in . . . Sometimes didn't say a word for hours.' Because these shots form the bulk of the very few images of Nick which are left to us, you are struck by their familiarity. And as I looked at a life in miniature, Keith told me about the first time he met Nick: 'It was in the Witchseason office in Charlotte Street. At that time, I was doing a lot of work for *Oz* and we had a thing about The Incredible String Band, and I had managed to wangle my way into Sound Techniques to take a roll of pictures which they really liked, and so I was summoned to meet this callow youth who Joe had just signed – I think he was still at Cambridge, and just about to begin work on the album.'

There is indeed something faintly familiar about the table from which Keith and I drink our tea, for this is where he photographed Nick for the shots used for the *Bryter Layter* advertisements; the table Nick is seated at on the cover of the *Brittle Days* tribute album. Wooden and gnarled, in the end it is still only a table.

And then that photo slides across the table: the 'running man' shot from *Five Leaves Left*. And seeing the whole contact sheet, you appreciate it as part of a sequence, with a whole series of shots either side of that particular photo. (The complete sequence can be seen in the booklet accompanying 1994's compilation *Way To Blue*.) Ian MacDonald felt this was the image that captured the essence of the man he had encountered in Cambridge: 'The back cover of *Five Leaves Left*, with him leaning up against the wall with the man running, that is absolutely Nick Drake. That is such a brilliant expression of who he was, except that it makes him appear a little more solid than he actually was in person. He was a little bit fading out himself, even though he was very still.'

The photos weren't taken off Charlotte Street as Joe Boyd remembered, but by a wall outside a factory called Morgan Crucible, in Battersea, south-west London. Neither the factory nor the wall is any longer there. The running man sequence was taken at the end of a working day, and the staff had begun flooding out of the factory gates, streaming homewards: 'The guy in the photo we ended up using was just running because he was late for his bus,' Keith remembered. Simple as that. Like the man who stopped to tie his shoe in Paris a century and a half before . . .

Flicking through the sequence, you can see Nick and his faintly bemused self, leaning against the wall that late afternoon in 1969, and all around him flock the factory workers, keen to get away, unaware that, at random, one of them will be plucked, and his fleeting, blurred image will endure on a record sleeve which will be pored over for years and years to come.

Keith Morris: 'One of the good things about Joe is that if he sees something he likes, he goes with it – there's none of this "Have you done an album before?" I'd never done an album sleeve before . . . It was "This is Nick Drake. Listen to the tape. Will you do the sleeve?" So that was *Five Leaves Left*. Nick and I went off and had a non-alcoholic extended lunch, and I said, have you got any ideas you want to do? . . . I always work better bouncing ideas off people, and between us we came up with a number of ideas that we then shot. So the actual session ranged from my studio over a lot of south London. The cover shot – the one looking out the window – was in a deserted house just off Wimbledon Common . . .'

Because of what we know is to come, perhaps there is a temptation to read too much into the front sleeve of *Five Leaves Left*. What you see is simply a young man looking out of a window, surrounded by a border of Lincoln green. For the many who have come to Nick long after his death, *Five Leaves Left* is an emblematic treasure, an icon. Taken three-quarters on, Nick is gazing hazily out, a half-smile playing on his lips. The black jacket would be familiar to Nick's Cambridge friends. Behind him, a half-open window looks out on to a shed (with a man in it?) Below the window, what looks like a carpenter's bench stands, empty save for wood shavings. It is the mundane transmuted into the iconographic.

Nigel Waymouth, who shot the front cover for *Bryter Layter*, was a co-founder of the Swinging London boutique Granny Takes A Trip. He came up through the English underground of the late sixties with his partner Michael English. As Hapshash & The Coloured Coat, they created psychedelic posters to promote albums by The Crazy World Of Arthur Brown, Soft Machine and events staged at Brian Epstein's Saville Theatre. English and Waymouth's posters have come to be regarded as definitive artefacts of the era, and examples were included in the Barbican's 1993 exhibition of 'The London Art Scene In The Sixties'.

Keith Morris: 'We did a few things for *Bryter Layter*, but we still hadn't got a front, and Nigel Waymouth, who I've got a lot of time for as a designer – I think I was out of town – and at the last minute they decided they had to get this thing done, so Nick was dragged in the studio for the front cover.

'The one on the back, on the motorway, was the one I did, on the Westway. It is Nick standing there, I've heard people say it wasn't him, but it was taken one evening . . . We did a whole series of ideas, which is why we'd never got on with the front . . . double exposures, shots looking out over a desolate city, which we did in black and white. I suppose that back shot is like the one on *Five Leaves Left* . . . Nick always cast himself as an observer, this solitary figure, a very romanticized idea of himself. I think that was how Nick thought of himself . . .'

During the time he spent with Nick in the studio and on location, Keith Morris got as close to him as anyone, and had the opportunity to observe him, and the cultivation of his image. Nick's surprisingly acute image-consciousness was something which friends from school and university had commented on, and Keith likewise noticed that Nick was quite astute in casting himself as the sensitive outsider: 'He was very shy . . . but he really wanted to be famous, which was quite bizarre, given how laid-back about his career he was. But he was very shy and diffident.

'He used to come round occasionally, sit at this table, have a cup of coffee. If he was up, yeah, you could have a conversation with him. He wasn't . . . an Elvis Costello, giving it all that all the time, but yeah, you could have a normal conversation with him. He'd play the guitar while I was setting up. If he was down . . . there'd be a knock on the door, I'd let him in, he'd sit there, have a cup of tea, and he wouldn't have said a word before leaving.

' "Vain" is a bit strong, but he knew what he wanted to look like, and I think one of the reasons he quite liked working with me was because I never tried to force things on him. I was quite happy to go with what he threw at me, try and work it different ways. You didn't have smiling pictures, but occasionally he would laugh if something funny happened on the set, and you'd be quick to get that. He was very much the sucked-in cheeks. He . . . posed naturally. I used to photograph Marc Bolan a lot, and Marc once said to me: "I'm not the greatest guitarist in the world, but I've got great movements because I practised in front of the mirror for years." I think in a funny sort of way, Nick knew what he was doing visually.'

Annie Sullivan's career was as vivid and colourful as the sixties themselves by the time she arrived at Island in 1970 to become Art Director. Annie had been a house dancer at *Ready, Steady, Go*; helped coordinate the infamous legalize marijuana advert in *The Times* in 1967; and worked on the backstage organization of the Woodstock Festival in 1969 – she still has the correspondence detailing Janis Joplin's requirements ('a case of Southern Comfort!')

Annie Sullivan: 'I bumped into Guy Stevens at Marine Ices opposite the Roundhouse, and he said come to work for me on Monday at Island . . . At the time Island had King Crimson, Free, Traffic, Spooky Tooth, Cat Stevens, Jethro Tull, Fairport, Sandy Denny . . . The sleeves were very much the lingua franca of the time. I always felt the artwork should be an extension of the contents, reflect it in some way.'

As Nick became more and more withdrawn, the likelihood of a third album grew ever more remote. Then, to Island's surprise, *Pink*

Moon appeared out of nowhere. Nick never stated that he didn't want his picture on the cover, but as with much of his communication at the time, it was just understood, and the album did appear with no picture of the artist visible anywhere. Annie Sullivan worked with Nick for the first and last time on *Pink Moon*: 'I'd been warned beforehand. Chris Blackwell said to me you're going to do the album sleeve for Nick Drake, but it's going to be difficult. And I thought, well, I've got a quite good, sensitive manner. But it was difficult.

'I remember going to talk to him, and he just sat there, hunched up, and even though he didn't speak, I knew the album was called *Pink Moon*, and I can't remember how he conveyed it, whether he wrote it down . . . he wanted a pink moon. He couldn't tell me what he wanted, but I had *Pink Moon* to go on. So I went to the Radio Times Hulton Picture Library and got lots and lots of pictures of moons. I got someone to photograph the moon and put a pink light over it. I got historic old pictures of the moon. And I commissioned an artist called Michael Trevithick – I'd seen his work and liked it, and he wasn't someone I'd used before.

'He was a painter, and I remembered his folio, quite surreal, which at that time was very unusual – nowadays, of course, everything is surreal. It was very different, very strange. I'm pretty certain he hadn't done any album sleeves before. I just had the feeling that he might come up with something, and he came up with the artwork. I would have given him the album to listen to. I went and showed Nick the different ideas – "Do you like this?" – and the best I could get was "Mm" . . . But at the same time I sensed he knew what he wanted. It was a challenge, I quite liked trying to find something that reflected him. I don't remember him talking about "Pink Moon", the song or the sleeve. I know he liked it. I don't remember him talking about anything.'

The Keith Morris photo used for the posthumous *Time Of No Reply* album is symptomatic of the time. The setting is Regent's Park, one spring day in 1969, with Nick seated beneath a tree. He is captured as the eternal student and nascent songwriter, with his bulky book, Chelsea boots and trusty guitar never far from his side. The *Time Of No Reply* inlay, the photo actually underneath the CD itself, is a familiar cropped shot from another Morris session. The three-quarter-face shot was taken on a day when the two men were trawling south London for locations. It was taken overlooking the urban desolation of New Cross, squeezed between Deptford and Peckham, with the green, leafy spread of Greenwich just round a curl of the Thames.

It has come to be believed that the striped blanket in which Nick is enveloped on the cover of *Way To Blue* was Nick's own special blanket, the blanket he wrapped himself in to keep warm while living so frugally in Hampstead. And over the years Joe Boyd has had patiently to point out that perhaps Nick's fans shouldn't take everything quite so . . . literally. 'The wrapped in a blanket shot,' he explained to Kevin Ring in *Zip Code*, 'was not because he lived wrapped in a blanket, it was just a blanket the photographer happened to have with him.'

But that blanket just won't go away. Early in 1997, following the appearance in *Mojo* of a feature I had written on Nick Drake, Gary Hill wrote in from Smile records in Dublin: 'Many thanks for . . . having the consummate good taste to put Nick on your cover. That very same photo was taken by a friend of mine, Julian Lloyd, and when he told me he still possessed the rug that Nick wrapped around him in that glorious shot, I was obviously fascinated. Julian kindly allowed me to hang the rug on the wall of my shop where it has attracted much attention and comment. Please find enclosed photographic evidence that a small corner of Dublin will forever be Tanworth-in-Arden!'

By the time of *Pink Moon*, Nick was visibly crumbling. Linda Thompson observed the decay during Nick's last months in London: 'Towards the end of his life, there were signs that everyone should have seen. He completely stopped washing I mean, he shut down. We all tried to help a bit, but . . . I was very shocked the last time I saw him, he really did look very ill, he wasn't eating. I don't know if he was doing any drugs, he was apparently on medication. I think there's no way that Nick could have survived. Absolutely no way at all. He had no survival skills.'

Keith Morris hadn't seen Nick for a while, and was pleasantly surprised to receive a call asking him to take some publicity photos to help promote *Pink Moon*. He too was shocked by the dreadful decline: 'I got a call saying would I do this session with Nick. I was really surprised because I hadn't seen him for months. They came round in a car to pick me up, then went to get Nick, and out to Hampstead Heath. It was the quickest session we ever did, barely an hour. We didn't talk about any ideas, I just snapped away.

'I had seen him before when he'd been very introverted . . . But that day at Hampstead, he wouldn't even look at me, let alone do anything. It was just "stand there, stand there, look over there". He just did it . . . My favourite photo of the session is him going down the hill, his back to the camera, with the dog jumping up. I think there's a tragic simplicity to those pictures. Anyone could have taken them, I just happened to be the person . . . I still remember that I felt if I'd said something at the time, it might actually have stopped him . . . Normally I was quite chatty and sixties: lots of "Yeah, man" and "beautiful" . . .'

Gabrielle Drake points to one of the Keith Morris photos from that final Hampstead Heath session as her most abiding image of her late brother. 'He used to do this thing of just sitting there, lost,' she told *Melody Maker*'s Kris Kirk. 'The most truthful photo I've ever seen of him is in the record booklet, where he is sitting on a park bench. Everyone, no matter how bad they are feeling, will try to pose when they are having their photograph taken, but here all Nick's desire to pose has gone – he's not even aware of the camera.'

Keith Morris: 'I have to agree with Gabrielle. She liked the ones of Nick in Hampstead on the bench; she says they're the most honest pictures of Nick . . . I think that's right, he was just sitting around, looking . . . uncomfortably Nick.'

The sense of bleakness and isolation which Keith captured on those final photos on Hampstead Heath are coloured retrospectively by the knowledge that it would be Nick's last-ever photo session. Even so, Nick's obvious detachment and frailty have him looking like a character left marooned by Samuel Beckett. There is nothing coming from the eyes. The photographic evidence is conclusive: here is a person barely capable of comprehending what is going on around or inside him. Nick Drake seated on Hampstead Heath that day is the sight of a man shutting down.

The only lightness to come from that final session is provided by the dog who bounds up, as Nick walks, back to the camera, away from the lens and towards the pond. Annie Sullivan remembers that day: 'Keith was brilliant with people. I think one of the keys of being a good Art Director is putting the right photographer with the right person, and not interfering . . . I had my dog Gus, a golden retriever with me. I'd brought him along because everybody liked Gus, and also dogs have a way of getting through sometimes, where people don't. Nick didn't talk to Gus, but he obviously liked him. And that's where that picture came from: Nick walking down the path, and Gus came rushing round the corner and looked up at Nick.'

Annie got a call from *Melody Maker*: 'They were asking, where's the ad? A space had been booked, and I had to make an instant decision because they were going to print "This space was booked by

Island Records", which would have been disastrous. I thought, I've got to put something in, and I had half an hour to make up an ad. I was looking at the pictures, and I thought, this picture says more about Nick . . . there was no point in using a full-frontal picture of him, because you'd just have had this rather shy, sad-looking person. I thought that was a kind of enigmatic image.'

For many, that image of Nick Drake with his back to the camera, walking away from . . . everything, is the one which endures. It is the one featured in the *Melody Maker* advertisement of 26 February 1972, and the one which Jason Creed has featured on the back of every single issue of his fanzine, *Pink Moon*. But as Annie points out, the reality wasn't that romantic: 'He wasn't fashionably down at heel, he was kind of sad. Such a shame, he was such a nice-looking boy. I never asked, but I suppose I presumed, at the time, it was drugs.'

Keith Morris was one of the few people close to Nick who had watched the arc of his short professional career, and for him that last meeting was memorable: 'I remember him in two ways: one was the first time I met him – incredible personality – and the other is the last – a grey day, a grey mac . . . Certain sessions you remember for their colour. I remember that one because I don't remember a single colour. Everything about it was grey. I don't remember green, I remember grey.'

19

If you want to mark the beginning of the cult which has sprung up around Nick Drake, 9 March 1979 is as good a date as any. On that day Island Records released the box set *Fruit Tree*.

Island fought shy of marketing Nick in the first few years after he died. Enquiries to the label were met with the response that all Nick's records remained on catalogue, to be purchased by interested parties. Island's then press officer, Richard Williams, had even gone so far as to write to the *NME*, following Nick Kent's feature on Nick Drake which appeared in February 1975, to make it plain that they planned no further releases: ' . . . we have no intention of repackaging Nick's recordings, either now or at any time in the foreseeable future. His three albums have never been deleted and they will remain available for those who wish to discover and enjoy them.

'Furthermore, Nick himself expressed dissatisfaction with the four songs he recorded late last year, consequently John Wood has destroyed the 16-track master tapes – with our full approval.'

As Sean Connery so wisely said: never say never again.

Before working for Island, Rob Partridge had been at *Melody Maker* and the trade paper *Music Week*. On his arrival in London in 1969, one of the first artists he saw performing was Nick Drake: 'The first thing I did when I got to Island as a press officer was suggest that perhaps we could put together a retrospective on Nick Drake – the studio albums plus whatever else was there – which eventually became *Fruit Tree*. I wasn't necessarily expecting massive vaults with millions of tunes, live recordings or whatever, but there was very little . . .'

The original press release announcing the Nick Drake box set came during 1978, headed 'Nick Drake The Complete Collected Works', and talked of a November release: 'If he won any battles in his short life, Nick Drake mastered the challenge of authenticity. He was of one piece. His songs, like his clothes, were melancholy to the point of morbidity. Yet somehow he escaped self indulgence. Elton John, who as a young studio musician cut a demo tape of Drake's songs, recalls their "beautiful haunting quality" . . . "listening to music so beautiful, you are shamed by the ugliness of the world" commented the prestigious American magazine *New Times*.

'Nick's three albums – plus four previously unreleased tracks, "Voice From The Mountain", "Rider On The Wheel", "Black-Eyed Dog" [*sic*] and "Hanging On A Star" – have now been compiled in a three-album box-set, called The Complete Collected Works (Island NDSP 100), released on November 10. The box-set, which will retail for £9.50, comes complete with an eight page booklet. Nick Kent of the *New Musical Express* has been commissioned to write the text for the booklet, which also includes Nick Drake's lyrics plus photographs and illustrations. The box-set also features three pencil drawings of Nick Drake.'

Nick Kent's sleeve notes were never used for *Fruit Tree*. Since arriving at the *NME* in 1972, he had been itching to write about Nick Drake, but the only opportunity he got was a posthumous appreciation: 'I was always waiting for a chance . . . Then he went back in '74 and recorded some songs with Joe Boyd, and we were just waiting for something to tie it all together so we could write about him.

' "Black Eyed Dog", it's all about mental illness, isn't it? It's about being there, and seeing your whole psyche overwhelmed by something that you can't control, and is sending you straight to a catatonic hell. You can't do anything about it and the very few moments of any kind of lucidity you write a song which expresses how you're feeling . . . It's like Syd Barrett's "Dark Globe", where it's obvious the guy knows what's happening.

'Even in the songs on *Bryter Layter*, this guy just doesn't seem to be able to relate to anybody. There's not even a flesh-and-blood woman that he is sexually or emotionally tied to. These are just images or dreams that he has of other people. I did write an 8000-word piece for *Fruit Tree* . . . It's not that much different from the piece I wrote for *NME*. The conclusion I came to was that he was this confused guy who was . . . a little confused and too sensitive for his time.'

Rob Partridge: 'Nick Kent was originally commissioned to write the booklet which he duly delivered; it was an extraordinary piece of journalism – if you've read his piece in *NME* on Nick, which questioned the verdict of suicide – but was felt to be inappropriate for a box set which celebrated the life and work of Nick Drake. I think we felt it would have been distressing to the family. It was completely legitimate to ask those questions in a magazine piece, but possibly not appropriate to appear in a box set.

'At that time an American journalist called Arthur Lubow was in town – there were always two or three journalists in the press office over from America every year in search of Nick Drake. I'd introduced Lubow to Molly and Rodney, and also to Gabrielle, and at the last minute, commissioned him to write the essay.'

What became *Fruit Tree* was one of the first-ever box sets devoted to the work of a single artist, in an attempt to put that artist's work into some sort of perspective, as well as allowing the release of previously unheard material.

There had been records in boxes before – George Harrison's *All Things Must Pass* and *The Concert For Bangla Desh* – but *Fruit Tree* was the first to try to gain an overview of a life and work, and could be seen as a template for what followed. Box sets are now seen as setting the seal on an act's integrity. Since *Fruit Tree*, Dylan, Clapton and The Who are just some who have seen their work remade and remodelled. But few artists have had a box set built on such a small body of work as Nick Drake.

To accommodate the four unreleased songs – there wasn't room on the vinyl album for them all – the final four tracks from *Pink Moon* had to be excised. The original sequence was restored on the revised and reissued four-LP *Fruit Tree* released by Hannibal in 1986, which incorporated the posthumous *Time Of No Reply* album.

The musical temperature had undergone severe changes in the seven years between *Pink Moon* and the release of the *Fruit Tree* box. Acts like Led Zeppelin, David Bowie and Bruce Springsteen, promising newcomers when Nick was still alive, now straddled the decade as its most visible icons.

The cosy camaraderie of mid-seventies pub-rock was just making an impact as Nick died, and from the remnants of pub rock came the Rottweiler impetus of Punk. Nothing could be further from the introspective, contemplative, balanced wistfulness of Nick Drake than the howling, cataclysmic, seething *Zeitgeist* of Johnny Rotten. A howl of discontent, Punk shaped the seventies and brought rock 'n' roll back to its roots.

In the incendiary wake of the Sex Pistols came The Clash, The Jam, Elvis Costello and all that America liked to christen 'New Wave'. Punk rewrote the musical rule book. It was a revisionist movement all by itself. The only music that the punks had any time for apart from their own three-chord manifestos was reggae. 'No more Elvis, Beatles or Rolling Stones in 1977' sang The Clash. Of Nick Drake, there was no mention from Punk lips, but his contemporary singer-songwriters had not weathered the storm any better. John Martyn continued to plough an idiosyncratic and increasingly solitary furrow; Cat Stevens converted to Islam, as did Richard Thompson, effectively removing himself for three years during the late seventies.

The fact that Television's Tom Verlaine could name-check Nick in *Fruit Tree*'s essay was not without interest at the time. Many of the Punk bands sprang from nowhere, fully formed, with no preconceptions of, nor appreciation for, rock history before Punk's year zero, so to see Tom Verlaine listed alongside Elton John and David Geffen as an admirer of Nick Drake was significant.

With the release of *Fruit Tree* came the realization that interest in the music of Nick Drake was just not going to go away. The set was put together in conjunction with the Drake family, by Joe Boyd and Island press officer Rob Partridge: 'In Nick's lifetime, there were probably more review copies around than there were actual sales. They were released at a time when Island had big hitters like Cat Stevens. Nick Drake was not a big hitter.

'I never met Rodney or Molly, although we had a great telephone relationship over the years. Whenever there was a journalist who wanted to interview them, I'd check it out, and they'd always be enormously accommodating. Nick's room was left exactly the way it was, which I guess is one way for them to deal with it.'

Molly: 'When I heard that they were going to make this compilation thing of all his albums, I said to Rodney I think it ought to be called *Fruit Tree*, because that to me is a terribly prophetic song. Several months later, Joe came and had lunch with us in London and was talking about this album, and he said I tell you the title I think it should be: *Fruit Tree*.'

Reviews for *Fruit Tree* were not widespread; the weeklies were preoccupied with disco frenzy and albums such as Blondie's *Parallel Lines*, Supertramp's *Breakfast In America* and Rod Stewart's *Blondes Have More Fun*. The anticipation of Led Zeppelin's first UK shows in two years was tangible, and there were new bands like The Police, Dire Straits, The Pretenders and U2 to contend with.

In his *NME* review of *Fruit Tree*, David Hepworth wrote: 'This box set brings together the three albums that he recorded for Island with four tracks put down near the end when his vulnerability had got past the point of melancholy and had become a crippling disease . . . Most songwriters use their sadness but with Nick Drake it was the sadness that used him and even music as rare and honest as this is never worth such tragedy.'

Rodney Drake did notice a slight dip in the sales of Nick's records around 1981, following the release of *Fruit Tree* in 1979, but apart from that sales remained steady and the three Island albums remained on catalogue, available for the curious of each successive generation.

The next upsurge of interest came in 1985 courtesy of Dream Academy, a trio consisting of Nick Laird-Clowes, ethereal oboist Kate St John and multi-instrumentalist Gilbert Gabriel. Their fifteen minutes of fame began with a haunting single, 'Life In A Northern Town', which was dedicated to the memory of Nick Drake. The single reached number fifteen on the UK charts in March 1985, and the following month Dream Academy were profiled in *Melody Maker*, where Nick Laird-Clowes explained about the dedication: 'I just felt the song has a strong connection with Nick Drake in a way I can't even explain. I held him in such high esteem – and still do. Mike Read played our single on the radio and mentioned that it was dedicated to Nick and since then he's apparently been deluged with letters from people who said they were fans and could Mike please play some of his songs for them!'

Nick Laird-Clowes was obsessed by the minutiae and memorabilia of the sixties. On hearing that the Guild guitar which Nick holds on the cover of *Bryter Layter* had surfaced, he immediately purchased it. Another of Nick's guitars now belongs to Brian Wells, who was given it by Rodney after Nick's funeral: 'I own Nick's Martin D28 . . . I don't think it ever appeared on an album, because I think a lot of *Pink Moon* was done with a gut string, I don't think it was done with a steel string . . . I think he bought the Martin after *Pink Moon*, because when he died it was quite new – perhaps he sold the Guild to buy it. It had a normal tuning, which was quite rare, as most of Nick's guitars were tuned to some funny tuning.'

Brian was also able to scotch another rumour concerning Nick's guitars: 'I actually talked to Eric Clapton about Nick, and he had never heard of Nick . . . I know Eric quite well because we're on the same charity things together, we're both in recovery from addictions, so Eric helps out by giving my charity some free concerts, and there was this rumour that his guitar-playing had been seriously influenced by Nick . . . There's a lot of this stuff: someone said Eric owned Nick's guitar, but Eric had never heard of Nick Drake.'

The success of Dream Academy's single in 1985 prompted Island into action, and within a matter of weeks they announced the first Nick Drake compilation. The title, *Heaven In A Wild Flower*, came from one of Nick's favourite poets, William Blake, and his 1802 poem 'Auguries Of Innocence'. Trevor Dann was asked to compile the fourteen-track collection: 'A guy called Nick Stewart who was working at Island in the mid-eighties mentioned Nick Drake, and I started waxing on, as I do, and then he just rang me up one day and said we're going to do a Nick Drake compilation CD, because there'd never been one – there was the box set *Fruit Tree*, but there had never been a single CD compilation – and would you like to compile it? I said I would be absolutely thrilled.

'So I just went home and recorded the album off my own copies of the records and said this feels nice, like it has "Hazey Jane I" and "II" put together . . . Even though it was specifically going to be a CD, I remember compiling it so it would work as a vinyl album, so that the beginnings of each side, and the ends of each side, felt good. From memory, it's completely chronological, except that Joe insisted that they change one of the tracks. He put in "Northern Sky", and they just plonked it in the middle; otherwise it's in perfectly chronological order.'

Paul Du Noyer's respectful review in *NME* was typical of those accorded *Heaven In A Wild Flower*, and demonstrated the sort of reverence Nick was beginning to attract: 'Rock has known a million morose young poets: bedsit brooders penning their pain, real or imagined, to angst-intensive refrains of frail pathos. What a bloody awful bunch. Yet, by the law of averages, they were bound to spawn at least one genuine genius. They did. His name was Nick Drake.'

A keen-eyed journalist on the *Birmingham Evening Mail* noted that *Heaven In A Wild Flower* was being released at the same time as Gabrielle Drake was making her debut in the popular long-running TV soap *Crossroads*. Under the headline 'Record "no link to *Crossroads*"', the probing piece continued: 'Island records' Rob Partridge denied any element of cash-in: "The Nick Drake album has been a project planned for some years, and its release now has nothing whatsoever to do with the TV series."' Partridge was further quoted, incorrectly, as saying: 'The group Dream Academy have a hit at the moment with "Life In A Northern Town" which was written by Nick years ago – and its success has sparked a lot of interest.'

The success of the Dream Academy single and the subsequent release of *Heaven In A Wild Flower* helped bring Nick Drake's name to a new decade, eleven years after his solitary death. Since *Fruit Tree* in 1979, there had been the real sense of a cult developing; it was a cult which, to everyone's surprise, would only grow during successive years.

Researching in the Island vaults during the summer of 1985 while he was compiling the Sandy Denny box set *Who Knows Where The Time Goes?*, Joe Boyd, in the company of fellow American Frank Kornelussen, found the original master tapes of all Nick's sessions. Master tapes are the first-generation reels, the tapes that roll in the studio, capturing what the artist is actually playing. They are the pristine originals. They are what all CD releases should be cut from. They are what the artist and the producer hear. They are the fly on the wall of the recording studio.

Island had deleted *Fruit Tree* in 1983, and Boyd had made an arrangement which allowed him to release the box set on his own Hannibal Records, though Island still retained the rights to release all three of Nick's individual albums. Having discovered enough previously unreleased material to constitute a 'new' Nick Drake album, Boyd took the opportunity to revise *Fruit Tree*. The tapes unearthed at Island would form a fourth, and in all likelihood, final Nick Drake album, *Time Of No Reply*.

Rodney, Molly and Gabrielle Drake were concerned that Nick's reputation should not be sullied by inferior recordings released under his name, and despite constant pressure from fans to release everything, the recorded legacy of Nick Drake remains pristine. What appeared on *Time Of No Reply* had been cleared by Boyd with the Drake family, and in 1986 it was put out as part of the amended *Fruit Tree* box set, with Nick's fourth album appearing as a bonus disc. The following year *Time Of No Reply* was released in its own right.

The fourteen-track album consisted of previously unreleased songs from the *Five Leaves Left* sessions: 'Time Of No Reply', 'Joey', 'Clothes Of Sand' and 'Mayfair'. There were also alternative takes of songs Nick had included on his debut album, 'Man In A Shed', a version of 'I Was Made To Love Magic', complete with original arranger Richard Hewson's setting, and 'The Thoughts Of Mary

Jane', with some subdued guitar from Richard Thompson. There were three songs which Nick had recorded at home in Tanworth: a solo version of 'Fly', which had appeared beautifully arranged on his second album, as well as two otherwise unreleased titles: the blues cover 'Been Smoking Too Long' and his own 'Strange Meeting II'. The final four tracks were Nick's last-ever recordings from 1974, which had previously been available on the original *Fruit Tree* box, tacked on the end of *Pink Moon*.

With so much known about so little, it was disconcerting, twelve years after his death, to hear Nick Drake singing again. The little fumble in his singing of 'Mayfair' which is laughed off; hearing 'Fly' performed solo as Nick committed it to a home tape recorder, with a recording contract still a distant dream. There is Richard Thompson's tentative electric guitar on a song only familiar from Robert Kirby's lavish string arrangement. And best of all were the new songs, 'Time Of No Reply' and 'Strange Meeting II' particularly, which were quintessential Nick Drake: reflective with a pervading air of melancholy, wistful and oh-so frail. What elevates the songs is that enduring hallmark of Nick's talent, his undeniable flair for melody. The melodies here flow off the disc and seep into your subconscious. 'Time Of No Reply' was one of the songs Nick recorded for his Radio 1 session in August 1969, and had been a regular fixture of his infrequent live appearances. The delay in its official appearance is therefore baffling; one can only assume that Nick was unhappy with some aspect of his performance.

'I Was Made To Love Magic' does not benefit from its polite alternative arrangement, and lyrically, with the attention drawn to the author's tragic solitude in the first verse, it acquires an air of self-pity which is uncharacteristic and unrewarding. Similarly, 'Clothes Of Sand' adds little lustre to the legend of Nick Drake. The home recording 'Mayfair' is widely believed to have been inspired by Molly Drake, an homage to her fondness for the sophisticated Mayfair drawing-room songs of Noël Coward and Ivor Novello. Both Rodney and Molly Drake were delighted with *Time Of No Reply*, singling out 'Clothes Of Sand' and 'I Was Made To Love Magic' as their favourite tracks.

Time Of No Reply was intended as the final Nick Drake album, but following the appearance of a 1994 bootleg of Nick's Tanworth home recordings, Joe Boyd was asked by reader Paul Hough in *Mojo* if there were any unreleased Nick Drake songs still to be released: 'Tricky question,' replied Boyd diplomatically, and went on: 'Nick

was his own severest editor. The only unreleased songs he tried
recording are the ones we put on *Time Of No Reply* . . . We put these
out because they were all songs that Nick decided at some point that
he wanted people to hear. But he never considered any of those very
early songs . . . Everything releasable has been released. The family is
very upset about the bootleg. It's important to everybody involved
that what comes out under Nick's name is up to the same standard as
the released material.'

Boyd feels strongly that anything substandard released in the name
of Nick Drake does his memory a disservice, but I still asked him the
question every fan of Nick's wants to ask: is there anything left in the
vaults? 'Not in the recorded vaults at Island, no. Gabrielle has some
home tapes, which we're going to listen to at some point . . . I'm not
interested in the fans who want takes one to a hundred of everything.
To me, what you release is what will enhance and expand Nick's
reputation, his legacy. That doesn't mean it all has to be perfect. But
it has to be *good*. To me, the tracks on *Time Of No Reply* are worth
having: there's nothing on there that Nick would be ashamed of. I'm
sure he would have hated the idea of it, but it doesn't make people
think any less of Nick listening to that album. There are some naive
things on it; I cringe when I hear the string arrangement on "I Was
Made To Love Magic". But it's historically interesting, and it's still a
beautiful song . . . The last four songs are essential to understanding
Nick.'

In his rooms at Cambridge and at Sound Techniques in London,
Robert Kirby sat and watched Nick Drake create his music over a
period of nearly five years. Was he aware of anything Nick had
recorded that had never been released? 'All I've got of Nick is this
tape of him sitting and playing the guitar for about thirty minutes –
the one with the "Things Behind The Sun" lick on it, but I can't find
it. It was an old reel-to-reel, and the last time I played it, about fifteen
years ago, it was almost ruined then. Sound Techniques closed down,
if they've got the eight-tracks, they've just got the eight-tracks of all
the albums. Where are all the out–takes? . . . If someone could find
out what happened to all the reels that were upstairs at Sound
Techniques, there might well be some out-takes there.'

In the decade which had elapsed since the first compilation, *Heaven
In A Wild Flower*, the overwhelming interest in Nick's life and work
continued unabated. Joe Boyd had always been unhappy about the
sound quality on the vinyl pressing of *Heaven In A Wild Flower*, and

upset that Island had not improved it for the subsequent CD pressing. With the material from *Time Of No Reply* included there were now more than forty songs to play with. It was an irresistible opportunity, and in 1994 Boyd compiled a new collection, *Way To Blue*, as 'An Introduction To Nick Drake'. Inevitably, though, there was duplication: *Way To Blue* contained ten of *Heaven In A Wild Flower*'s tracks.

Advertisements to promote *Way To Blue* appeared with a testimonial from The The's Matt Johnson: 'Nick Drake is one of a trio of singer/songwriters from the late 1960s/early 1970s (the other two being Syd Barrett & Tim Buckley) forever linked together in my mind for no other reason than that tragedy struck all three early in their lives.' When I asked Matt Johnson to expand his thoughts on Nick Drake, he told me: 'He was one of those people who transcended fashion, who made music that spoke to your soul. There was a dignity which isn't there in a lot of contemporary music . . . Someone like the Velvet Underground, who only sold six thousand records when they were together, their stuff has lasted. Why did it last? Certain artists are still alive, Leonard Cohen, Neil Young, Van Morrison. Maybe Nick Drake, if he'd lived, there would have been a comparison with Van Morrison. *Bryter Layter* is very similar to *Astral Weeks* . . .

'For someone to create something of such beauty, even the instrumental pieces on *Bryter Layter*, even if he was that depressed, there was an energy to that music, which is not depressing. I find the music you hear on the commercial radio stations, that is what I call depressing. I find it sad that people think there is a glamour to an early death. It means that the media can do what they want to dead heroes, like Nick Drake and James Dean; they can reinvent them.'

Way To Blue was compiled and designed with an eye to attracting potential young buyers – those who were drawn to Nick because of comparisons with Ian Curtis and Morrissey, or because Peter Buck and Matt Johnson dropped his name. It was a successful package, remaining on catalogue after sales settled down at around 35,000 in the UK. In America, *Way To Blue* was runner-up in the 1994 *Rolling Stone* Music Awards for 'Best Reissue'. Coming second behind Marvin Gaye was a position Nick Drake would not have minded.

In *NME*, Iestyn George drew comparison with Nirvana's Kurt Cobain, who died just a month before *Way To Blue* was released: 'Nick Drake only released three albums before overdosing on tranquillisers in 1974, at the age of 26. This may read like some grizzly blueprint for the decline of Kurt Cobain 20 years later, but the circumstances which led to Drake's death were very different. Every last detail of Kurt Cobain's sorry decline was charted in interviews, reviews and hearsay, whereas Drake's death went virtually unreported . . .'

In the year which saw the release of Oasis's debut album, George concluded his review: '*Way To Blue* shows that we were robbed of a phenomenal talent. Completists might question the artistic value of re-releasing material which is already widely available, but that's little more than a minor quibble. If Nick Drake means nothing to you, go buy this album. It could be the best musical discovery you make this year.'

20

One Monday afternoon in Seattle, Peter Buck, guitarist with REM, The World's Biggest Rock Band, bounces baby daughter Zoe on his knee as he crackles down the transatlantic line. It was the week that REM officially became TWBRB, after faxing confirmation of an $80-million deal with which Warner Bros secured the band's services for five albums and on into the next millennium. But what drew Buck to the phone was not megabucks or REM hype, it was his fondness for the work of Nick Drake.

. 'As a teenager growing up in Georgia, before punk came along, it was all those Allman Brothers, Lynnyrd Skynnyrd . . . Marshall-Tucker were huge. I saw Ten Years After play. It was all fine, but it wasn't what I wanted. Folk music to me, then, was all 100-year-old guys playing bluegrass music incredibly fast.

'What got me into Nick Drake was Led Zeppelin. I got that fourth Zeppelin album, liked the girl singing, and a friend said she's in Fairport Convention, so I bought that record, liked that. It was a time when Duane Allman was God, and, you know, you're a kid and you want to be different . . . The first Nick Drake record, I remember, was *Five Leaves Left*. I got it in a bargain bin, I guess he was still alive. I wasn't drawn to it because of the . . . lonely adolescent thing. There was just something to me, as a teenager growing up in Georgia, incredibly sophisticated about it – the way the strings came in, that baroque sound, the guitar, that frail voice.

'I guess I knew Joe Boyd's name from the Fairport Convention records, Richard Thompson albums, saw he produced the Nick album, so thought that must be OK. We worked with him on *Reconstruction Of The Fables* because we wanted to use horns and strings for the first time, and liked the way he had achieved that, particularly on Nick's records. At the time we came to work with Joe I was familiar with the myth, I had the *Fruit Tree* box set and had read the essay by then, and there had been articles in *Crawdaddy*.

'To my mind, there is a line you can draw between *Bryter Layter*, *Sketches Of Spain* and *Astral Weeks*. I didn't identify with the pained adolescent aspect, I was a teenager then, I didn't recognize it. It was the . . . quality of an album like *Five Leaves Left*. What's interesting about the guitar-playing is that he's playing blues, but in a folk kind of way. We tried to do that on *Automatic For The People*, blues signatures, but disguised them.'

Clive Gregson is another musician who was aware of Nick's work while he was still alive. Like many others, Clive first heard him on the Island *Bumpers* compilation, but it is Nick's final album to which Clive is drawn back, again and again: '*Pink Moon* is my all-time favourite record. I think it's just timeless music. If you listen to music from the early seventies – from any period actually – the fashionable, pop-orientated records usually only live best within that period.

'I think the thing about *Pink Moon*, it still sounds great, just a voice and a guitar – apart from a tiny bit of piano on one track – I love the songs, I love the way it sounded. I thought it was incredibly well recorded: the closeness of everything. I'd never heard an acoustic guitar sound that good on any record. I think with Nick's records, and *Pink Moon* particularly, you are always trying to figure out how they did it. And with that record, I can't begin to imagine how they did it – any of it. I've talked to John [Wood] about it, and he just says: "Well, we stuck a microphone there, and that was it." And you think, no, it can't possibly be that simple.'

Peter Buck and Clive Gregson are fairly unusual in that they discovered Nick's music while he was still alive; many, many more have come to it only posthumously. A trawl through the cuttings on the short life and career of Nick Drake would show that 99 per cent are posthumous, features full of retrospective wisdom and knowing hindsight. In 1993 a panel of experts at *The Times* chose the Top 100 rock albums of all time, and *Five Leaves Left* made a surprise appearance at number sixty, beating Michael Jackson's *Thriller*, Wings' *Band On The Run*, Pink Floyd's *The Wall* and The Eagles' *Hotel California*.

In a feature for the *Scotsman* in 1995, Brian Pendreigh charted

Nick's posthumous appeal: 'Literature and painting have thrown up numerous examples of people whose work was recognised only after their death: few of Emily Dickinson's poems were published in her lifetime and Vincent Van Gogh only ever sold one painting. But Nick Drake is probably the first rock singer to be discovered after his death. Death certainly boosted the careers of Jim Morrison, Jimi Hendrix and others, but they were already major stars. They were too wild to get through life. Drake was the opposite: Drake was too delicate.'

Pendreigh also asked Joe Boyd how Nick could have developed had he lived. Boyd replied: 'His fatalistic view of his life and career was very much part and parcel of his view of the world, which is not to say he was always fated or doomed to a short life. But it's very hard to say "Right, let's assume Nick was a healthy, optimistic . . . person" . . . I don't think Nick was hanging on as tightly as others of us do.'

Inevitably, you have to ask just what it is about Nick's music which sees it endure, so long after his death. I was curious what Boyd, who worked so closely with him, felt were the reasons his music has persisted for so long, in an industry renowned for its appreciation of the ephemeral: 'He wasn't observing other people, he was mostly observing *himself*, which is what makes his songs so interesting, his acute observations of his own predicament, which are full of humour and irony. I think it is partly in the structure of the songs; partly in the intelligence of the lyrics – because I think the two go together, the thing already fits together well, just with the guitar and the voice, and it's just so well constructed that the more things you add, the better it gets. I find the more I listen to the records, the more . . . startled I am by the incredible high quality of Nick's guitar work.'

Besides working closely alongside Boyd at Witchseason, Anthea Joseph knew Dylan, Paul Simon, Richard Thompson, Sandy Denny and Nick Drake. 'I don't think Nick had the chance to develop . . .' she reflected. 'But there was something about him which was special . . . The early death and unrealized potential, I believe, are absolutely factors. No question. And the fact that he was romantic, he looked romantic. You look at those sleeves . . . It's Byronesque, isn't it? Or Shelleyesque, actually . . .

'But this is Joe, I suppose. Joe's vision. The way he produced those records, the sleeves, and so on. They're extraordinarily romantic. But you do wonder, had things been slightly different, because there's undoubtedly a wonderful talent, given growing up, growing older, kicking the shit, what he would have developed into?'

Trevor Dann went on to produce the BBC coverage of Live Aid, and head Radio 1, but his enthusiasm for the music of Nick Drake remains undimmed: 'What is it about his records that makes them last? The first record is a gloriously complete album, it's one of those records that doesn't have a weak track, it's very consistent; very coherent, and contiguous in its mood. It's one of the great mood records; it doesn't try and have variety. This is not: here's a mixed portfolio of my talents. It's: this is what it is. And many of the great albums are like that . . . *Astral Weeks* being another example where it's really one thing all the way through. *Five Leaves Left* is one of those records where if you're in that mood, you put it on, and it stays there in that mood.

'I guess the other thing is, most introspective raincoat student music is pretty twee, and you grow out of it. But there is something about the spare lyrical quality that means even when you've grown up, it doesn't feel embarrassing. You have to remember back to the kind of lyrics that people were writing back in that era. They were, for the most part, hogwash . . . It was a particularly bad phase: hey, I've taken some drugs, and now I'm going to write a fairy tale. Here was a man who didn't do that. To my mind, he wrote about how he felt, and they're completely direct and personal.'

As a student, Iain Dunn was lucky enough to hear Nick Drake sit down and play the songs he had just completed: 'That sense of alienation in his music is something that speaks very strongly to people in that age group, between your late teens and your late twenties . . . And I think Nick was very, very accurate in replaying what he was going through, and synthesizing it into his songs . . . which was art in its own right, but also spoke to people. I think that by its nature, it's very direct, it's very personal, and I think it can still speak to people at quite a profound level, because you can say quite complex things through that sort of structure, which you can't necessarily say when it's production-based.'

While Jerry Gilbert has long been associated with Nick Drake because of his *Sounds* interview, he was also in a position to appreciate the developing talents of Richard Thompson, Sandy Denny, Al Stewart, Cat Stevens and John Martyn: 'I remember talking to Joe . . . just before Nick died when I was trying to get a story together . . . I know he'd laid down four tracks, and that Joe had definitely said to me how upbeat he was, and how he really felt this was almost like a renaissance for Nick, and how enthusiastic he felt about these four tracks. So in that sense I was shocked . . . It was like somebody who was terribly ill, and then suddenly started to get better, and then the next day they're dead, and it's like: so what happened then?

'I suppose Nick's reputation is built on a flimsy body of work. I don't remember Nick being anything other than someone who was sucked along in what ultimately became a really good movement of contemporary English folk performance. A really accomplished player, but almost – and it's an awful thing to say – a bit-part player.'

Nick's close friend John Martyn found the myth-making wore him down, and talking to Brendan Quayle he admitted: 'It gets a bit morbid at times, especially in America. It's awful, you get these dreadful people with spaced eyes going: "Hey, wanna talk about Nick?" . . . The first couple of times you feel sorry for them, but after four or five of them you go: "Not another nutter. He's dead, you fool. Dead! Dead! You're alive. Rejoice! Rejoice!"'

Danny Thompson also tires of the obsessives: 'I've had Italians who drive me mad. "Oh, you work with Nick Drake, tell me . . ." and they're always tortured souls. I look at the faces of, yet again, tortured people. I say: "Look, he wanted to top himself, and he topped himself. That's it!" Very irreverent, and they look at me in absolute horror as if I've just shot the Pope. I'm fed up with all this precious . . . There are still people alive who need writing about. I said to Joe, all these albums with, bless their hearts, Sandy, Nick . . . I said: "Joe, I'm still alive, how about giving me a deal?" People like Davy Graham, great talents, who are overlooked.'

Like it or not, premature death does bestow an extra degree of greatness. Life gets in the way of the myth. If Richard Thompson had died immediately after the release of *Henry The Human Fly*, would he have become Nick Drake? It is no reflection at all on the inherent quality of Nick's work to suggest that it was his premature death which guaranteed him his current cult status.

Late in 1996 Donovan played a showcase at Dingwalls in Camden Lock. He was magnificent. Opening the evening was singer-song-writer Beth Orton. Hailed as that week's next big thing, she was nervous and edgy. She wasn't captivating the crowd – she works better on record. As she tuned her guitar, she introduced one of her own songs, 'Galaxy Of Emptiness'. Hello, I thought, here's someone who likes Nick Drake.

While he was in London, I took the opportunity to speak to Donovan about Nick Drake. He too was wary about the cult which has labelled Nick as doomed: 'Tim Buckley, Nick, Tim Hardin. You get these figures who didn't quite make it, and they're there, and they're influential. There are those who like those cult influences, who would have preferred Nick not to have made it. They prefer it that he was dark and doomed. And yet he was like me in many ways, he was very isolated, and I felt isolated as a child and as a songwriter, until I got the support.'

After Nick's death, Robert Kirby carried on working with Joe Boyd and John Wood, on albums for Julie Covington and Any Trouble. He kept busy arranging until 1975, when he joined The Strawbs, and toured America with them for two years. For someone who died in 1974, like the moon on the tides, Nick Drake still exerts a strong pull on fellow singer-songwriters. Kirby, though, is still very much alive and working: 'Elvis Costello approached me to conduct the RPO at the Royal Albert Hall in January 1982 because of my work with Nick Drake. Jake Riviera's office contacted me and said that Elvis was really into the Nick Drake albums, and the arrangements, and wanted me to do the arrangements – they thought I was dead! For a long time, when Nick died, a lot of people thought I was dead.'

There is a roll-call of Nick Drake disciples that musters Kate Bush, REM, The The's Matt Johnson, Mark Eitzel, Beth Orton, Lucy Ray, The Cardigans, Belle & Sebastian ('They sound like Nick Drake fronting the BMX Bandits,' said the *NME*), Folk Implosion ('Nick Drake goes Trip Hop' – *Mojo*), Tom Verlaine, The Black Crowes, The Cure's Robert Smith, Nervous's Justin Travis and September 67. Stephen Duffy, who had flirted with Duran Duran and pop success as Stephen 'Tin Tin' Duffy in the early 1980s, came back in 1987 with a new band, The Lilac Time, who took their name from a line in Nick's 'River Man'.

Everything But The Girl were particularly keen on the legacy of Nick Drake. Selecting *Five Leaves Left* as one of his all-time favourite albums, Ben Watt told *Q* in 1994: 'It's the art of understatement – English folk-rock understatement I suppose. I love them as mood pieces as much as anything else, and again the fact that they have influences that are not directly from rock 'n' roll, and an un-embarrassed ability to mix almost semi-classical string arrangements with acoustic basses and acoustic guitars. I also like what I've read about Nick Drake – that he was terribly frustrated that he wasn't more popular than he was. He genuinely believed that what he was doing was potentially intensely commercial, which I find quite charming, because it so obviously isn't. But he really felt that he was saying something that was direct and would appeal to people in an open-hearted way. Rock 'n' roll needs grander gestures, unfortunately.'

Without carbon-copying Nick, one way to pay homage is to cover one of his songs, but to date, incredibly few have been covered. It is not as if they are unwieldy word-orgies, like Dylan's 'It's Alright Ma . . .' or wilfully arcane like Richard Thompson's 'Don't Sit On My Jimmy Shands'. Nick's songs are open and accessible, melodic and rhythmically memorable. The lyrics are not challenging or abstruse. Yet, aside from the 1992 tribute album *Brittle Days*, Nick's catalogue remains largely unplundered.

Five years after 'My Boy Lollipop', Millie became one of only two acts to cover a song by Nick Drake during his lifetime, when 'Mayfair' appeared on her *Time Will Tell* album in 1970. Nick's former labelmates Tir Na Nog included 'Ride' on their 1973 Chrysalis debut, *Strong In The Sun*; and singer-songwriter Lucinda Williams recorded 'Which Will'; but otherwise, covers of Nick Drake songs are rarer than rocking-horse droppings.

For years, Joe Boyd has cherished the idea of a Nick Drake tribute album, on which contemporary acts would cover their own favourite song of Nick's. The concept reached its high watermark in the early 1990s, when tributes appeared to Leonard Cohen (three times), Elton John, Jimi Hendrix and Richard Thompson (twice), among others. Among the names pencilled in for the Nick tribute were REM's Peter Buck and The Psychedelic Furs' Richard Butler together on 'Pink Moon', John Cale and Britain's premier pedal-steel player, B.J. Cole ('River Man'), All About Eve ('Clothes Of Sand'), The Black Crowes ('Black Eyed Dog') and Everything But The Girl ('Northern Sky'). Plans have been in the air since at least 1990, but at the time of writing, the Nick Drake tribute remains unreleased.

The kudos which is wrapped around the late Nick Drake manifests itself in the oddest ways and the strangest places. The 1996 catalogue for Polygram/Island music, representing the publishing interests of some of the greatest songwriters of the rock 'n' roll era (Elton John, Bob Marley, U2, Van Morrison), boasted a reproduction of Nick's original handwritten lyrics for 'Fruit Tree'.

In *Record Collector*'s poll of collectable artists, the second highest-climbing name in 1997 was Nick Drake, up 138 places to number eighty-seven. A sharp-eyed *Mojo* reader noted that the back sleeve of

Five Leaves Left was just visible in a scene in the film *Grace Of My Heart*. But surely the most bizarre rumour recently to attach itself to Nick Drake was that one of his songs had been used as background music for a Nike ad screened on MTV; according to Nike's advertising agency, there is absolutely no truth in the rumour.

By the beginning of 1997 *Heartbeat: Number One Love Songs Of The 60s*, which features 'Fruit Tree' as its closing track, had sold over 300,000 copies, to become the eighth-best-selling compilation album of 1996. As well as providing a good selection of golden oldies from pop's most fondly remembered decade, the record obviously sold on the back of the enormously popular retro TV drama. Its success meant that in the space of just a few months roughly ten times more people heard Nick Drake than ever bought his records while he was alive.

Unquestionably, Nick Drake has been pigeon-holed; safely slotted into the template of tragic, doomed young poet, whose talent went unappreciated by record company and public at large, leading to depression, and ultimately, premature death. But that is all too pat, and it does the life and memory and work of Nick Drake a grave disservice.

So strong has the morbid myth become, and so delicate the body of work, I asked Peter Buck if he thought that Nick's death was in danger of suffocating the innate quality of the music: 'I don't buy the posthumous appeal thing. The guitar player from Chicago died, and I don't remember legions of fans going out and buying the first four Chicago albums. The thing with Nick is I couldn't see him around now, or in the future, aged sixty-five, and doing the fourth farewell tour. I mean, hindsight is a great thing, isn't it? – all the symbols that are there on the records and in the lyrics.'

Dave Pegg, who watched Nick opening the show for Fairport early in 1970 and worked with him on *Bryter Layter*, said: 'It's awfully sad what happened to Nick . . . he obviously did want to be successful, it's all that stuff, you don't know anything about people at the time. He was the last person I would have thought would have taken it that seriously . . .

'Nick was a great talent, and it's great that people appreciate him. It's great that young people do; the only cred I get is that I played on a Nick Drake album. Which is quite good when you look like I do. If you were clever enough to analyse why people like something that much, I'd have retired thirty years ago. They are just great songs, and they sound good. Without knowing anything about the personality behind the songs, if you heard *Bryter Layter* for the first time, and you didn't know who it was . . . I think most people would really like it. As a guitarist, he is so complete . . . He was really good. He could do stuff in one take. There was never a problem, and rhythmically he was incredibly sound.'

Clive Gregson: 'It's kind of hard to imagine what he would have carried on doing . . . It was totally unfashionable then. It is, in many ways, totally unfashionable now. The fact that so many people come to it, is to do with the timeless quality. It's just basically very, very good music, very good songwriting. There's also the air of mystery surrounding his life and his death. There's so little that's really known about Nick . . .

'The cult is certainly associated with the premature death. The fact that there will be no more records. It's a very finite thing you can look at and say, well, there's basically three records, a compilation of out-takes . . . But I do think that Nick was a great artist as well. There is something about *Pink Moon*. I don't understand it. There's something intriguing, it's fascinating. I can always find something new in it even after listening to it all these years. Nothing feels out of place. To do something so personal, so sparse and simple, for me, I can't think of any other record that captures that sound.'

Hidden in the hinterland of Shepherd's Bush, Nomis Studios is a big rehearsal and recording complex where, early in January 1997, I went to talk to Paul Weller about Nick Drake. Weller struck many as an unlikely convert to the cause: there appeared to be little to connect the fiery leader of The Jam and epicene co-host of The Style Council with the quietly introspective music of Nick Drake. But since the relaunch of Weller's career as a solo act in the early 1990s, his own music had taken on a more reflective edge, and Weller is always careful to cite sources. While contemporaries in The Clash and Sex Pistols had railed against what had gone before, in pugnaciously punk fashion, Weller has always shown an appreciation of pop, R&B and soul history. He was turned on to Nick by hearing 'River Man', and when he began name-checking Nick as an influence in interviews, Weller's fans also began taking an interest in the music of the singer-songwriter who had died before they were born.

Preparing for his fourth solo album, Weller sat alongside cappuccino compadre and Oasis biographer Paolo Hewitt, and talked about Nick Drake: 'For me it's quite simple: it's the melodic side that attracted me. I only heard his stuff three years ago maybe, that was the first I ever heard of him. The first thing I heard was "River Man", which I think is just fantastic. The melody is so brilliant. So that's what hooked me . . . Intimate, the voice, the guitar, the melody . . . As a guitarist, I like the open tunings, which is probably a standard folk-music tuning, but I don't know that stuff, so he was my introduction to that style. I'm not a "disciple" of Nick Drake. I just heard his records and liked them, liked that very distinctive thing he was doing.

'The fact he died young, that always adds to the myth, plus the fact he only ever made three albums, and they're all really good albums. He didn't get to make the fourth or fifth shitty one . . . "At The Chime Of A City Clock", *Bryter Layter*, is brilliant. The instrumental stuff on that, mixes it up a bit. "Hazey Jane", "Northern Sky", they're just great melodies, moody and menacing. Great songs, that's why they're timeless, that's why he lasts. There is an Englishness, pastoral . . . There's a classical style in his music as well, which is very English.

'With Nick, it was that one particular song, "River Man", that did it for me. The arrangement, the strings, that alone. I like great melodies, songs. It's really hard to come up with an original melody, to come up with something that you haven't heard before. He's got at least half a dozen that are real classics, as soon as you hear them, so distinctive. I don't pay an awful lot of attention to his lyrics, because they're so samey, but on top of the melodies, they take you somewhere else: they transcend a lot of that sadness.'

Weller was intrigued when I mentioned Nick's virtual invisibility. With the prospect of recording a new album, resultant promo videos, the endless cycle of interviews and concerts to promote the album . . . With the next two years of his life effectively bound up, he seemed envious of the way things were back then. 'So he only ever made three albums, a dozen gigs, never played America and one interview? That's the way to do it!'

After Nick's death in 1974, Rodney and Molly Drake were touched by the continuing interest shown in their son's music, and were always welcoming to fans and admirers. Far Leys was open house to those who travelled to see the house where Nick grew up and died. Nick's music was what drew them there, and his parents were clearly delighted by anyone who was touched by it. Only too aware of how neglected Nick felt during his lifetime, their joy in the lasting, even escalating, interest in his music was heartfelt.

Molly: 'We always appreciated music, even if we didn't understand the technicalities – the extraordinary ability on the guitar – neither of us played the guitar, so we didn't understand. People come from far and wide and say: "How did Nick tune his guitar?" and of course we have to say we don't know.'

Rodney: 'It's not surprising that we didn't really appreciate his music, we were of a different generation, and even his own generation didn't appreciate it at the time. I think he was ahead of his time, wasn't he?'

In 1986, twelve years after Nick's death, a young American guitarist called Scott Appel wrote to Rodney and Molly Drake, expressing his appreciation of Nick's music. Scott was particularly fascinated by the unusual guitar tunings which Nick had used, and wondered if his parents could help clarify them. Neither could, but his enquiry opened up a correspondence which continued until Molly's death. Scott was clearly an aficionado of Nick's work, and both his parents responded to his knowledge of, and enthusiasm for, their son's music.

A *Daily Express* profile of Gabrielle in 1997, published to coincide with her West End opening in *Lady Windermere's Fan*, dubbed Nick 'Britain's answer to Bob Dylan' and quoted Gabrielle on the people who made pilgrimages to Far Leys: 'After he died, youngsters from all over the world would turn up at my parents' home to talk about Nick. They were welcomed. His fans were delightful. Some had the kind of problems which used to trouble him. My parents were destroyed by his death, but it never dominated their lives. They didn't become sad. They took pleasure in the interest young people showed in Nick. That was a great help to them.'

They came from Europe and America, drawn to the neat and tidy house in the tiny village of Tanworth. Rodney and Molly were largely unaware of how valuable Nick's possessions were to his fans, but they were touched by the continuing interest, and consequently, irreplaceable manuscripts, photos and other items were handed over in good faith, never to be returned. Joe Boyd and Island Records advised them, but they too were probably unprepared for the enduring intensity of interest in Nick's music.

Scott Appel's initial contact with Rodney and Molly coincided with the release of Nick's posthumous fourth album, and Molly wrote to him just after they had received a finished copy of *Time Of No Reply*: 'Knowing that young people still love and play Nick's music has been our only comfort since he died . . . Rodney and I feel the more Nick's music is given out to the world the happier we shall be.'

In their continuing correspondence with Scott Appel, the Drakes sensed someone with a real affinity for Nick's music, and they wrote to him about some 'work tapes' which Nick had left behind: 'Some time in 1974 Nick, who was by then *very* withdrawn and uncommunicative, went over to Suffolk to see John Wood who used to own a recording studio of his own and also recorded for Island and understood Nick and his problems. Nick returned with this tape but never told us what was on it – he just put it away with the other tapes he had. I did not discover it till after his death by which time Island had the recordings of his last four songs, complete with words.'

Through a mutual love of Nick's music, Scott and the Drakes began to discuss the idea of Scott working from Nick's tapes to develop the fragments, a prospect which delighted his parents. They were, however, very clear about how it should be handled: 'provided the songs are kept the same in essence and not made unrecognizable – and providing too that it is always clear – and I know with you at the helm it always *would* be made clear – that these are Nick's songs'.

True to his word, Scott sat down and began transposing snippets of tape, and trying to figure out the tunings, which were unique to Nick. It was like trying to crack the Enigma code. Nick's friend Robert Kirby understood the problems Scott faced: 'I defy anyone to sit down with a Nick Drake song and try to figure out how to play it,' he was quoted as saying on the sleeve of Scott's finished *Nine Of Swords* album, 'the songs just don't follow the ordinary rules of composition.'

Talking to me in 1997, Kirby was still keen to sing Nick's praises as a guitarist: 'When he first came into my room . . . as soon as he played the guitar, I've never heard anything like it before or since, in terms of virtuosity. Maybe some people play faster, maybe some people play more complicated pieces, but he never gave a bad performance . . . I know for a fact that he practised a phenomenal amount. When he was at home alone, he practised and practised and practised. He had to, just to maintain that technique. Even on the first album – something like "River Man", or something like "Three Hours", where there is a very complicated guitar part – it was always note for note the same. He might vary tempi sometimes . . . but every string, every fingernail connected at the same microsecond, each time he did it.

'All five of the fingers on his right hand could be used equally for playing a melody . . . the thumb would come up and do the tenor part on the D and A strings. But he wouldn't just get the notes right, he would control the tone and timbre . . . He'd got the technique of a virtuoso classical guitarist.'

At the core of *Nine Of Swords* are Nick Drake originals which he never lived to record. The record opens with 'Bird Flew By', one of the first songs Nick ever wrote; a wistful lament, and in Scott Appel's hands, quintessentially Nick, with its rhetorical refrain 'What's the point of a year or a season?' The song evokes the haunted territory which Nick had made his own, with its 'list of false starts and crumbled broken hearts'. Though long in his repertoire, Nick had never felt happy enough with 'Blossom' to record it. It is one of the most optimistic songs in his canon, with the influence of Joni Mitchell's 'The Circle Game' and 'Both Sides Now' faintly evident.

Concerned that the release of *Nine Of Swords* would sully Nick's memory, Joe Boyd was reluctant to grant Appel permission to tamper with Nick's music. Nick's parents, however, had no doubts: 'I'm sure there can be no objection whatever to your developing the piece you are interested in – indeed, as far as Molly and I are concerned we should welcome it,' wrote Rodney in 1986. The following year he confirmed: 'On the legal position over your making use of Nick's music (developing his themes and so on) I do not see that there can possibly be any restriction on your using songs that have never been published, beyond getting our agreement, and that you have.'

There is no knowing how Nick himself would have tackled these works in progress, or indeed if he would have chosen to develop them at all. But Nick's fans are insatiably hungry for any crumb of unreleased music, and if the only way they can hear 'Bird Flew By' or 'Blossom' is to hear them interpreted by Scott Appel, then they will happily settle for that.

Having spent so much time assimilating his unique musicianship, Scott Appel wrote a revealing article on Nick's guitar playing for *Frets* magazine: 'Drake's right hand technique was considerable. He produced a dreadnought-like sound with a small-bodied Guild M-20 – the only guitar he ever used to record. He fingerpicked with a combination of flesh and nail, and used only his nails for strumming. He never used picks of any kind. The recorded sound of Drake's guitar was also partly due to the miking techniques of his sound engineer John Wood, who already had recorded British musicians Richard Thompson, John Martyn and Robin Williamson, using a four microphone setup for Drake's acoustic. One ambient mike was placed all the way across the room. Power was not the only characteristic of Drake's right-hand technique. He played unusual and irregular patterns with his thumb, contrary to the clearly defined bass rhythms played by the thumb in most fingerpicking patterns (the alternating bass, for example).'

Paul Wheeler, who had innumerable opportunities to observe Nick and his guitar technique, smiled when he remembered those Cambridge days: 'There was a professionalism about Nick . . . I don't remember many gigs, but even just sitting round people's rooms, if he'd written a new song or something, if he played through something, he would always get it absolutely right. He would wait until people were listening before he played it. He would never play it twice. There was always a sense of professionalism. He never played a bum note. He wouldn't do the washing-up because it might break his nails. So he was conscious of his reputation.'

As a fellow guitarist, Paul Wheeler studied Nick's playing closely; he too felt that the unique strength lay in his right hand: 'As a guitarist, Nick used his right hand in a way that I don't think anyone like John or Bert used it . . . You see, even someone like Richard Thompson doesn't use his right hand that subtly . . . Speaking as a guitarist, it's his right hand that's interesting. Synchronizing your fingers, most guitarists only use two fingers on the right hand. Nick definitely used his whole hand, and he used it in a very interesting way. Listen to "River Man", and get a guitarist to explain to you what's happening, and he won't be able to!'

Over the years, Nick Drake's inimitable guitar playing has contributed hugely to his enduring appeal. While the songs are timeless and beguiling, for musicians Nick's tunings, his fluent fingering and playing are transcendent. An accomplished singer-songwriter and nimble guitarist himself, Clive Gregson is fascinated by Nick's playing: 'I cannot figure out the guitar tunings, I don't know what the guitar's tuned to 99 per cent of the time; the chords, the fingerings, the way his voice sounds that good, it's so dry. It's a complete mystery. But at the end of the day, it's just a bloke playing the guitar and singing. But it doesn't sound like anything else I've ever heard.'

Just what is it about Nick's guitar tunings which continues to fascinate people?: 'I think it's incredible technique, for a start. He's finger-picking in really odd rhythms . . . "River Man" is in 5/4, and the rhythmic part, the playing on that, is just astonishing. And in some ways it sounds simpler than it really is. I can sit down, and pick out certain things, but it never sounds . . . right. It's a technical facility way beyond . . . I guess it's a very musician thing, and a lot of the latter interest in Nick is from musicians and players. It's terribly understated, it's very tasteful. "The Road", off *Pink Moon*, that is just rhythmically so complex, and yet it's not hard chords. There are aspects of it that are simple . . . There's a little instrumental called "Horn". The way he plays it, tiny little thing, most people wouldn't even think that way. The comparison with Richard [Thompson] is interesting, because having worked with Richard, I can rationalize, I can understand what Richard does, because I've seen him do it a lot – I can't do it, I can't begin to do it – but I kind of understand it. Whereas with Nick, there's a lot of it that I don't understand.'

No mean guitarist himself, Nick's friend John Martyn was equally fascinated by his guitar tunings. Martyn had watched Nick first-hand, but was still baffled by just how he did it. He spoke in 1986 of his memories of watching him hunched over his guitar, endlessly tuning and retuning: 'Nick was extraordinarily secretive about all that. I could probably work them out for you . . . he used seconds quite a lot, very strange tunings, diminished as well, so when you applied just two fingers you'd change the thing in a very radical way. I remember his fingering here – he had the most beautiful fingers when he played, and they were made even more beautiful by the fact that the shapes that he'd play were not those you would normally see when other people play. Very interesting little shapes . . . I just never asked him, I was too busy toddling off on my own and doing my own stuff. He's a much-underrated player.'

Jeremy Mason was there, in early 1967, as Nick Drake developed his guitar tunings. Nick had learned the basic guitar chords from David Wright at Marlborough only a few years before, but in Aix, Jeremy was driven mad by Nick's endless tuning and retuning of his guitar. Because there was nothing else to do, Jeremy began drawing, and because there was nobody else to draw, his first subject was the teenager on the bed opposite: 'What was probably my first attempt at drawing was a drawing of Nick playing his guitar, which I turned into a linocut. And bad as I was, that was the way I remember him sitting. He always wore those moccasins. He always looked at the guitar. The guitar picking, the sound that you hear now on the records, he developed in Aix . . . He sat for hours on his bed. I knew then he was getting pretty serious about it.

'He used to sit on his bed, and loosen the strings on his guitar, completely, as I recall. I think he had now obviously started to smoke – marijuana – and he would strum away, and tighten them up as he went. I think he formulated it there, because the sound I hear on the records now is the sound he was getting then.'

At Cambridge and at Sound Techniques, Robert Kirby watched Nick develop his unique guitar style. He was also one of the few people with whom Nick ever discussed the actual mechanics of songwriting. For Nick, the genesis of a song came from playing the guitar, and finding a phrase which he could make his own and develop. With memories of Nick in London and Cambridge, Kirby remembered: 'What he'd do is play for fifteen or twenty minutes, non-stop, moving from figure to figure, and the figure that I'm thinking of is the introduction to "Things Behind The Sun". That was going for years before he recorded it on *Pink Moon*. I think a lot of Nick's writing came from the fact that he would experiment with a detuning, experiment with a figure within it, and that would give him the basis for a song . . .

'He did talk about the music, when we were at Cambridge, or when we were doing *Bryter Layter*. He would come up with strong guitar phrases, harmonic sequences, tunings . . . He would have these parts in his head for a long time, and then as lyrics came, he'd got a library of parts that would go with that. It makes it sound a bit mechanical, but I believe that's the way they came . . . I'm sure there must have been plenty of songs when he was sitting there and a lyric came, and then he wrote some music for it, but all of his experimentation came with the guitar. He took the guitar to extremes.'

Both Rodney and Molly Drake were delighted with what Scott Appel had achieved with Nick's music on *Nine Of Swords* and they continued to correspond for years. When Molly moved to a smaller house after Rodney's death in 1988, Scott suggested donating Nick's manuscripts to a museum archive, but Molly's reply confirms what many still fail to understand: 'there is *so little* that Nick left behind him – apart from the legacy of his music. He never wrote anything down, never kept a diary – hardly even wrote his name in his own books. It was as if he didn't want anything of himself to remain except his songs – to quote from one of those songs – I have always described him to myself as "a soul with no footprint" . . .

'The only written thing I have of Nick's is one exercise book (from Cambridge University) in which he put down the words to most of his songs. This is one of my most precious possessions and I could not part with it . . . Apart from this all I have are his letters from school – Marlborough College – every single one of which I have kept. But these are just schoolboy letters talking of football, hockey and cricket matches, athletics, lessons or lectures etc – and nothing about music whatsoever, except an occasional reference to a classical lesson.'

At the beginning of their correspondence in 1986, when the Drakes sent Scott Appel the tape containing over four hours' worth of works in progress, which Nick had recorded but never released, his mother Molly noted poignantly that 'Bird Flew By' was 'one of Nick's earliest songs, played on his old original 20 dollar guitar. It has never appeared on any record – I love it and it reminds me of the very young – and still happy – Nick before the shadows closed in.'

21

As you trawl through the life, at the end and in the end, in Churchill's words, 'the terrible ifs accumulate'. If Nick had sold more records while he was still alive, it might have tempered his depression . . . If the anti-depressants hadn't been dished out as freely as chocolates at Christmas . . . If Nick had been born with a thicker skin . . . In the end, though, Nick Drake was born, and died, the way he was. The sadness and introspection gave birth to the music. Had he been less contemplative, it is unlikely that he would have produced such inimitable music. And music was very important to Nick.

Was it the music industry which killed him? It is a popular scapegoat – an industry which is venal in its pursuit of profit. There have been sacrifices, but they are outnumbered by the survivors. For every Janis or Jimi, there have been hundreds who made it through: from Wee Willie Harris to Keith Richards, and back. Friends who knew him during the early stages of his life, right up to the time he began making a career of music, emphasized the normality of the Nick they knew, but somehow I think it is too easy to blame an industry for his very personal problems.

It is conceivable that drugs accentuated and made even more frail an already fragile personality. A precursor was Syd Barrett, the archetypal acid casualty. But with Syd too there is evidence that the drugs simply exacerbated problems that were already there. Drugs were certainly tacitly understood to be part and parcel of rock 'n' roll life. Island Records' David Betteridge had plenty of experience dealing with fragile egos, dealing with 'young human beings working under very difficult social circumstances'. Island's Art Director, Annie Sullivan, remembers the last time she saw Nick, at the Hampstead Heath photo shoot for *Pink Moon*, and assumed his shabby condition was due to drugs. David Sandison, Nick's press officer at Island, told me: 'I suspect he smoked a lot of dope – everybody did. But then if you are inclined to introspection, hash certainly is not inclined to make you come out of yourself.'

Simon Crocker had sunny memories of Nick at Marlborough. He also saw him six months before he died, and was shocked at his deterioration. By then, Crocker was in the music business himself, managing Pete Atkin, who had fashioned a career singing the lyrics of Clive James. As he had been around the music business and was aware of the drug question, I asked him if he assumed Nick's condition was drug-induced. 'Yes, at the time I did . . .' he told me. 'But I don't know how involved in drugs he got at that period. I don't know how far drugs contributed to his problems . . . Robert Kirby had seen it all gradually happen; for me it had been this huge jump. He was very shaky . . . I thought it seemed to be a kind of stoned . . . He probably wasn't. Looking back, he'd been taking anti-depressants, which have the same kind of effect, making you . . . confused.'

Nick is known to have smoked dope, suspected to have dropped acid and rumoured to have tried heroin. The only difference between Arthur Lubow's piece on Nick Drake for *New Times* in 1978 and his essay which accompanied the *Fruit Tree* box set in 1979, was the four lines excised for the latter ('He told one friend he was "looking to score – the big one". Heroin? "I've tried everything else," he said. "There's nothing else left." He never got any'). When the censored lines were spotted, it only fuelled the rumours that heroin was a contributory factor. It is easy to understand how such rumours sprung up: in those days people – particularly music-business people – who died of overdoses invariably had taken drugs supplied by a dealer rather than a doctor.

Rumours of Nick's use of heroin persisted long after his death and the 'heroin chic' of the nineties saw them gain even more ground. In fact, the only occasion when Brian Wells remembers Nick showing any interest in heroin, owes more to Cheech & Chong than *Trainspotting*: 'I remember Nick coming round to a flat where I lived [in 1973] . . . with my wife saying: "Look, I really want to try smack." So I said: "Are you sure?" because neither of us had ever done any . . . He said: "Yeah, I really think . . . I want to try it", and it was all slightly hesitant. It wasn't: "I'm *really* determined to try it."

'So I said, well, do you want to give this guy a call? I knew someone who was doing smack, and he said: "Yeah, OK." We'd maybe had a joint . . . and it was quite late, but he'd suddenly introduced the subject: "I want to try smack." It wasn't: "There's nothing else left for me, I want to do it." It's just: "I've been thinking about it, and I *think* I want to try the big one."

'I was a bit wary of this, because I was smoking dope and getting drunk, but not into taking heroin. And I phoned this guy who'd got a flat in Soho, and they picked the phone up and I was looking at Nick and said: "There's nothing to worry about", and this guy said: "What do you mean, there's nothing to worry about?" I was saying to Nick: "Just relax, man." And this guy, whose number I'd got, was getting really freaked out at the end of the phone . . . Nick started laughing and I just put the phone down. We fell about laughing.

'I said I didn't ask him for any gear, he just freaked out at the other end of the phone, God knows what he's stuffing himself with . . . So I called back and said: "Look, I called a minute ago . . .", and the guy says: "Who the fuck are you?" I said: "Look, I'm sorry, I didn't know what to say to you. I just wondered if you'd got any smack." He said: "Don't ever ring this number again. Never, never, never ring this number again!" and he slammed the phone down. And so that was that . . . As far as I know, Nick never took heroin. He wasn't really a big drug user.'

Perhaps if he had become an engineer like his father, or a surgeon like his grandfather, Nick's life would have been less troubled. Maybe a less privileged upbringing would have toughened him, made him a degree more street-wise, a little less sensitive. Or was there simply something there in Nick all along? So that whichever path he took, a sense of failure and of worthlessness would have dogged him to the end of his days? There might have been more days, but would they have been better or brighter days? Or maybe he was just a poor, sad, lost boy, brought down by illness, who didn't find a cure in time.

It is fascinating, but fruitless to speculate. We will never know. Even those closest to him could never know. It seems likely that not even Nick knew. But Nick's death cannot be elevated to any heroic stature. We have to accept that an overdose of prescribed medicine was the method of his tragically premature death; and by investing false heroism in his death we only undermine the very substantial achievements of his life.

Any valour and heroism in Nick's all-too-short life came in the courage of his living. It can be seen in his proud but foolhardy determination to try to beat his illness on his own, and in the will to go back and record even after he had apparently given up hope and retreated to Tanworth. It came in the day-to-day battles with despair, the acceptance of a life unfulfilled and empty, and the continued, weary living of that life.

In the tireless quest for an answer, an explanation, Nick's lyrics have been dissected as systematically and painstakingly as a corpse on a mortuary slab. With the easy wisdom of hindsight, you can sift through Nick's work and find eerie premonitions and chill forebodings by the bucketload. But this is treacherous territory: analyse the lyrics of any introspective young songwriter, and you are unlikely to divine plump, pragmatic, middle-aged contentment; and yet, for most, that was the more likely fate. John Martyn pointed out the dangers in conversation with Andy Robson: 'Nick was neither generous nor outgoing. I sound like I'm having a pop at him now, don't I? . . . But I'm just trying to deflate the myth. I hate that myth-making. You could listen to my music and say I was a fucking lunatic, or a really romantic soul. Yet neither of those are true. And maybe it was the same for Nick.'

Stuart Maconie's *Q* review of *Way To Blue* also tried to disabuse the myth-makers: 'Eulogies about Nick Drake often make romantic noises about his being "not of this world" and the like while ignoring the fact that he was mentally ill. To treat him as some super cultural sage rather than a gifted, sick, unhappy young man is both to cheapen his tragedy and undervalue his music.'

The combination of Nick's looks, body of work and premature death conspires against all rational objections, to reinforce the romantic myth of the doomed and tragic poet, who in dying young achieved the acclaim which was denied him in life. The very Englishness of his work places Nick in a line which stretches from Byron and Shelley through to Wilfred Owen and Rupert Brooke. These are not easy temptations to avoid.

But no life worth the name is ever that simple, and even the brief life of Nick Drake abounds with contradictions: the boy who seemed to personify the corrosive effects of loneliness, though he never really left his parents' home; who found communication such an effort, but reached out so fluently, to so many, through his work. The artist who valued integrity above all, yet grew increasingly bitter at his own lack of commercial success. To cast Nick in the role of doomed poet, first you must reconcile that image with his avowed prowess at athletics.

To paint Nick as a perpetual outsider, you must explain away his conviviality at Marlborough. To blame the record industry for Nick's failure, you must consider whether Nick's own unwillingness to gig was not a major factor in his lack of recognition.

Try as you might, it is hard to reconcile the athletic schoolboy in the C1 House rugby XV with the gaunt and haunted figure pictured on Hampstead Heath only a handful of years later. But always the dark side is taken for the *real* Nick Drake. The truth of a whole life is sought solely in those last few years, dominated by depression, when Nick himself had all but forgotten who he really was. His death has become his defining moment, like a prism which distorts the way in which we look at the whole short life. And yet his overdose, whether accidental or deliberate, was probably no more than the impulse of one lonely, confused, pre-dawn moment.

If Nick Drake was doomed during his lifetime, how much worse that he should now be doomed again in death; his life defined not by what he was, nor even by what he achieved, but simply by the nature of the illness that cursed him.

Nick Drake remains a luminous presence – the very stuff of legend. But as is so often the case, the myth clashes with the life. Nick's sad, solitary death, after a prolonged bout of depression, sealed his reputation as prophet of the disaffected, the outsider's outsider. But the truth is equally that of a shy boy, popular and successful at his public school, who ran races and set records, passed exams and bunked off down to London to listen to music. He wrote songs and tried them out on friends, and he practised and practised and practised on the guitar. Such base reality humankind cannot bear.

In researching and writing this life of Nick Drake, I found myself cutting across borders and boundaries: of the English public-school system, and the freewheeling London underground scene; of a close-knit family in rural England, and a gifted golden boy who came adrift. Of an artist who never achieved commercial success in his lifetime, but won the pyrrhic prize of posthumous fame. Of gregarious survivors and a reclusive casualty, and the difficulty of telling them apart. All the strands converged in the short, bitter-sweet life of Nick Drake.

At times, though, the myth has threatened to drown out the melodies. So insubstantial are the facts of Nick's life that his audience have imposed their own flaws and fantasies on to a virtually blank canvas. The cult of Nick Drake is, to paraphrase Oscar Wilde, Narcissus glimpsing his own reflection, unable to tear himself away from the beauty he finds in the mirror. For some, the real beauty lies in the emptiness.

There are no easy answers. Perhaps in the end facts can only diminish the myth, but ultimately the life is more important. For whatever the truth about Nick Drake's death, it remains a tragedy – just as his legacy of extraordinary songs remains a triumph, and a joyful one at that.

DISCOGRAPHY

For all that has been written, said and sung about Nick Drake, what made him so special is to be found in the three records he wrote and recorded between 1968 and 1972. Island Records supplied the current catalogue numbers and original release dates of these albums:

FIVE LEAVES LEFT
ILPS 9105, 1 September 1969 (CD: IMCD 8, March 1987)
'Time Has Told Me', 'River Man', 'Three Hours', 'Way To Blue', 'Day Is Done', 'Cello Song', 'The Thoughts Of Mary Jane', 'Man In A Shed', 'Fruit Tree', 'Saturday Sun'.

BRYTER LAYTER
ILPS 9134, 1 November 1970 (CD: IMCD 71, May 1987)
'Introduction', 'Hazey Jane II', 'At The Chime Of A City Clock', 'One Of These Things First', 'Hazey Jane I', 'Bryter Layter', 'Fly', 'Poor Boy', 'Northern Sky', 'Sunday'.

PINK MOON
ILPS 9184, 25 February 1972 (CD: IMCD 94, April 1990)
'Pink Moon', 'Place To Be', 'Radio', 'Which Will', 'Horn', 'Things Behind The Sun', 'Know', 'Parasite', 'Ride', 'Harvest Breed', 'From The Morning'.

FRUIT TREE
NDSP100, 9 March 1979
Island's three-LP box set of the original albums, but with the last four
tracks of *Pink Moon* replaced with Nick's final recordings:
'Rider On The Wheel', 'Black Eyed Dog', 'Hanging On A Star',
'Voice From The Mountain'.

FRUIT TREE
HNBX 5302, August 1986 (CD: HNCD 5402, December 1991 in LP-
sized box; reissued August 1996 in CD-sized box, same catalogue
number)
Hannibal's revised and expanded four-LP box set, which restored
Pink Moon to its original format and added the new album *Time Of
No Reply*.

TIME OF NO REPLY
HNBL 1318 (CD: HNCD 1318, March 1987)
Posthumous fourth album including seven new songs and the four
tracks from the final session, initially only available as part of the
revised box set.
'Time Of No Reply', 'I Was Made To Love Magic', 'Joey', 'Clothes
Of Sand', 'Man In A Shed', 'Mayfair', 'Fly', 'The Thoughts Of Mary
Jane', 'Been Smoking Too Long', 'Strange Meeting II', 'Rider On The
Wheel', 'Black Eyed Dog', 'Hanging On A Star', 'Voice From The
Mountain'.

NICK DRAKE COMPILATIONS
HEAVEN IN A WILD FLOWER
ILPS 9826, 28 May 1985 (CD: IMCD 91, April 1990)
Compiled by Trevor Dann from Nick's three original albums.
'Fruit Tree', 'Cello Song', 'Thoughts Of Mary Jane', 'Northern Sky',
'River Man', 'At The Chime Of A City Clock', 'Introduction', 'Hazey
Jane I', 'Hazey Jane II', 'Pink Moon', 'Road', 'Which Will', 'Things
Behind The Sun', 'Time Has Told Me'.

WAY TO BLUE
(IMCD 196, 31 May 1994).
Compiled by Joe Boyd from original three albums plus *Time Of No Reply*.
'Cello Song', 'Hazey Jane I', 'Way To Blue', 'Things Behind The Sun', 'River Man', 'Poor Boy', 'Time Of No Reply', 'From The Morning', 'One Of These Things First', 'Northern Sky', 'Which Will', 'Hazey Jane II', 'Time Has Told Me', 'Pink Moon', 'Black Eyed Dog', 'Fruit Tree'.

MULTI-ARTIST COMPILATIONS
NICE ENOUGH TO EAT (IWPS6, 1969) Includes 'Time Has Told Me'.

BUMPERS (IDP1, 1970) Includes 'Hazey Jane I'.

EL PEA (IDLP1, 1971) Includes 'One Of These Things First'.

VOICES (HNCD 8301, 1990) Includes 'Black Eyed Dog'.

FOLK ROUTES (IMCD 197, 1994) Includes 'Road'.

Latterly two compilations appeared within weeks of each other, each featuring a Nick Drake track:
AND I WRITE THE SONGS: 34 SINGER/SONGWRITER CLASSICS
(Debutante 553 062-2, 1996)
Chris De Burgh finally appears on disc with Nick, alongside Richard Thompson, Tim Hardin, Sandy Denny and John Martyn. Nick is rather bafflingly represented by the instrumental 'Bryter Layter'.

HEARTBEAT: NUMBER ONE LOVE SONGS OF THE SIXTIES
(RADCD 46, 1996)
CD spin-off from enormously popular TV series. This forty-four-track double CD sold over 250,000 copies in the UK, thereby allowing Nick Drake to reach his widest-ever audience. 'Fruit Tree' was included (along with Jim Croce's 'Time In A Bottle') as 'the music featured in the episode where Nick lost Kate'. Thirty-nine of the tracks were number-one hits - in the column for highest chart position, alongside 'Fruit Tree' stands the legend 'N/A', indicating 'not applicable'.

RELATED RELEASES
NINE OF SWORDS by Scott Appel
(Schoolkids' Records, SKR 1521, 1995)
Includes four instrumentals, 'Bird Flew By', 'Blossom', 'Our Season',
'Place To Be', which Nick never released; 'Parasite', which appeared
on *Pink Moon*, and 'Nearly/Far Leys', Appel's reworking of a Nick
Drake original.

BRITTLE DAYS: A TRIBUTE TO NICK DRAKE
(Imaginary Records ILLCD 026, September 1992) Deleted.
'River Man' (The Changelings), 'At The Chime Of A City Clock'
(The High Llamas), 'Pink Moon' (Loop), 'Road' (No Man), 'Cello
Song' (The Walkabouts), 'Joey' (Shellyann Orphan), 'From The
Morning' (Scott Appel), 'Fruit Tree' (The Times), 'Know' (Martyn
Bates), 'Voice From The Mountain' (The Swinging Swine), 'Time
Has Told Me' (Nikki Sudden & The French Revolution), 'Fly' (Tracy
Santa), 'Northern Sky' (Clive Gregson), 'Hazey Jane' (Scott Appel),
'River Man' (R. Stevie Moore)

Nick Drake and associated CDs can be obtained from: Rock Relics,
PO Box 50, Houghton-le-Spring, Tyne and Wear DH4 5YP, UK.

Scott Appel's *Nine of Swords* available from: Glassfinger Inc, PO Box
141, Lincoln Park, New Jersey, 07035-1217, USA.
   Pink Moon is a quarterly Nick Drake fanzine. Details from: Jason
Creed, 34 Kingsbridge Road, Walton-on-Thames, Surrey KT12 2BZ,
UK.

ACKNOWLEDGEMENTS

First of all, Penny Phillips at Bloomsbury had the kind imagination to commission this book, so thanks to her for the start, and to Peter Hogan for the end.

Along the way, a great many people helped shape this book. Will Bennett, the intrepid 'Bennett of the Telegraph', and Mark Seaman provided illumination and encouragement when all around was darkness.

Thanks to the Freewheelin' Jeremy Mason for the first step on a great journey and Robert Kirby for the last piece of the jigsaw; to Paul Wheeler for his memories and introducing me to Nick's Cambridge; and to Brian Wells, who took the time for repeated consultations above and beyond the call of duty.

Françoise Hardy spoke for the first time to me about her memories of Nick. *Merci bien. Merci, aussi* to Juliet Love for her translation, and to Kelly Pike and Romain Vivien at Virgin records for making the connection.

For the background to the Drake family in Burma and Tanworth, I would like to thank Steven Button of Churchill & Sim, Mr James of The Timber Trade Federation, R.W. Samuel of Wallace Brothers & Co., Walter Snadden, Mr Stanbridge of the British Library, John Maloney, Revd. Canon M.W. Tunnicliffe, Johan Asherton and invaluable transatlantic allies T.J. McGrath, Larry Ayres and Scott Appel.

Information about Nick's prep-school days was kindly supplied by Maxine Craig, who had gone down this road a decade before. Johnny Black, David and Jean Allen, John Uzielli, E.J.H. Gould, and particularly Marlborough College archivist Terry Rogers, provided the Marlborough connection. Dennis Silk was Nick's housemaster, and to him I extend warmest thanks for finding time in his hectic timetable to meet me and share his fond memories of a former C1 House pupil.

The following Old Marlburians were generous in sharing their memories of N.R. Drake during the time he spent at the college between 1962 and 1966: Simon Crocker, Arthur Packard, and David Wright, who dipped back over thirty years to recall the first guitar chords he taught the teenage Nick. Thanks also to Michael Maclaran, who shared memories of his trip to France with Nick in 1967, and to Richard Charkin in London 1997, for Morocco 1967.

For Nick's university career at Cambridge, sincere thanks to Christopher Pratt, Roger Brown, Iain Cameron, Iain Dunn, Ian MacDonald, and Trevor Dann, who, in between running Radio 1, provided revealing insights into Cambridge in the late sixties.

And so to London . . . In the beginning there was and always shall be Ashley Hutchings. Anthea Joseph and Nick's press officer at Island, David Sandison, were enormously helpful and generous – someone should get them to write their memoirs. Jerry Gilbert, Chris Carr and Pete Frame, all of whose enthusiasm oils the dry wheels of nineties rock 'n' roll. For memories of photo sessions, long ago and far away, and for support today, many thanks, Keith Morris.

Fly-on-the-studio-wall stuff came courtesy of Mike Kowalski, Dave Pegg and Danny Thompson; and invaluable background on Island Records in the early 1970s from David Betteridge, Tim Clark, Martin Satterthwaite, Annie Sullivan and, in memoriam, Gus the Dog.

Deep in his basement, Phil Lawton is the Radio 1 archivist; thanks to him, Pete Ritzema, Jonathan Dann, Alec Reid and Garrell Redfearn for radio waves.

Thanks to *Mojo*'s Jim Irvin for commissioning the feature which was my first foray into Nick Drake waters, and to Mat Snow for making it Nick's first appearance on a magazine cover. Post-publication, Dave Burrows, Dave Crewe, Paul Cullum, Paul Donnelly, Steve Aparicio and Mick Stannard were kind enough to write in with their memories of seeing Nick perform; Alex Skorecki shed valuable light on the origin of *Five Leaves Left*, with a little thanks to O. Henry; and Brian Cullman was particularly evocative of times long gone.

For help, information, advice, cuttings, contacts, clarification, amplification and encouragement, grateful thanks to Ian Burgess, Peter Doggett, Johnny Rogan, Paddy Forwood, Dave Gardner, Bernard Doherty, Pippa at Go! Discs, Mark Jones, Mark Perry, Dylan Winter, Chas Keep, Jason Creed, Alan Robinson, Greg Van Dike, Levent Varlik, Alannah Hopkin, Luca Ferrari, Andy Robson, Koen Hottentot, Mike King, Wesley McDowell, Alan Hewitt, Dave Brown, Peter Curd, Yoshifumi Yakiyama, Maurice Shannon, Mark Rogers, George Taylor, Barry Lazell, Anthony Trotter, Tony Reif, Mikael Ledin, Liz Thompson, Chris Groom, Richard Prout, Rupert Hunt, Kevin Howlett, Colin Harper, Jeremy Harmer – sorry we never got to meet, Allan Jones, Maggie Simpson, Justin Bairamian, Fred Dellar – ever a font, Paula Shutkever, Annie Cleghorn and Lawrence Morphet for surfing the net, and special thanks to Kevin O'Neil and Paolo Hewitt – we'll always have Sorrento.

It's good to talk. Many thanks to Linda Thompson, who always finds time to chat; and also to Jeroen Berkvens, Nick Kent and Rob Partridge.

For first-hand memories of the hurly-burly folk scene of the late 1960s, Michael Chapman, Bruce 'Brewster' Fursman, Steve Tilston, Bridget St John and Ralph McTell. And for the genesis of Genesis, Anthony Phillips.

Chris Blackwell spoke for the first time about his memories of Nick Drake; for this and for his pioneering work at Island Records over the years – and to Cathy Snipper and Trevor Wyatt – thank you.

To the indefatigable Mark Lewisohn, thanks, and for the future, nothing but the best. John Martyn for ringing to tell me he'd said everything he had to say about Nick, but wishing me good luck. Jonathan Morrish, for exemplary contacts and unflagging enthusiasm over the years.

To Martin and the little Loves - Liberty and Rufus - for reasons to be cheerful. Sue Parr for sorting the wheat from the chaff, fifty thousand thank yous; and Richard Dawes for his sense and sensitivity in turning that into this.

Finally, Paul Weller, Peter Buck, Clive Gregson, Matt Johnson and Donovan all talked about why they felt Nick's music was so special to them. For their time and enthusiasm, I say thank you. To those I might have missed, apologies, and thanks all the same. As the Master once wrote: Take care of your memories, said Nick, for you cannot relive them . . .